Thomas C. Mann

THOMAS C. MANN

*President Johnson, the Cold War,
and the Restructuring of
Latin American Foreign Policy*

Thomas Tunstall Allcock

UNIVERSITY PRESS OF KENTUCKY

Editorial and Sales Offices: The University Press of Kentucky
663 South Limestone Street, Lexington, Kentucky 40508-4008
www.kentuckypress.com

Library of Congress Cataloging-in-Publication Data

Names: Tunstall Allcock, Thomas, author.
Title: Thomas C. Mann : President Johnson, the Cold War, and the
    Restructuring of Latin American Foreign Policy / Thomas Tunstall Allcock.
Description: Lexington, Kentucky : The University Press of Kentucky, [2018] |
    Series: Studies in conflict, diplomacy, and peace | Includes bibliographical references
    and index.
Identifiers: LCCN 2018027841| ISBN 9780813176154 (hardcover : alk. paper) |
    ISBN 9780813176178 (pdf) | ISBN 9780813176161 (epub)
Subjects: LCSH: Mann, Thomas C. (Thomas Clifton), 1912–1999. | United
    States—Foreign relations—Latin America. | Latin America—Foreign relations—United
    States. | United States—Foreign relations—1963–1969. | Latin American—Foreign
    relations—1948–1980.
Classification: LCC F1418 .A47 2018 | DDC 327.7308092 [B]—dc23

This book is printed on acid-free paper meeting
the requirements of the American National Standard
for Permanence in Paper for Printed Library Materials.

Manufactured in the United States of America.

Member of the Association
of University Presses

For Caitlin

Contents

Abbreviations

ARA	Bureau of Inter-American Affairs (State Department)
BGLA	Business Group for Latin America
CACM	Central American Common Market
CIAP	Inter-American Committee on the Alliance for Progress
ECLA	Economic Commission for Latin America (United Nations)
IADB	Inter-American Development Bank
IAPC	Inter-American Peace Committee
IAPF	Inter-American Peace Force
IPC	International Petroleum Company
LAFTA	Latin American Free Trade Association
MNR	Movimiento Nacionalista Revolucionario (Bolivia)
NSC	National Security Council
OAS	Organization of American States
ODECA	Organization of Central American States
PRD	Partido Revolucionario Dominicano (Dominican Republic)
PRI	Partido Revolucionario Institucional (Mexico)
UFC	United Fruit Company
USIA	US Information Agency
USAID	US Agency for International Development

Introduction

Lyndon Johnson, Thomas Mann, and Latin America

We have problems everywhere.
—Thomas Mann to Lyndon Johnson, June 1964

On 11 April 1967, President Lyndon Baines Johnson made a rare foray outside the United States to spend three days in Punta del Este, Uruguay, attending a conference of American presidents. Six years previously, that same coastal resort town had been the location from which John F. Kennedy's ambitious cooperative aid program, the Alliance for Progress, had been launched, yet Johnson hoped the meeting could be more than a celebration of his predecessor's achievements. Having played a leading role in organizing the hemispheric summit, he pushed his aides to draft a wide-ranging series of proposals intended to launch a renewed and reinvigorated Alliance for Progress, focusing on regional economic integration through a common market and cooperative infrastructure projects. His public dedication to renewed efforts at hemispheric development would result in a rewarding trip, with constructive private and public meetings followed by a joint declaration that incorporated all his key proposals. The United States, he told the gathered presidents, was committed "by history, by national interest, and by simple friendship to the cause of progress in Latin America."[1]

Unfortunately for Johnson, the struggles he would face in effectively implementing those proposals would ultimately demonstrate many of the fundamental challenges facing both inter-American relations in the 1960s and his own presidency. Indeed, the satisfying nature of the conference was a rare bright spot for a president widely perceived to have struggled in the arena of international diplomacy. The US delegation would return from Punta del Este to a Washington where the fallout from the disastrous conflict in Vietnam was already threatening to consume the administration and related clashes with Congress threatened the funding required for any new aid initiatives to succeed. By the time Johnson left office in January 1969, the promise of the 1967 conference of the presidents would appear but a minor footnote in a controversial and divisive presidency.

Assessments of Johnson's foreign policy record remain, on the whole, poor. One recent poll of scholars ranked his presidency a remarkable third overall for domestic leadership but a lowly thirty-second in foreign affairs, a legacy dominated by legislative achievements at home and the disastrous military campaign waged under his command in Vietnam.[2] Despite highlights such as Punta del Este, assessments of his record in Latin America have typically done little to moderate such views. Notably, a clumsy intervention in the Dominican Republic in April 1965 and the related fallout support the impression of a president overly invested in notions of global credibility, one who overestimated the threat of Communist insurgencies, was hypersensitive to criticism, and was quick to seek military rather than diplomatic solutions to crises.[3] Whereas Johnson's handling of Vietnam is often blamed in part on his overreliance on a cadre of like-minded advisers, his management of Latin American policy is usually linked to one particular individual, Thomas Clifton Mann. A long-serving Foreign Service officer from Texas appointed as Johnson's chief Latin American aide in December 1963, Mann is often assigned responsibility for overseeing disastrous diplomacy, such as in the Dominican Republic, and dismantling the Alliance for Progress. According to the Kennedy aide and historian Arthur Schlesinger Jr., Mann "eviscerated" the program.[4]

On the face of things, then, Johnson's Latin American policy may not seem like a promising subject for a book that could be grouped with the small but growing number of revisionist works on foreign affairs during his presidency. Indeed, both Johnson and Mann were complex, often difficult characters who seemingly made enemies easily and whose fundamentally flawed responses to certain challenges suggest their reputations are well earned. Yet, as the president's successful summit diplomacy and attempts to reinvigorate the Alliance for Progress in April 1967 suggest, that perspective is only part of a more complex and multifaceted story. Working from three fundamental positions regarding Mann, Johnson, and the nature of development thinking during their administration, this book makes an argument for revising assessments of several aspects of US policy in Latin America during the 1960s.[5]

The first is that Thomas Mann's career is in need of a detailed and balanced assessment that goes beyond existing characterizations of a reactionary, conservative figure concerned largely with the fortunes of US corporations and dismissive of the interests of other countries. Mann's career in the State Department encompassed one world war and five presidencies, a period during which inter-American relations shifted from wartime cooperation under the Good Neighbor policy, to early Cold War neglect, to economic and political engagement inspired by a fear of Communist gains in the wake of the Cuban Revolution. His positions remained markedly consistent throughout. Primarily concerned with protecting the interests of the United States, Mann was, like almost all his policy-making contemporaries during the Cold War, a committed anti-Communist who believed in the importance of private industry and international trade. Yet he also favored sustainable aid programs and regional integration initiatives that could make long-term contributions to Latin American development and regularly counseled for the establishment of fairer business practices on the part of US-based corporations. His consistency would see him considered a liberal, progressive figure during the 1950s, when he regularly pushed for increased aid to and cooperation with Latin American governments, but his views were grounded in the New Deal and Good Neighbor era of the 1930s and 1940s, and he would find himself out of step with the liberal internationalists and modernization theorists who abounded in the Kennedy administration. His occasionally blunt manner and doubts regarding theories of development would result in clashes with those Kennedy loyalists that would see him accused of introducing the "Mann Doctrine," which undermined the progressive gains of the early Alliance, and his dearth of skill at political infighting and lack of media savvy would leave him ill equipped to defend himself. His resulting reputation has hindered an accurate understanding of his policy-making contributions, particularly during Johnson's presidency.[6]

The second fundamental position of the book is that, while Johnson was not a president overly concerned with foreign affairs, Latin America was a region that retained more interest for him than most and to which he dedicated significant time and resources. His record in Latin American affairs should therefore play a more integral role, for good or ill, in assessments of his presidency. Both the Kennedy and the Johnson administrations operated from a genuine desire to see the creation of a prosperous, safe, and democratic Latin America, believing that this would benefit the hemisphere as a whole and that the US government had a major role to play in bringing it about. That dedication was always underpinned by a constant fear of Communist influence and the possibility of another Cuba in the hemisphere, and Johnson retained an interest in Latin America even as Vietnam consumed increasing amounts of his time and energy. Within the context of US Cold War presidents, his record in the region should be viewed as mixed, containing mistakes and misjudgments, particularly in his handling of crises, but also some moderate achievements. Despite the struggles faced by the Alliance, Johnson's presidency still compares favorably to others in the Cold War era in terms of the scale of financial aid provided to the region and the priority given to encouraging Latin American economic development.[7]

The third central argument of this book flows from the first two, reflecting the manner in which both Mann's and Johnson's worldviews intersected with development policy during the latter's presidency. The Punta del Este conference of 1967 represented the culmination of the Johnson administration's concerted efforts to reshape the Alliance for Progress into an effective and sustainable aid program grounded in both Mann's and Johnson's experiences with the New Deal and the Good Neighbor policy of the 1930s and 1940s. The Johnson presidency briefly saw a new framework emerge that retained the modernizer's faith in economic development while embracing inter-American multilateralism to push an agenda of regional integration. While it was ultimately unsuccessful, it offered a genuine alternative to the path laid out during the Alliance's founding.

Taken together, these three positions provide the foundation for an exploration of US policy during a critical period in inter-American relations. Political crises, coups, and economic disputes in the hemisphere all had to be managed within the context of running battles with the press and domestic political rivals, all of which played out against the backdrop of an increasingly global Cold War. While many of these challenges would be of the administration's own making, it was with some justification that Mann would warn Johnson: "We have problems everywhere."[8]

Thomas Mann enjoyed two periods of particular influence in Washington policy-making circles. The first was in the late 1950s as Dwight Eisenhower sought to modify his economic policies in the hemisphere and looked to his

State Department experts for their views. The second occurred under Lyndon Johnson in the mid-1960s, when Mann was handed a substantial degree of control over all aspects of Latin American policy. That second period—during which Mann would implement bureaucratic restructurings and oversee the Alliance for Progress while becoming a close confidant of the president's, being promoted to undersecretary of state for economic affairs, and being twice offered the position of national security adviser—would be the peak of his career. His contributions during those periods were fundamental to shaping many aspects of US economic and political engagement with Latin America, but the phases of his career when he was not so influential are, in their own way, just as revealing.

Mann's appointment as ambassador to Mexico in 1961 by John F. Kennedy is particularly notable in that regard. He would make a success of the posting, but his departure from Washington nonetheless reflected the fact that the pragmatic diplomat whose economic views were grounded in the New Deal era and whose experiences in the field had rendered him cautious regarding the limits of US influence was an awkward fit with the youthful energy and faith in the modernizing potential of foreign aid that characterized the early months of Kennedy's administration. Mann's subsequent return to a position of power in December 1963 following Kennedy's assassination consequently reawakened those tensions and exposed divisions within Johnson's inherited administration. Several of Kennedy's most dedicated aides viewed Mann as a threat to both their own positions and their former president's progressive legacy and would make their feelings well-known. Those tensions have done much to shape subsequent narratives of Mann's career, with particularly critical accounts portraying him as a Texas crony of Johnson's, a political and economic conservative who believed that Latin Americans responded best to "a kick in the ass."[9] Limited accounts from some contemporaries aside, Mann's legacy is portrayed as almost entirely negative.[10]

In reality, the changes Mann introduced in 1964 and 1965 were gradual, often reflecting processes that were already under way, and were designed to strengthen, not undermine, existing policy. Nonetheless, his career is intrinsically linked to the changing nature of Latin American relations in Washington as well as the internal battles that marked White House politics and the Democratic Party in the 1960s. An exploration of his career therefore provides an important foundation for an assessment of US policy in Latin

America over a number of years and is particularly revealing regarding the presidency of Lyndon Johnson.

In terms of foreign affairs, Johnson's presidency was in many ways a transitional one. In part this was due to his initial feeling that he was a "stand-in" president, there to continue Kennedy's policies at least until he won an election in his own right, as well as his decision to retain the majority of his predecessor's key advisers. Yet Johnson also failed to articulate a grand unifying vision for foreign affairs, with his global policy lacking an identity comparable to the Nixon administration's form of realpolitik or Jimmy Carter's association with the language of universal human rights.[11] John F. Kennedy had expanded the scope of American international engagement, promising to "pay any price and bear any burden," and Johnson would find himself attempting to manage a bulging portfolio of global commitments largely on a case-by-case basis. This lack of identity has contributed to the image of Johnson as a talented domestic politician with little feel for the intricacies of foreign affairs. In the journalist Paul Geyelin's famous articulation, LBJ was "king of the river and a stranger to the open sea." The complex challenges of the 1960s required subtlety, patience, and skill to negotiate, the standard viewpoint has posited; yet in Johnson the United States possessed a leader keen to focus on his ambitious domestic agenda and willing to neglect foreign affairs in the process, with often disastrous results.[12]

For Johnson, Latin American policy would prove a particular challenge. Kennedy had combined a heady mix of the most inspiring elements of social-scientific thinking on national development, his administration's youthful vigor, and his own gift for exhilarating rhetoric when launching the Alliance for Progress early in his presidency. By the decade's end, a controversial military venture in the Caribbean would undermine political cooperation in the hemisphere, and the Alliance would be largely discredited and languishing under a president, Richard Nixon, for whom Latin American development ranked somewhere near the bottom of his list of global priorities. Unsurprisingly, then, Johnson's handling of hemispheric affairs—often criticized as reactive and seen as achieving little other than abandoning the social and political aspects of the Alliance in favor of narrow economic and security concerns—has done little to improve his reputation as a foreign policy leader. Despite his public statements to the contrary in the wake of Kennedy's death, most accounts suggest that Johnson soon lost what little interest he possessed in hemispheric affairs, with few paying much attention to the events that followed the clumsy intervention in the Dominican Republic in April 1965. While the Kennedy administration does not escape blame for muddled and contradictory policies either, any hope for the Alliance is typically seen as evaporating by 1965 at the latest, the program declining steadily thereafter until its ultimate demise under Nixon.[13]

Yet in many ways Latin America should stand out as a region to which Johnson dedicated time, attention, and money and in which he attempted to wed aspects of Kennedy's legacy to a vision at least partly his own. Indeed, the efforts of the administration to fashion a functioning Latin American policy in the shadow of Kennedy and within constraints imposed by the Cold War—initially coordinated by Mann but continued following his departure from office—offer a glimpse of an alternative path never fully explored. Retaining the dual commitment to containing Communist influence in the hemisphere while also attempting to stimulate economic development, Johnson and Mann would first streamline the Alliance bureaucracy before pursuing an approach that relied less on the transformative power of direct aid and instead envisioned more gradual development built on greater inter-American integration. These changes would see them accused by Kennedy loyalists of abandoning the Alliance, but, in his embrace of economic integration, Johnson wedded New Deal ideals, aspects of modernization thinking, and traditional summit diplomacy to propose a new direction for hemispheric affairs.

The Alliance for Progress had initially been born from a melding of policy-making and academic theory. Positing that enough foreign aid and technical expertise could eventually transform any country into a modern society in the mode of the United States, theories of modernization migrated from academic to policy-making circles throughout the 1950s and 1960s, heavily influencing the planners of the Alliance.[14] Neither Mann nor Johnson was heavily invested in such theoretical frameworks, but neither did they abandon the goals of the Alliance. Instead, their New Deal–era beliefs in political nonintervention and properly regulated private economic growth supported by public infrastructure investment met the grand modernizing sweep of the Alliance for Progress and briefly resulted in a hybrid of the two. Although much of modernization thinking had its roots in New Deal liberalism, the transformative goals of the Alliance went beyond what most policy makers of that era, Johnson included, would have envisaged possible.[15] Following early setbacks in the implementation of programs like the Alliance, by the mid-1960s many leading modernization theorists—some of them based in Johnson's administration—were thinking along similar lines and adjusting their positions to downplay the global applicability of their models.[16] In focusing on private investment, economic and agricultural development, and infrastructure projects while downplaying the potential for social and cultural transformation, the Alliance under Johnson reflected both the influence of a president and a chief Latin American aide schooled in New Deal–era politics and broader trends in modernization thinking. These efforts met with mixed success, but Johnson and Mann certainly did not set out to dismantle the Alliance. It would be the collapse of Johnson's presidency into the mire of Vietnam, congressional hostility toward funding major aid programs, and the Nixon administration's lack of interest that would instead see it die a quiet and largely unlamented death.

In presenting a balanced account of Johnson's and Mann's records that acknowledges both positive contributions and damaging failures, this book provides a history of US–Latin American relations that also speaks to a wider reassessment of foreign policy during the Johnson administration. Several relatively recent works have challenged traditional accounts by widening analysis to incorporate Johnson's record beyond Vietnam, resulting in a more complex assessment of America's thirty-sixth president that acknowledges the scale of the challenges he faced and his occasional successes in addressing them.[17] Until now, this process has rarely extended to his record in the Americas. However, while the account provided here of Latin American policy under Johnson is more positive than most, it is far from celebratory. The travails of the Alliance were accompanied by a series of political crises that were handled with varying degrees of success. While riots and a subsequent political crisis in Panama in 1964 would be resolved relatively smoothly, the rash decision to intervene in the Dominican Republic the following year demonstrated the paranoia regarding Communist influence that pervaded the administration. Despite Mann's often-stated commitment to the nonintervention promise of the Good Neighbor policy, Cold War security fears trumped all. Just as it had been in the Eisenhower and Kennedy eras, any form of Communist influence was considered intolerable, and the speed with which left-leaning political movements were condemned and in many cases actively undermined continually hampered any chance of real progress in the hemisphere throughout the 1960s. Many conservative Latin Americans also realized the power that anti-Communist rhetoric possessed in securing support from the United States in their domestic political struggles and were not afraid to invoke the specter of Fidel Castro when seeking Washington's approval and assistance. By the administration's end, some policy makers—the president included—would at least partially recognize this fact and their own culpability for the continued prevalence of military coups d'état, but by then it would be too late. Considering the political violence and brutality that marred many Latin American nations in subsequent decades, any praise for the achievements of the Kennedy-Johnson era remains qualified.

It is also important to note what this book is not. It is not a comprehensive account of inter-American relations or the Alliance for Progress during the 1960s. An in-depth and detailed assessment of US relations with all its southern neighbors in both a bilateral context and a regional context is beyond the scope of this, and perhaps any, single-volume work of history. This is particularly true in relation to the Alliance, a vast, sprawling enterprise involving several executive departments in Washington as well as multiple, ever-changing inter-American boards and committees. The historian Jeffrey Taffet has, for instance, described the Alliance as being defined by its complexity, and, of the sheer amount of often-contradictory statistics produced by its various bodies, the economist Enrique Lerdau has observed: "I doubt that any one person in the world has read them all, and if such a person existed he would probably have even greater difficulties in deriving valid generalizations than do the rest of us." Instead, Mann's career and the major developments of Johnson's presidency provide a framework that contextualizes notable shifts in policy and responses to key crises, enabling an assessment of their impact and position within a longer history of inter-American relations.[18]

This approach also means that the book is not a work of Latin American history. Much of the best recent scholarship on inter-American relations in this period shifts analytic focus away from Washington and toward the rest of the Americas. This includes studies of Cold War interactions between Latin American nations and accounts of bilateral relations with the United States highlighting the complexities of a vast and diverse region during a time of widespread social and political turbulence. These works also serve to emphasize that the United States was far from omnipotent in the hemisphere during this or any other era. Nonetheless, policies adopted in Washington often had wide-reaching effects throughout the hemisphere, and US interventions in various forms retained the potential to affect the course of another country's future substantially. Thus, while this book is ultimately a study of how policy in Washington was formulated and enacted, it draws on scholarship that provides multinational perspectives on inter-American affairs and fully embraces the position that US agency was not absolute.[19]

Finally, while containing its share of criticism of US actions, this book is not a moral history. The study of US–Latin American relations has traditionally lent itself to value judgments, providing ample opportunities to criticize policy makers for greed, aggression, ignorance, or plain indifference. Such an approach was vital in moving the field beyond simplistic assessments of American noblesse oblige, and its persistent relevance is evidenced by heated debates and provocative works that continue to draw attention to the worst excesses of American policy.[20] That the economic and security interests of their own nation were always paramount in the thinking of US policy makers is taken as a given; greater consideration is given here to the methods employed to achieve those interests. If any value judgment of that policy is present, it is that flexibility and a willingness at least to consider the interests of other nations is a position preferable to one of neglect or domination. As Thomas Mann once commented: "Love and affection is not what foreign relations are based on. . . . [But] I don't think self-interest has to be selfish or it has to grind somebody else under."[21]

In order to provide the fullest assessment of Lyndon Johnson's and Thomas Mann's influence on Latin American policy, the chapters that follow range in chronology from Mann's pre-Johnson career to the final year of Johnson's administration. Chapter 1 therefore begins by establishing important details of Mann's early life and career, particularly the experiences in the State Department that would be drawn on in later years. For Johnson and most of his advisers, similar details are covered exhaustively elsewhere, but this is not the case for Mann.[22] Establishing his core beliefs regarding policy and diplomacy, his role as an early champion of increased economic aid and cooperative measures to assist the economies of the hemisphere under Dwight Eisenhower, and his successful tenure as Kennedy's ambassador to Mexico is vital for understanding the positions he would later advocate under Johnson. The chapter also outlines the broad pattern of inter-American relations in the late 1950s and early 1960s as, largely prompted by Fidel Castro's Cuban Revolution, the Eisenhower administration's "trade not aid" position shifted to early efforts to promote economic modernization, efforts supported by Senate majority leader Lyndon Johnson. The chapter concludes with the culmination of this process, the creation of John F. Kennedy's Alliance for Progress.

Chapter 2 studies the tumultuous period 1960–1964, incorporating analysis of Kennedy's management of the Alliance, and focusing in particular on the challenging transition period that followed Johnson's tragic elevation to the presidency. In assessing both Johnson's and Mann's difficult relationship with Kennedy's chief Latin American aides, deep divisions within the administration are revealed that would have damaging consequences in the coming years and do much to establish Mann's lasting reputation. The new president's efforts to establish authority over Latin American policy were taken by some as an attack on Kennedy's legacy, culminating with the controversy over the Mann Doctrine speech. For the most part, however, policy would remain remarkably consistent, as Johnson's and Mann's experience and New Deal–era views gradually began moving aid policy and its management in a more efficient, albeit less inspirational, direction.

Following that difficult transition period, chapter 3 covers Johnson and Mann's handling of Latin American policy in the first full year of the new administration. The year 1964 began with a major international crisis in the Panama Canal Zone and would prove to be challenging, featuring military coups in Brazil and Bolivia, Mann's attempts to reshape Alliance bureaucracy, and former Kennedy aides contesting the legitimacy of Johnson's leadership and Mann's liberal credentials. Particular attention is given to the skillful manner in which the Panamanian crisis was resolved and the improvements in the performance of the Alliance for Progress. These are contrasted to the administration's controversial response to the coup in Brazil, with the complex relationship between the Brazilian military, the US ambassador in Brasília, and State Department and National Security Council (NSC) officials in Washington representative of the increasingly problematic and intertwined nature of security and development goals.

April 1965 witnessed the most controversial and destructive incident of Johnson's Latin American policy—the intervention in the Dominican Republic—and the majority of chapter 4 is dedicated to the fateful dispatch of US Marines. By considering the decision to intervene, the period of occupation, and the Organization of American States (OAS)–supervised elections that followed, the impact and significance of the first use of US forces in the hemisphere since the 1930s is thoroughly unpacked. A turning point in Johnson's presidency, the intervention was in many respects a success, with few casualties and the eventual election of a US-friendly government. However, it also severely damaged relations with Congress and the press, alienated many Latin Americans, undermined trust in the OAS, and convinced Thomas Mann to leave government service after more than twenty years. Occurring almost simultaneously with the introduction of US troops in Vietnam, this use of force in the Caribbean had global relevance that is readily apparent.

The final chapter considers the period following the Dominican Republic intervention and Mann's departure from the administration, highlighting the 1967 Summit of the Presidents of the Americas as the centerpiece of efforts to revive the Alliance for Progress. In particular, Johnson's emphasis on integration—both physical, through the development of inter-American infrastructure, and economic, through the envisaged expansion of common markets—which had grown from the mixture of New Deal and New Frontier thinking within his administration, represented a potentially more viable framework for modernization than the initial direct-aid-centered approach of the Alliance. While these positive efforts undermine the traditional narrative of an administration that had all but given up on Latin America post-1965, Johnson's efforts to create a safer and more prosperous hemisphere that benefited ordinary Latin Americans while serving his own country's interests were at best only partially successful. Furthermore, coups in Argentina, Peru, and Panama also serve to highlight the continuing failure to encourage democratic progress, the damaging impact of military-assistance programs, and the scale of the problems that would continue to plague Cold War inter-American relations.

1

Trade, Aid, and the Cold War in the Americas

Thomas Mann and Latin America

Thomas Mann's government career began under President Franklin Delano Roosevelt and came to an end twenty-five years later under Lyndon Baines Johnson, encompassing several State Department roles in Washington and postings abroad. During a period that witnessed US policy develop from FDR's Good Neighbor stance of improving relations and establishing wartime cooperation, to the relative neglect and occasional interventions of the Truman and early Eisenhower years, followed by the increasing engagement and ambitious aid programs of the late 1950s and the 1960s, Mann's career was almost entirely focused on Latin American issues. This long experience would provide the foundations for many of his views on economic, social, and political aspects of inter-American relations, even as he in turn contributed to altering attitudes and policies in Washington. His varied career in the years before his elevation to a position of substantial power by Lyndon Johnson—particularly his apparent transformation from respected and progressively minded diplomat to outdated irrelevance during the Eisenhower-Kennedy transition—reveals much about his character and the changing nature of Latin American policy throughout this period. This chapter therefore provides the vital foundations, in terms of both Mann's views and wider political developments, necessary for a balanced and detailed understanding of the events that would follow once Johnson took office.

The Younger Mann

Thomas Clifton Mann was born on 11 November 1912 in Laredo, Texas, a town on the border with Mexico known for its importance as a point of trade, tourism, and immigration and separated from its Mexican twin, Nuevo Laredo, only by the Rio Grande. The young Mann was raised to be bilingual, claiming to have "learned Spanish before English," and cognizant of events south of the border. One of his earliest memories was the fight for control of Nuevo Laredo during the tail end of the Mexican Revolution. Typically, however, the Mann household was a quiet one. Thomas Sr., a lawyer, was devoutly committed to the Southern Baptist church, and, in addition to a strict moral code, the younger Mann also gained from his father a deep respect for the practice of law. Hence, following a law degree at Baylor University, where he met and married his wife, Nancy, Mann returned to Laredo, joined his father's firm, and became, in his words, a "Texas country lawyer." There he might have remained had his life, like so many others, not been irrevocably altered by his nation's entry into World War II.[1]

Thomas Mann had just turned twenty-nine when the Japanese attack on Pearl Harbor took place, and his attempts to sign up for active military service in early 1942 were rendered problematic by his thin frame and vision that required him to wear thick spectacles constantly. However, Mann's legal and linguistic skills marked him out for a different kind of warfare— combating the economic threat of the Axis in Latin America. "I was sent to Montevideo to help to advise the Embassy and the Uruguayan Government on freezing of German and Japanese trade credits," Mann later recalled. He was next moved to Washington to assess individuals suspected of aiding the enemy and, if necessary, freeze their US assets and declare them enemy nationals.[2]

His involvement in the war effort in Latin America set his career on a path Mann had never anticipated. Economic warfare was largely run from the State Department, and that gained him access to the Foreign Service and the potential for a career in diplomacy. Remaining in Washington after the war's end, he made the best of his unexpected opportunity, initially as head of River Plate Affairs, a role that involved locating Nazi fugitives in Argentina and arranging their deportation. He subsequently served as special assistant to Assistant Secretary of State Spruille Braden before he was transferred to the US embassy in Caracas in 1947 to assist with negotiating disputes over oil contracts between the Venezuelan government and US corporations. Drawing on his legal training and the guidance of the Good Neighbor policy, Mann viewed his role as that of an intermediary, attempting to find common ground that benefited all parties. The success of this approach, which sought to support US investment but not at the cost of damaging relations with the host country, would be drawn on regularly later in his career. In January 1950, he was recalled to Washington to take control of the Bureau of Middle American Affairs and, by November, would be promoted to serve as deputy to Edward Miller, the assistant secretary of state for inter-American affairs.[3]

His approach to the Venezuelan oil dispute reflects the fact that US involvement with Latin America during the period in which Mann built his unanticipated diplomatic career was characterized by Roosevelt's Good Neighbor policy, which renounced the long-held right of the United States to intervene at will in the affairs of its neighbors. Proclaiming that the United States would be "the neighbor who respects himself and, because he does so, respects the rights of others," the Good Neighbor policy was a shrewd move on FDR's part. It cost the United States very little; it was largely a promise *not* to carry out certain actions rather than a guarantee of political cooperation or financial assistance, yet it appeared to admit the mistakes of the past and suggest a future for the hemisphere based on a more equal footing. It also resulted in a series of economic agreements, largely to lower tariffs, that greatly increased US trade within the hemisphere. "It didn't cost us one red cent," one State Department official mused, "[but] the Latin Americans . . . loved Franklin Roosevelt." During World War II, Roosevelt's stance paid off handsomely. While the United States became "the arsenal of democracy" and then entered the conflict outright, the supply of raw materials at artificially depressed prices that flowed northward was indispensable. "We courted the Latin Americans during World War Two, we couldn't live without their products," one official recalled, "and as soon as the war was over, we dropped them."[4]

Latin America was indeed "dropped" as a priority in Washington once the war had ended. The occupations of Japan and Germany and the rebuilding of Western Europe were the more pressing concerns. Once tensions with the Soviet Union coalesced into the Cold War, inter-American issues fell even further down Washington's list of priorities. Although a hemispheric consultative body, the OAS, was created in 1947, the Truman administration paid little heed to Latin American issues, rejecting calls for increased economic assistance and commodity agreements, and delivering occasional lectures on the importance of free trade and investment. "The institution of private property ranks with those of religion and family as a bulwark of civilization," intoned Spruille Braden, Mann's boss and a future lobbyist for the United Fruit Company (UFC), when commenting on economic policy. "To tamper with private enterprise will precipitate a disintegration of life and liberty as we conceive and treasure them." The economic rewards that many countries had been led to believe would follow their wartime cooperation failed to materialize; there was to be no equivalent to the Marshall Plan in Latin America.[5]

Mann's swift rise through the ranks in this period was not particularly surprising. In the postwar Foreign Service, Latin America was not a prized posting. Europe was still seen as the preferred location in which to pursue a diplomatic career, and the prominent New Dealer and former assistant secretary of state under FDR Adolf Berle noted that the head of the Latin American Division held "a job with more responsibility and less administrative authority to discharge it" than any other.[6] Within an underpowered bureau, talent stood out. Fluent in Spanish, a surprisingly rare commodity among Foreign Service officers based in the newly christened Bureau of Inter-American Affairs (ARA), and eight years of experience practicing law, Mann was a prized asset. The Republican Dwight D. Eisenhower would win the presidential election of 1952, and, after a slightly rocky start in the new administration, Mann would go on to establish himself as one of his country's most influential Latin American experts and ultimately help guide the changes that would set the scene for the bolder developments of the 1960s.[7]

An Eisenhower Policy for Latin America

For Deputy Assistant Secretary of State Thomas Mann, the Truman years had been an often-frustrating period as unprecedented levels of aid were sent to Europe and Asia while he was left to bemoan the lack of financial assistance available for inter-American projects and argue unsuccessfully for more flexible trade policies.[8] The advent of a new administration, albeit a Republican one led by the hero of World War II, Dwight Eisenhower, in January 1953 offered hope of a reappraisal of the importance of the Americas and a concurrent adjustment in aid levels. Indeed, Mann noted in February that he intended "to recommend to [Assistant Secretary of State for Inter-American Affairs John Moors] Cabot that . . . the lending policies of the World and Exim [*sic*] banks should be liberalized and made more responsive to our foreign policy requirements in Latin America or, if this is not feasible, an economic grant program for the area comparable to that for the rest of the world."[9] Not calling for a radical policy overhaul, Mann simply wanted the new administration to relax some of the more restrictive policies of the World and Export-Import banks and bring the amount of financing available to Latin America in line with that available to other regions.[10] By favoring a slightly more progressive attitude toward Latin American development, Mann soon found himself part of a small group that included John Cabot and the president's younger brother and former New Dealer Milton Eisenhower.[11]

Unfortunately for Mann and his like-minded colleagues, Dwight Eisenhower's regional policies appeared to differ little from those of his predecessor. Despite attacking the Truman administration during the election campaign of 1952 for its failure to deal effectively with Latin America, the fundamental goals of political stability and free trade remained firmly in place, and Latin American issues quickly faded into the background. The "New Look" approach to foreign policy that the administration developed emphasized fiscal responsibility in foreign policy; substantial new aid initiatives were not a priority. Secretary of State John Foster Dulles summarized the effect of this approach on hemispheric affairs when he told an aide that he wanted "an imaginative program for Latin America, but one that does not cost any money."[12]

The administration's policies were certainly low cost, but it would be a stretch to describe them as imaginative. The fundamental principle was "trade not aid," as policy consisted largely of ignoring calls for greater assistance while encouraging trade opportunities for US businesses.[13] Politically, the Good Neighbor approach of nonintervention largely held sway, with little concern for the nature of Latin American governments, provided they were not Communist. The result was that dictatorships like those of Rafael Trujillo in the Dominican Republic and Anastasio Somoza in Nicaragua were firm US allies. The open and friendly cooperation with these generally stable, staunchly anti-Communist, and authoritarian regimes would be a distinguishing feature of US policy for much of the decade. "Do nothing to offend the dictators," Dulles reportedly once remarked. "They're the only people we can depend on."[14]

Although Mann's hopes for a new approach to the economic problems of the Americas were not to be fulfilled, he did not give up entirely. Occasional victories, such as securing a $300 million loan to Brazil over the objections of several colleagues, indicated that there was a level of awareness among senior administration figures of the potential benefits of increased financial largesse.[15] The issue most likely to garner the attention of senior policy makers, however, was the potential for Communist incursion into the hemisphere.[16] Two nations were of particular concern but would be dealt with in strikingly different ways. The first of these was Bolivia, where throughout the 1950s the government received around $200 million in direct aid from Washington. In this case, it was decided that aid to the Movimiento Nacionalista Revolucionario (MNR) government that came to power via a revolution in April 1952 could provide enough leverage to keep radical elements out of positions of influence.[17] The other case was Guatemala, where Washington instead exercised influence through a CIA-sponsored coup rather than economic assistance. The Eisenhower-era CIA operation, known as PBSUCCESS, would encapsulate much of the administration's dominant approach to foreign affairs, including reflexive anticommunism, concern for US corporate interests, and enthusiasm for covert operations.

The principal cause for concern regarding Guatemala was President Jacobo Árbenz, whose land reform programs and lack of deference to major US corporations such as the UFC earned him plenty of enemies in Washington. In December 1952, Árbenz officially legalized the Guatemalan Communist Party, and disputes between his government and the UFC reached new heights in February 1953 when the expropriation of 234,000 acres of the company's land was announced. By the end of 1953, key policy makers in the United States were convinced that Árbenz's views went beyond mere tolerance of subversive elements, with Ambassador John E. Peurifoy reporting on 17 December: "If President [Árbenz] is not a Communist he will certainly do until one comes along." For John Foster Dulles, final proof that Árbenz was a stooge of the Kremlin was provided in May 1954 when Guatemala purchased a large shipment of arms from Czechoslovakia, an Eastern Bloc nation. The following month, the signal was given to proceed with an operation to remove an elected president of a foreign nation from power. On 18 June, a small exile force—overseen largely by the CIA, led by former Guatemalan army colonel Carlos Castillo Armas, and organized and trained in neighboring Honduras—launched an attack while American intelligence operatives executed a concerted campaign of confusion and misinformation over the radio waves. Convinced that, if Armas's troops were defeated, a US invasion would follow, much of the Guatemalan military refused to fight, and on 27 June Árbenz resigned the presidency.[18]

Thomas Mann's involvement with Guatemalan policy began during the Truman administration, while he was chief of the Middle American Section of the State Department's ARA, and would reveal the growing tension between belief in the Good Neighbor policy of nonintervention and the demands of the Cold War. For much of the Truman period at least, this resulted in support for actions designed to weaken Árbenz's support base, such as building closer links with the Guatemalan military, while also rejecting "ill-concealed" overtures from would-be coup plotters.[19] Despite his later reputation as a friend of American big business, Mann also regularly demonstrated frustration with the inflexibility and clumsy plotting demonstrated by the UFC in response to Árbenz's reforms. When Robert M. La Follette Jr., a UFC lobbyist and former US senator, telephoned Mann in September 1951 to complain about Árbenz, he was advised that the UFC should reconsider its position. If the company forced the Guatemalan government—or any government for that matter—to choose between the interests of its own population and those of a foreign investor, Mann warned him, simple political expediency suggested that the UFC would not emerge victorious. The most sensible option, in Mann's opinion, would be to offer Árbenz "a middle course in the form of a new contract with . . . higher income taxes" and to open negotiations on all other outstanding disputes.[20]

Mann repeated his calls for compromise in November, when La Follette and three UFC executives visited the State Department for consultations. After listening to their litany of complaints, Mann responded that "the apparent reluctance of the company to publish its financial figures made a bad impression since it led people to the assumption that the company was making so much money that the release of the figures would be embarrassing," allowing "demagogues" to demonize them. Furthermore, had the company considered a solution such as the one he had helped negotiate in Venezuela under which foreign investors split profits evenly with the national government? Such an arrangement, Mann suggested, would "make the company's and the government's interests mutual" and avoid most of the current disputes. The meeting ended almost immediately.[21]

Impatience with arrogant US investors did not necessarily equate with sympathy for the Guatemalan president, however. Throughout the Truman administration and into the Eisenhower administration, Mann would continue to pressure the Árbenz government to seek a reasonable solution to its disputes with the UFC, warning that more needed to be done to assuage American concerns about the degree of Communist influence within the Guatemalan leadership. Nonetheless, he and many others within the State Department remained unwilling to endorse regime change, with Mann informing the notorious Washington lawyer and lobbyist Thomas "Tommy the Cork" Corcoran that he "considered special action unnecessary." Mann would also play a role in halting one early Truman-era CIA plan, known as PBFORTUNE, to topple Árbenz, drafting a memo to Secretary of State Dean Acheson in November 1952 informing him: "President Somoza of Nicaragua apparently has gained the impression, however mistakenly, that a military venture directed at the overthrow of the present Guatemalan government would have the blessing of the United States." The memo also suggested that Somoza may have gained such an impression through conversations with Neil Mara, a military aide to President Truman. While it remains unclear how well informed Truman was regarding the plot, once Acheson learned of it, a shipment of arms due to sail from New Orleans on a UFC-owned vessel was canceled and the entire operation abandoned. One CIA memo reflected that "as a result of a policy decision by State . . . all of the action planned in support of the opposition was off," placing the blame firmly on the indiscretion of Nicaraguans who had apparently "confirmed our general belief that no Latin American can be trusted to keep his mouth shut."[22]

Mann's last notable contribution to precoup Guatemalan policy was a memo in February 1953 arguing against intervention or more aggressive sanctions as this would be "divisive and counterproductive" for US relations with the rest of the hemisphere. That Mann had largely been a voice of moderation, urging his government to pressure both the UFC and Árbenz into finding some form of compromise and helping derail PBFORTUNE reflected his faith in the philosophy of the Good Neighbor and his more detailed understanding of Latin American politics and society than many of his contemporaries possessed. In late 1952, he had drafted a detailed memo emphasizing that Latin American nationalism—and associated demands for improvements in economic, political, and social conditions—was likely to grow more intense during the Cold War and should not be automatically conflated with Communist agitation. While he would grow increasingly suspicious of and impatient with Árbenz, he was certainly not as quick as some colleagues to denounce him as a Communist and advocate his removal.[23]

Under the Eisenhower administration, Mann's influence on the matter lessened as the CIA took greater control over Guatemalan policy at the expense of ARA and began planning for Operation PBSUCCESS. It appears that Mann gradually became more convinced of Árbenz's radicalism, later defending the intervention on the basis that, by the time of his downfall, "the Communist party actively controlled the presidential palace." He received some briefings during the early stages of CIA planning, but he would ultimately have little input into the operation itself. Assigned to Greece for a relatively brief field posting in August 1953, he would still be in Athens when Castillo Armas launched his attack the following year. That no US forces were officially involved in the Guatemalan operation allowed the administration to claim technical adherence to the principle of nonintervention while still sending a clear message that Communist influence would not be tolerated in the leader of the free world's own backyard. The tragedy for most Guatemalans, of course, was that a democratically elected president whose programs of land reform had begun to address the nation's glaring inequalities would be replaced by a series of corrupt and incompetent military leaders who would lead their nation into a decades-long spiral of brutal internal conflict.[24]

Árbenz's downfall was widely celebrated in Washington, with John Foster Dulles privately declaring himself "delighted" and a hastily assembled House select committee investigation lavishing praise on Castillo Armas as a hero, citing "irrefutable evidence" that the Árbenz government had been "Communist controlled," and concluding that Guatemala had been serving as a Soviet "beachhead" for almost a decade.[25] Eisenhower and Dulles hoped that an economically successful and politically stable Guatemala would serve as a showcase, demonstrating the wisdom of American intervention and the folly of challenging the status quo. They would be disappointed, however, as Mann soon discovered when he was appointed counselor to the American embassy in Guatemala City after several uneventful months in Athens. Despite substantial US aid, largely aimed at improving infrastructure through highway construction projects and resettling those farmers displaced as Castillo Armas set about ripping up his predecessor's land reforms, Guatemala was far from the desired showcase, with widespread food shortages and accusations of corruption. US aid and technical assistance and the steady reintroduction of private investment proved no substitute for competent government, but, having initially backed Castillo Armas to rescue

Guatemala from Árbenz, there was no abandoning him when he demonstrated little ability as president.[26]

After an unhappy year working with an increasingly erratic and repressive Castillo Armas, Mann turned down an offer to move into the number one slot at the embassy in Guatemala City, instead taking on the role of ambassador to El Salvador in November 1955. On paper, the relocation did not seem a much less challenging assignment, given that El Salvador was ranked by the State Department as the primary "Central American target for subversive infiltration." A report prepared for Mann the month before his arrival warned that threats of subversion were heightened by "the intense pressure of increasing population on very limited natural resources, . . . widespread discrepancies in distribution of wealth, . . . and ill health, poverty and ignorance leading to low productivity and bad living standards of [the Salvadoran] people." Although Mann found himself able to do little to assist the struggling Salvadoran economy while in this post, the experience would solidify his convictions that more should be done to assist and diversify the export-based economies of the region and inform many of the initiatives he would push for in subsequent years.[27]

During his time in San Salvador, Ambassador Mann would regularly remind his staff not to interfere in the complex and often-combustible world of Salvadoran politics, not least because it would rarely result in the desired effect. "We are a sort of punching bag during elections," he would later observe. "Everybody likes to take a swing at us, and makes sure he does every time you say something."[28] He was also able to observe firsthand many of the economic problems that much of Latin America faced to varying degrees. The vast majority of El Salvador's agricultural production focused on two crops, corn to feed the population and coffee for export. As in much of Central America, the majority of the land utilized for producing these crops was owned by a tiny percentage of the population, concentrating wealth among an elite whose upper stratum was known as "the fourteen families." As Mann was regularly reminded in orders from Washington, his role as ambassador was not to resolve long-standing inequalities in El Salvador but to further US interests, that is, stability, trade, and investment opportunities. Nonetheless, he was concerned about the dangers of an export-based economy that relied on only one or two commodities, increasingly aware that "a 30 percent drop in the price of coffee would mean in effect an immediate need to cut back the budget 30 percent, and to cut back imports by 30 percent." The experience confirmed the depths and structural nature of the economic problems faced by many countries outside the United States and would see Mann push for price commodity agreements and other adjustments to economic policy on his return to Washington.[29]

Mann departed El Salvador in September 1957, recalled to a State Department post after four years in the field. During that time, he had implemented the Cold War–driven policy of the Eisenhower administration to support an unconstitutional but anti-Communist government in Guatemala but had also witnessed firsthand the economic deprivations of much of Central America and the growing hostility toward North American support for dictatorships. The fundamentals of Eisenhower's Latin American policy had changed little during Mann's years abroad. Even as the Soviet Union sought to increase its ties with developing nations through the offer of generous aid and assistance packages, high-level policy makers considered substantial adjustments to their detached trade-not-aid stance unnecessary. Indeed, despite having been produced in response to this "Soviet Economic Offensive," policy document NSC 5613/1 endorsed a continuation of the current approach as, owing to US vigilance, there was "no danger of overt Communist attack . . . [and] Communists have no present prospect of gaining control of any Latin American state by electoral means."[30]

Mann was, to an extent, guilty of sharing in this complacency, but he also thought it necessary to at least reassure allies in the hemisphere that the United States remained committed to nonintervention in their internal political affairs. One of his last acts as ambassador to El Salvador was to draft a lengthy article reaffirming the wisdom of the Good Neighbor policy that he hoped could be "published under the name Mr. X or something similar" and widely reproduced throughout Latin America. Conveniently ignoring the CIA's recent activity in Guatemala, the article attacked past US interventionism under James Monroe, Teddy Roosevelt, and Woodrow Wilson, among others, as "unilateral," "patronizing," and "degrading." Moreover, Mann also believed it to have been a failure, noting: "It is precisely some of the states which we occupied and in which we 'supervised' elections that are currently under the heaviest criticism for being undemocratic." Furthermore, he argued, the most important developments since those dark days were the institutions of inter-American law and the renouncement of unilateral interventions, clear evidence as far as he was concerned that most Latin Americans would prefer to have some nondemocratic nations in their midst than the United States interfering at will throughout the hemisphere. His only break from Good Neighbor–style detachment was to endorse opposition to the worst dictatorial regimes, but even then only if action were taken multi-laterally through the OAS. While recognizing the logistic difficulties of such undertakings, he argued that this would be the only way in which the United States could take action without violating either its principles or its treaty obligations.[31]

Although the article was most likely crafted with his imagined Latin American audience in mind, the views on US interventionism and the impor-tance of respecting inter-American law were ones that Mann would repeat on multiple occasions. In contrast to the reputation he would gain during his later career, his distaste for past US aggression and his commitment to a cooperative, noninterventionist relationship with the other nations of the hemisphere appeared to be genuine. He was also returning to Washington at a time when adjustments in policy appeared possible. The Soviet Economic Offensive had prompted some minor concern regarding Latin America's position within the Cold War and coincided with important changes in per-sonnel. Ultimately, it would be events beyond Washington's control that led to fundamental reassessments of policy, but the bureaucratic changes, includ-ing Mann's new role, would allow the Eisenhower administration to readjust its priorities and fashion a new approach to hemispheric issues that would do much to set the course for the grander developments that followed.[32]

Shifting Priorities

When Mann was appointed assistant secretary of state for economic affairs in September 1957, he joined a much-changed State Department bureau-cracy that would begin a slow process of reshaping the administration's hemi-spheric policy. Roy Rubottom had been appointed to head ARA in June, and the following month Clarence Douglas Dillon became the new undersecre-tary of state for economic affairs, the third most powerful position in the department. All were essentially moderate figures, Mann and Rubottom career Foreign Service officers and Dillon a successful banker, active in Republican politics, who had served as ambassador to France from 1953. Crucially, however, all were interested in exploring ways to improve foreign economic policy. Indeed, Dillon has recalled that he handpicked Mann for the specific reason that he "knew Latin America" and "was not opposed to

. . . commodity agreements and things like that his office . . . had always been opposed to."[33]

Dillon's appointment and the departure of the economically conservative Treasury secretary George Humphrey, replaced by the more moderate Robert Anderson just a few weeks later, created an environment in which attitudes that varied from the trade-not-aid approach could be influential rather than marginalized, and both Mann and Rubottom sought to take full advantage of the situation.[34] In the wake of a conference that Rubottom believed convinced Dillon and Anderson of the scale of Latin America's economic problems, he and Mann began actively to explore the possibility of widespread price-stabilization agreements for key export commodities such as coffee.[35] Fully aware that this contradicted the administration's free market principles, yet believing that the benefits outweighed the costs, the two badgered Secretary Dulles to relax his stance while simultaneously drawing up potential agreements. As Rubottom recalled it: "Mann and I got a group of Latin American ambassadors together . . . and said, 'we don't have the authority to do this, but we're prepared to move with you if you want to take the initiative, and we will support the idea.'" Although an arrangement on coffee prices would not be reached until September 1959, discussions and the formulation of potential solutions began in late 1957 and represented a significant, if limited, departure from Washington's previously held opposition to any such agreements.[36]

Despite this minor success, changing the entrenched attitude that private investment was the only remedy for economic problems proved challenging, with Mann and Rubottom forced to endure a parade of meetings where they would "face the opposition of a lot of the old time economists and legal experts" resistant to substantial changes in policy. Neither Mann nor Rubottom wanted to curb US private investment, but they did discuss ways of restraining the worst excesses of ruthless corporate interests. Having witnessed firsthand the actions of the UFC in Guatemala, Mann in particular hoped for a system in which investors operated "within the framework of local laws and customs instead of seeking to remake them in the image of the United States" and sought to combat the appeal of extreme nationalists and Communists by "adopting fair attitudes towards labor, taxation and other problems" and thus positioning themselves "in the forefront of social progress."[37]

Furthermore, while still hoping to increase the volume of private investment, Mann and Rubottom differed from many of their colleagues by arguing that the US government should be prepared to "provide the dollars which are needed for sound projects for which private capital is not available." During an off-the-record speech at a dinner for the Council on Foreign Relations in January 1958, Mann emphasized the need for private and public capital to work together as neither alone would be sufficient to meet the development needs of the hemisphere. In doing so, he believed, the United States had to "identify . . . with Latin American economic aspirations . . . by insuring that Latin America receives its fair share of the economic aid funds appropriated by Congress." Ignore restrictive doctrines, he urged, and simply do what works. While no large-scale policy changes were implemented, the language used in the communications of this eight-month period demonstrates that at least among the State Department's Latin American experts, backed by the influential Dillon, there was a growing recognition of the need for at least a partial policy overhaul that incorporated targeted, case-by-case financial assistance, limited commodity-stabilization measures, and a reining in of the worst excesses of US investors abroad.[38]

Mann and his like-minded colleagues within the State Department were far from alone in their belief that inter-American relations required reexamination. A prominent Latin American voice was that of the noted Argentine economist Raúl Prebisch, head of the UN's Economic Commission for Latin America (ECLA). Prebisch was a charismatic, dynamic figure who had long advocated a transformation in the relationship between struggling nations on the periphery and those at the industrialized center. Under his leadership, the ECLA repeatedly criticized US economic policies as reinforcing the Latin American dependency on exporting primary goods, pointing to declining terms of trade as evidence that these policies were hindering the growth of nations throughout the developing world.[39] US-based critics, such as Senators Wayne Morse (D-OR) and John F. Kennedy (D-MA), focused less on economic issues but began publicly to question Eisenhower's failure to place his support more fully behind the fledgling democracies of the hemisphere. The influence of such criticism should not be discounted, but it is safe to say that it was not the primary factor in the administration's slow realization that its policies required an overhaul. Demands from Latin America for more favorable economic treatment had been successfully rebuffed by Washington since World War II, and, while Senate liberals began to voice their discontent, they did not go so far as to instigate any investigations into hemispheric policy until October 1958.[40]

It would take much more dramatic interventions to prompt substantial change, the first of which occurred in May 1958 with a disastrous tour of Latin America by Vice President Richard Nixon, during which his motorcade was attacked in Venezuela and he and his wife spat on. In the aftermath, prominent Latin American politicians increased calls for practical change, notably Brazilian president Juscelino Kubitschek, who seized on the public reaction to the Nixon trip as evidence of a desire for increased US support for political and economic development. Kubitschek proposed "Operation Pan-America," a cooperative development effort largely funded by the United States and similar in scope to the Marshall Plan. Criticism was also forthcoming from Senate majority leader Lyndon Johnson, usually a reliable supporter of the administration's foreign policy, who lamented the "neglect of our close neighbors to the south" that had so damaged hemispheric relations. Calling for New Deal–style programs of road building and rural electrification allied with closer trade ties, Johnson invoked the spirit of Franklin Roosevelt when he concluded: "[A] good neighbor realizes that unless the whole community is prosperous, ultimately none of it will be prosperous."[41]

A harassed Eisenhower dispatched Dulles for talks with Kubitschek and announced in August 1958 that his administration opposed "authoritarianism and autocracy of whatever form." Unwilling to go so far as to endorse Kubitschek or Johnson's proposals, Eisenhower nonetheless acknowledged Latin American desires for development assistance through the creation of the Inter-American Development Bank (IADB). Announced by Dillon in the same month that the president affirmed US support for democracy, the IADB would provide development loans to national governments, sometimes in the form of soft loans, and almost half its funds would be provided by Washington. Although the amounts available were initially relatively small, the IADB would go on to play a critical role in later aid initiatives and represented a significant departure from the trade-not-aid approach.[42]

Although the changes in personnel and Nixon's disastrous tour had prompted some readjustments in Washington, it would take Fidel Castro's victory over the dictator Fulgencio Batista in the Cuban Revolution of January 1959 to truly focus the administration's attention on hemispheric affairs. The historian Lars Schoultz has argued that Castro's triumph, followed by his increasing ties to the Soviet Union, served to "dynamite the logjam" in US attitudes toward Latin American policy, and the Cuban Revolution certainly eclipsed Nixon's tour as a wake-up call in Washington. The loss of a nation to communism in Washington's own hemisphere prompted responses ranging from a reduction in sugar-purchasing quotas to the CIA's planning of an operation in the mold of PBSUCCESS to bring down Castro's fledgling government.[43]

Mann shared his government's hostility toward Castro and supported the decision to slash the sugar quota, although he did advocate for a more multilateral approach to economic sanctions. He and Rubottom would find themselves less involved with direct action against Castro, however, instead tasked with developing policies that would prevent other Latin American nations following the same path as Cuba.[44] Attempts to forge good relations with democratic leaders and to appear less rigidly committed to the trade-not-aid policy that had begun in 1958 would be given renewed impetus. Complaints from US corporations about host governments, for example, were often met with advice to compromise and offer better deals, while new secretary of state Christian Herter set about reassuring allies, democratic and authoritarian alike, that requests for increased military assistance would be met "promptly and favorably." Advising Herter on how best to address the topic of hemispheric aid programs such as Operation Pan-America that the administration had opposed for so long, Mann informed the secretary in February 1960 that it was time a new tone was adopted. The United States should now accept a "collective responsibility" for "improving the living standards of the masses," he counseled, noting: "The important thing is *not* whether public or private capital is the most appropriate; it is that we need *all* the capital, public and private, domestic and foreign, that can be generated." Finally, he cautioned that, despite the new importance of Cuba to US policy, this should be mentioned as little as possible as "it is better to counterpunch than attack."[45]

The administration's counterpunches consisted of the announcement in July 1960 of the $500 million Social Progress Trust Fund, which would distribute soft loans through the IADB for health, education, housing, and land reform programs, swiftly followed by the Act of Bogota, the closest that Eisenhower was willing to get to an endorsement of Operation Pan-America. Emerging from a series of meetings held by an OAS committee led by Dillon, the Act of Bogota announced a multilateral program of development aid for the hemisphere, including measures for social improvements, housing, education, and public health as well as suggestions for economic development. In doing so, it reflected both the long-standing demands of many Latin American nations as well as the growing influence of modernization theorists in the United States who posited that, through aid and technical assistance, developing countries could be guided on a path toward American-style capitalism and democracy.[46] According to Mann: "[The act] gave a social dimension to our economic and financial relations with the hemisphere for the first time. That was a great achievement." While neither initiative was on the scale of Operation Pan-America, both nonetheless seemed to demonstrate a crucial shift in attitude, with Mann able to reflect that the Bogota meeting was "the first inter-American conference in which the U.S. did not take a dissent or reservation on anything." Recognizing the crux of this shift, he felt emboldened enough to inform the Committee on Foreign Economic Policy and its formidable chairman, Clarence Randall, in October 1960: "The fact is . . . foreign private enterprise is in very bad grace in Latin America today. New outside capital will have to come, for the most part, through government channels."[47]

As 1960 drew to a close, so too did the Eisenhower administration near the end of its term of office. John F. Kennedy had narrowly defeated Richard Nixon in the 1960 election and was due to enter the White House in January 1961. Having been appointed assistant secretary of state for inter-American affairs for the final few months of the administration amid rumors that Vice President Nixon was bitterly disappointed in Rubottom's leadership, Mann would find himself overseeing the transition of hemispheric policy. Unsure who would be replacing him in the new administration, he prepared a lengthy memo for his successor, outlining current US objectives and policies in Latin America. Highlighting the twin threats of Castro and economic underdevelopment, he argued strongly that the Act of Bogota offered the best course of action and should be implemented swiftly; otherwise, Latin American leaders were "likely to become discouraged" and "the valuable momentum" that the act had generated could be lost. Central America was singled out as being in particularly urgent need of US assistance, and Mann recommended full support for OAS actions against dictatorships such as Rafael Trujillo's in the Dominican Republic.[48]

As Mann's memo made clear, by 1960 Latin America was definitely considered a Cold War battleground in Washington. Castro's emergence had sharpened vague worries about unrest and poverty in the region into deep concern that communism could make significant gains in "the closest of the emerging areas" and heightened public awareness of the problems of the hemisphere. That international communism had gained a beachhead in a region long neglected by Eisenhower makes it unsurprising that critical voices such as Senator William Fulbright (D-AR) referred to the Social Progress Trust Fund and the Act of Bogota as the administration's "death bed confession."[49]

Yet there remains debate as to whether the administration was offering little more than token efforts, as Fulbright contended, or the developments at the close of the decade reflected a substantial reorientation of policy.[50] While it is difficult to praise too fulsomely programs that required a vice president to be nearly stoned to death and a revolution in the Caribbean to occur in order to get off the ground, it is unquestionable that Latin American policy looked quite different at the end of the Eisenhower administration than it had in 1953. Although owing much to external catalysts, it was also due to the changing personnel within the administration, which produced a more flexible and sympathetic attitude within the State Department toward Latin American issues. Fear of more nations taking the same path as Cuba allowed the more progressively minded members of the administration to shape a policy that incorporated increased aid levels, programs of social development, and greater restrictions on the behavior of US investors abroad. Concurrently, those very same Cold War concerns meant that plans were under way to topple Castro's nascent regime, and political developments in the hemisphere were closely observed for any sign of Communist influence. As had been the case with Bolivia and Guatemala earlier in the decade, the Cold War provided opportunities to follow very different paths, either supporting Latin American development in the hope that nations would choose the path of democracy or using covert and overt strength to crush any seeds of radicalism. In attempting to do both, a pattern was set that would play out throughout the following decade, often with less than positive results.

On a more personal level, Mann ended the Eisenhower administration as the State Department's senior Latin American expert and with a burgeoning reputation, both within the United States and abroad. The *Washington Daily News,* for instance, noted that he was the preferred choice of Latin American diplomats to represent the United States on inter-American economic committees, owing to "the high respect in which he is held following his successful advocacy of . . . an inter-American regional development bank" and his success "in negotiations to stabilize prices for basic commodities." Tad Szulc of the *New York Times,* who would later be highly critical of Mann, was equally fulsome, noting that US interest in Latin American problems during the Eisenhower administration began "largely on the initiative of Thomas C. Mann." Criticism was harder to find, although, following a US decision to withdraw support for his regime, one of Dominican dictator Rafael Trujillo's cronies did declare dramatically: "It is well known that Señor Mann has diabolical intentions and is effeminate."[51]

Despite his role promoting new directions in administration policy, annoying dictators, and enthusiastically supporting the Act of Bogota, Mann nonetheless remained cautious regarding the nature and scale of US commitments in the hemisphere. During a cabinet meeting in February 1959 in which he emphasized the desperate need to address the "9 to 1 disparity in per capita income between U.S. and Latin American citizens" by "'constantly seeking new and imaginative ways to make our cooperation more effective," he also warned of promising too much, too quickly. A program on a Marshall Plan scale would simply be unsustainable in Congress and flounder in Latin America as "governments would not find it politically possible to ask commensurate sacrifices of their people." Such a failure—particularly if specific growth targets had been set and subsequently missed—would only cause resentment among Latin Americans, who would eventually feel "deceived." Mann also appeared suspicious of both entrenched economic dogma and the growing influence of modernization theorists, warning that, for a new initiative, "the test ought not to be whether it squares with some particular doctrine, but whether it is sound and will really promote western hemisphere and free world economic progress." Mann would enter the Kennedy administration with a reputation as a respected and progressively minded diplomat and policy maker, but the scale and speed of the changes to come under the new president would evoke many of his fears regarding unrealistic promises and the inflexibility of social-science-driven modernization thinking, with decidedly mixed results for his career.[52]

A New Era

On 20 January 1961, John Fitzgerald Kennedy was sworn in as president of the United States of America, having been the youngest man as well as the first Catholic to win the country's highest political office. He was also the first for many years, if not the first ever, to enter the White House possessing wide popularity throughout Latin America. While this owed much to his faith, it was also because of a campaign that had promised a fresh and energetic engagement with international affairs, a stance he would confirm in a famous inaugural address that vowed the United States would "pay any price, bear any burden" for the cause of global freedom. As early as December 1958, Kennedy had expressed solidarity with the hopes and aspirations of the people of the Americas, supporting the Eisenhower administration's consideration of commodity agreements and creation of the IADB while also chastising the president for not acting quickly enough.[53] Seeking a campaign platform that would distinguish Kennedy from his opponent, Vice President Nixon, one of his speechwriters, Richard Goodwin, coined the term *Alianza para el Progreso* or "Alliance for Progress." Although Kennedy was vague on details, he began to use the phrase in relation to Latin America during speeches in October 1960. That same month, the Democratic nominee used the platform of the fourth and final televised debate with his opponent to utilize one of his most potent weapons, the "loss" of Cuba. Just as the Republicans had blamed the Truman administration for the loss of China during the 1952 campaign, so Kennedy was able to paint a Republican administration as weak and slow to respond to Communist infiltration in its own historic sphere of influence.[54]

Given the role that Latin American issues had played in the campaign, Mann fully expected that the new president would shake up the inter-American bureaucracy and had consequently spent the last weeks of the Eisenhower presidency preparing to hand over the reins of ARA to an as-yet-unnamed successor. Kennedy did indeed plan to make changes, agreeing with his foreign policy adviser Chester Bowles that, while Mann was "an outstanding civil servant . . . [who] should be replaced only when and if we find a person of even greater ability," a clean break with the Eisenhower presidency would be advisable. The president-elect found it harder than expected to locate his "person of even greater ability," however, and had not done so by the time he entered office. To his surprise, Mann would be in Washington for another presidential transition.[55]

Initially, the old hand was not impressed by many of Kennedy's youthful White House staff, who seemed eager to direct foreign policy yet possessed precious little experience. Mann's status as a holdover meant he was largely sidelined, later reflecting: "Well, somebody comes in, and you're an 'Eisenhower appointee' and, therefore, you're a reactionary." Comparing the experience to the previous transition, he noted: "Eight years before we were all communists, and we're the same people. It's really absurd." Writing to Rubottom, now ambassador to Argentina, on 31 January, he expressed his belief that he would not be in Washington long, six months at most, and signed off with: "I hope to join you in the field before too long." As a stopgap secretary, Mann had little influence on the broad direction of policy, a status made clear by his efforts to question the nascent plan to invade Cuba with a CIA-trained exile force. He had attempted to breach the ban on bureaucratic consultation between the period of election and the inauguration to discuss the matter but had found Kennedy's chosen secretary of state, Dean Rusk, unwilling to communicate. Other long-term ARA employees found themselves in a similarly weak position as, while most were still thinking in terms of how to implement the Act of Bogota, Kennedy was already formulating a program to supersede it.[56]

Well before his inauguration, Kennedy had established a task force to outline a new policy for Latin America. Chaired by former assistant secretary of state Adolf Berle, it included future members of his presidential staff such as Richard Goodwin, the representatives of the Puerto Rican government Arturo Morales-Carrión and Teodoro Moscoso, and academics like Lincoln Gordon, who would later serve as ambassador to Brazil. Noting that Kennedy's campaign had "aroused high hopes in Latin America" even as the Soviet Union and the People's Republic of China targeted the region for subversion, the task force's initial report dramatically concluded: "The present Communist challenge in Latin America resembles, but is more dangerous than, the Nazi-Fascist threat of the Franklin Roosevelt period and demands an even bolder and more imaginative response." Following the inauguration, representatives of various executive agencies, including Mann, were added to the group, although, according to Goodwin, detailed input from ARA was neither offered nor requested. As Kennedy's aide recalled in his memoirs: "The lone representative of the State Department . . . [was] Tom Mann, a holdover from the Eisenhower administration, who sat in wordless acquiescence as we condemned and prepared to overturn the policies he had so faithfully administered." That Mann contributed little is hardly surprising; the meetings were effectively convened to help Goodwin translate the task force's preinauguration ideas into a speech, but they appear to have convinced the talented young aide that any holdovers from the previous administration had little to offer in the formulation of a new direction in inter-American relations.[57]

A more influential voice in shaping Goodwin's speech was that of another of Kennedy's young White House staffers, Arthur Schlesinger Jr. A former

Harvard historian who had left the academy to become a special assistant to the president, Schlesinger agreed with the task force consultant Lincoln Gordon's view that Goodwin should focus on the message that the Alliance would aim to create "a decade of democratic progress, to demonstrate in this Hemisphere that economic growth, social equity, and the democratic development of societies can proceed hand-in-hand." He also believed that the rhetoric employed would be just as important as the content. In order to grab the attention of the hemisphere, he argued, Goodwin should "go in for a certain amount of high-flown corn," which would "thrill the audience south of the border, where meta-historical disquisitions are inordinately admired."[58]

The fruits of Goodwin's labors were unveiled on 13 March as Kennedy gathered the Latin American diplomatic corps, select members of Congress, and Vice President Lyndon Johnson together in the White House Rose Garden. The speech he delivered provided some substance to his promises of an Alliance for Progress, along with enough "highflown corn" to satisfy Schlesinger. In order to fulfill the region's potential and to protect it from outside threats, he announced, the Americas must unite in "a vast cooperative effort, unparalleled in magnitude and nobility of purpose." If this were done, the fundamental needs of the people—"homes, work and land, health and schools"—could be met, and all could "live out their lives in dignity and freedom." While no specific programs or targets were outlined, Kennedy spoke of greater political freedom and fundamental social change through the medium of land and tax reform.[59]

The Alliance would be given form and substance the following August at a special meeting of the OAS in Punta del Este, Uruguay. The fundamentals of the Charter of Punta del Este promised a cooperative framework in which the United States and all the nations of Latin America, barring Cuba, would contribute finances toward programs aimed at modernizing the economic, political, and social life of the hemisphere. Various targets, such as an annual 2.5 percent per capita GDP growth rate, were set, and the United States pledged to contribute $20 billion through public and private means over the course of ten years. Douglas Dillon, now secretary of the Treasury, represented the administration in Uruguay and outlined just how ambitious the Alliance would be. Echoing his president's rhetoric, Dillon promised that the Alliance could "modernize our economies and provide employment, [create a society] in which no man wants for food and all have access to education, . . . wipe out disease, . . . eliminate poverty, [and] do away with social and economic injustice." He continued: "All this and more is within our power if we dedicate the creative energies of free men to the cause of progress."[60]

For many of Kennedy's supporters, the Alliance for Progress speech marked a watershed in US–Latin American relations. For Goodwin, it signi-fied that the administration had placed itself firmly "on the side of change; become the ally of justified discontent, a spokesman and weapon for the oppressed and impoverished against . . . unjust social structures." For Wil-liam Rogers, who would work on aid policy for both Kennedy and Lyndon Johnson, the very phrase *Alliance for Progress* meant "the end of an era": "U.S. policy—in style and substance—would never be the same." Mann offered a differing interpretation. While agreeing with Rogers that the *style* of policy making had altered, he felt: "Aside from the rhetoric, all of the programs were anticipated and initiated by the Eisenhower administration." He may have been correct that Eisenhower's programs provided an initial framework for the Alliance for Progress, but it is also clear that Kennedy's approach differed significantly from that of his predecessor. Most obviously, the language and rhetoric used by Kennedy eclipsed that of the far-more-low-key Eisenhower administration. The inspirational phrases that accompanied the announce-ment of the Alliance captured the imagination and fit perfectly with Ken-nedy's image as a young, dynamic leader. The promises of hemispheric prosperity and cooperation made, as Rogers observed, "the steps taken before 1961, important as they were, seem grudging, improvised and inadequate." There were also practical differences. Specific economic targets were now being set, something Mann had specifically discouraged, and the sheer scale of promised funding made the $500 million Social Progress Trust Fund look trifling. The focus on promoting political freedom throughout the region—although not the freedom to be a Communist—also went beyond Eisenhow-er's rather tepid preference for democratic leaders and seemed to promise a new morality to US foreign policy.[61]

In short, Alliance rhetoric appeared to place development aid and inter-American cooperation at the forefront of the administration's global engage-ment instead of being a reluctant afterthought, introduced in response to unpleasant events. Much of the impetus for that shift can be traced to the Kennedy administration's more enthusiastic embrace of theories of modern-ization, popularized throughout the late 1950s by prominent political scien-tists such as Walt Rostow and Max Millikan. Essentially suggesting that all nations were at various stages along the same linear path of economic development, theories of modernization posited that the rate at which a nation developed, or modernized, could be increased rapidly by outside assistance in the form of investment and technical expertise. Furthermore, stages of growth were also linked to political developments, suggesting that nations would move toward stable democracies as their economic situation improved.[62] The primary appeal of modernization theory to policy makers was that it appeared to offer a solution that could combat the appeal of communism in Latin America without the need for a conventional military commitment.[63]

While Kennedy himself was too much of a realist to buy into the theory wholeheartedly, the possibilities obviously intrigued him, as evinced by the fact that he appointed Rostow as a campaign adviser and later head of the State Department's Policy Planning staff. In response, Rostow would pen Kennedy lengthy memos full of the language of modernization, identifying which nations were closest to the takeoff stage, and suggesting sound bites such as the "economic development decade." While Kennedy was not always entirely convinced by all Rostow's policy suggestions, describing some of them as "not merely unsound, but dangerously so," on the issue of foreign aid the former Massachusetts Institute of Technology professor was a valued adviser who played a substantial role in the drafting of the Alliance charter.[64]

Observing these developments from his insecure position in the State Department, Mann could be forgiven a few mixed feelings. Many of the core tenets of modernization theory had their intellectual roots in New Deal liberalism, and, in prioritizing investment in and cooperation with the nations of Latin America, the Alliance reflected positions that he, Dillon, Rubottom, and others had worked hard to advocate. Yet Mann also remained wary of the ambitious promises made by the Alliance and the reliance on what he viewed as oversimplified theoretical interpretations of complex economic and political issues. "This is my objection . . . to theorists," he later reflected. "They get a theory and then they just want to apply it across the board without reference to changes that take place here and abroad." The sheer scale of the transformation promised by the Alliance went far beyond the more modest policies Mann had supported during the previous administration.[65]

Undergirding the scope of the Alliance, then, was a sense that Eisenhower and his advisers had reacted unconvincingly to new challenges in a changing Cold War. The program was intended to stabilize the hemisphere and thus prevent further Communist infiltration, with Adolf Berle reminding Kennedy in April 1961 that Latin American policy had to be placed "on a cold war basis—thereby recognizing the actual situation."[66] The president required few reminders, however, and, alongside the economic and social programs, funding for military assistance increased by more than $200 million over Eisenhower's final budget. Particular importance was given to counterinsurgency training, with Cuba paramount in the administration's thinking. Nowhere was this clearer than in Kennedy's decision, despite misgivings, to continue planning for Operation Zapata, more commonly known as the Bay of Pigs invasion. CIA plans for the operation were almost fully formed by the time Kennedy came to office and called for a US-trained force of Cuban exiles to invade the island nation, at which point the population was expected to rise up against their supposed oppressor. The invasion was launched on 17 April 1961, with disastrous results. The massively outnumbered exile force was killed or captured almost immediately, and the Cuban people demonstrated no signs of taking to the streets. Kennedy refused air support for the supposedly covert operation, and the United States was made to look simultaneously aggressive and weak, with the Soviet Union condemning an imperialist invasion by "American hirelings."[67]

The failed invasion was a low point of Kennedy's presidency, although defenders of his reputation, such as Schlesinger, have tended to dismiss the decision to land American-armed and -trained Cuban exiles on the isolated beachhead as a CIA-driven holdover from the Eisenhower administration and a plan for which the new president had little enthusiasm.[68] It is a view with some merit, but it is also notable that one of the few dissenting voices regarding the plan was that of Mann, another of those holdovers from the previous presidency. In a memo to Secretary Rusk dated 15 February 1961, Mann argued that "it is unlikely that a popular uprising would take place in Cuba," meaning that US forces would be required for the operation to be a success. He elaborated his opinion of the effect of such an intervention: "At best our moral posture throughout the hemisphere would be impaired. At worst the effect on our position of hemispheric leadership would be catastrophic." After noting that Cuba currently posed no active threat to US national security sufficient to justify an invasion, he concluded: "It would not be in the national interest to proceed unilaterally to put this plan into execution."[69]

The memo caused a few ripples but made little real impact, "like a stone falling in water" its author recalled. After all, Mann was not one of "the best and brightest" but a temporary seat warmer while State Department posts were filled. In this instance, his issues with the operation were also more practical than principled. Castro was a Communist and therefore, in Mann's opinion, not covered by the doctrine of nonintervention. His detailed objections to the plan instead demonstrated his experience and knowledge in comparison to that of many of Kennedy's aides and advisers, recognizing the damage a failed operation would do to the administration's reputation and the ridiculousness of a plan that relied on "an uprising of the Cuban people, sort of 1776 style, where everybody grabbed a musket."[70] Mann's pragmatic assessment of the situation, weighing up the likelihood of success versus the damage caused by failure, contrasts to the near-delusional recommendations of the CIA and the acquiescence of the majority of the president's staff. It also left him isolated, and, finding little support for his views, he backed down and ultimately joined the unanimous vote in favor of the invasion. Unsurprisingly, this was a decision he would later claim to regret, albeit one that reflected his fundamental belief that his job required absolute loyalty to each president under whom he served, a position that would leave him in good standing in the next administration.[71]

Mann's objections to and eventual endorsement of the Bay of Pigs invasion marked his last significant contribution as assistant secretary of state in the Kennedy administration. On 29 April 1961, he was named the new ambassador to Mexico, and, in June, Robert Woodward, another career Foreign Service man, would be assigned to head ARA. Mann's move to Mexico signaled the end of an unhappy, if brief, period in his career. While the new administration planned its Latin American policy, the State Department had been largely sidelined. Dean Rusk had little interest in hemispheric affairs, leaving inexperienced young White House staffers and outside consultants to shape administration policy. To Mann, new advisers like Schlesinger, who believed that because of the Alliance for Progress "the slate [had] been wiped clean of past neglect and error" and envisaged a "middle class revolution" in nations that possessed little to no such social stratum, or Goodwin, who freely admitted to having never traveled farther south than Texas, seemed hopelessly naive. For their part, they saw Mann as tarred by his association with the Eisenhower administration, an unimaginative holdover to be ignored until a suitable replacement could be appointed.[72]

The State Department as a whole was struggling to make its voice heard in the early months of the Kennedy administration. Despite the plans for an invasion of Cuba being effectively an open secret, ARA had barely been consulted; Rusk and Mann had been privy to the plans, but that was as widely as the information was shared. One department official later recalled requesting to see the ARA files on the operation and being handed a stack of copies of the *Miami Herald*. "That's how we kept up with the planning," he was told. Wymberley Coerr, who oversaw the period between Mann's departure and Woodward's arrival, certainly felt sidelined. His bureau now exercised little influence over significant decisions yet would still take much of the public blame for disasters like the Bay of Pigs. One colleague recalls Coerr pointing out the window of his office at a small group of people in the parking lot, explaining that it was the Mann family departing for Mexico, and then sighing: "The lucky son of a bitch."[73]

Mexico

Mexico in 1961 was, as it remains at the time of writing, a crucial economic partner of the United States, with the United States providing around 60 percent of Mexican imports and receiving over 70 percent of its exports. The relationship was not without its tensions, however, and, as Mann took up residency in the embassy in Mexico City, it was clear that these went beyond traditional historical grievances and border disputes. While President Adolfo López Mateos of the ruling Partido Revolucionario Institucional (PRI) was described by State Department reports as "left-of-center" but not radical enough to alienate the more conservative elements of the party, concern was growing in Washington regarding the apparent Mexican tolerance for political extremism and the potential for such indulgence to make it "a major center for the international Communist movement in Latin America." López Mateos did little to assuage these fears, often joking that he was more scared of the Catholic Church as he at least had the option of cracking down on Communists. The desire to demonstrate that Mexico could not be bullied into compliance by Washington also caused particular tension in international organizations like the OAS and the United Nations, where Mexico regularly declined to support US initiatives and ignored pressure to sever relations with Cuba. Mexican economic policies also caused consternation in Washington, with the Commerce Department believing that the PRI's "Mexicanization" of many industries stopped just short of expropriation and that its tariff policies resulted in "excessive protectionism."[74]

Despite these concerns, the Kennedy administration viewed Mexico as a potential showcase for the Alliance for Progress. Stable politically, the country had already undergone a period of tumultuous land reform and seemed to offer a relatively risk-free climate for private investment, provided that corporations were willing to undertake joint ventures with the PRI. Accordingly, it received a significant amount of Alliance funding. From May 1961 to March 1962, for example, assistance from the United States totaled around $525 million through a combination of loans and grants. The US Agency for International Development (USAID) calculated that aid during Eisenhower's final year in office had totaled around $32 million. The position of ambassador to Mexico was, then, a prominent diplomatic posting, and Mann's appointment allowed the Kennedy administration to strengthen relations with America's closest neighbor by sending an experienced and well-respected envoy to Mexico City. It also allowed Kennedy to remove a prominent link to his predecessor's policies and appoint his own man to run ARA. Happy to be free from an executive branch bureaucracy in which he retained little influence, Mann would throw himself into his new role with gusto, proving to be one of the most successful ambassadors in the history of US-Mexican relations, and earning a return to the corridors of power in the process.[75]

Despite his years of experience, Mann could have been forgiven some trepidation regarding his new posting, with the *Waco Herald-Tribune* noting that he was the first Texan ever to be appointed ambassador to Mexico and that, owing to cultural touchstones like the Alamo and continuing border disputes, for decades it had appeared that "no Texan could or ever would be named to that country." Fortunately for Mann, he had other factors in his favor. His bilingual upbringing, his record in the later years of the Eisenhower administration, and friendships with Mexican politicians, in particular Foreign Minister Manuel Tello, that he had developed in Washington all served to make his appointment relatively uncontroversial. The *Mexican American Review*, for instance, made Mann's arrival its May cover story, praising the appointment of an ambassador who was "sympathetic to [Mexicans'] way of thinking" and reserving special praise for the fact that he spoke "perfect Spanish."[76]

One of Mann's most important tasks as ambassador was to advise the White House on how best to manage Mexico's position on Cuba and apparent intransigence regarding US embargo initiatives. While certainly not approving of López Mateos's stance, Mann advised Washington not to push the Mexican president too hard, lest the effort result in a Perón-style blow-back. Writing in December 1961, he warned that the best the United States could hope for from Mexico in an upcoming meeting of foreign ministers vote on sanctions against Cuba was an abstention. This should not be a cause for concern, he cautioned, and "should not be interpreted as Mexican Gov-ernment sympathy for Castro regime." Rather, it was a demonstration of Mexico's desire to plot a course independent from either Cold War bloc. Expressing public disapproval would only stir resentment and possibly push López Mateos further to the left of his party, he advised; it would be best to keep any criticisms private. Similarly, he cautioned that economic disputes also be kept as low-key as possible, suggesting that pressure could be exerted through delays or cancellations of aid or loans, as long as this was done subtly and in private. The Mexican government, Mann believed, fully understood the use of leverage in this manner and was surprised that the United States did not follow this course more often. What had to go, he argued, was the public blustering that "belonged to another age" and would only embolden the PRI's more radical elements.[77]

Just as he had during his time in El Salvador, Mann repeatedly cautioned his embassy staff to steer clear of local politics, reminding one junior officer to "be like Caesar's wife, above suspicion on intervention in . . . internal affairs." His attitude did not reflect support for the Mexican electoral system, however. In one notable telegram to Washington, he described the PRI's political system as falling short of a dictatorship "only because of the consti-tutional requirement that elected office holders change positions periodically, as in a game of 'musical chairs,'" and referred disparagingly to a social system that kept vast amounts of the population "in a state of grinding poverty which has many of the earmarks of peonage." Such comments were only ever meant for Washington, however; around his Mexican colleagues, Mann appears to have been a consummate diplomat.[78]

His quiet effectiveness was reflected in the almost uniformly positive media coverage that Mann received during his first year in Mexico City. His arrival had been greeted warmly by conservative publications such as *Excel-sior* and the more liberal papers like *El Popular,* which both praised him for possessing a detailed understanding of the economic problems of Latin America. Mann would continue to be praised north of the border as well. In July, the *Houston Post* commented that he had "turned Texanhood to his advantage" by displaying a sensitivity and understanding of the Mexican people and Mexican culture that had been beyond his predecessor, the more boisterous Robert C. Hill. Proving that awareness of Mann's popularity spread beyond the borders of Texas, in November and December 1961 the *Chicago Tribune* published a number of articles addressing US-Mexican relations. Mann and his Mexican counterpart, Antonio Carrillo Flores, were credited with relations between their nations reaching "a better level than they have been at in years," with Mann given particular praise for having "dedicated himself to upsetting the communist myth that anyone who is against Castro must be against democracy." The *Tribune* articles portrayed Mann as popular with López Mateos and firm friends with Foreign Minister Tello and noted that, in terms of experience in Latin American affairs, he was "an unusual career officer": "There is probably no-one like him in the diplomatic service today."[79] Placed in historical context, Mann happened to be ambassador at a time of relatively low tension in US-Mexican relations, but this does not mean that such praise was undeserved. His time in Mexico was one of the high points of a lengthy career and would reflect the fact that his diplomatic abilities probably outstripped his aptitude for policy making.

Two major events in 1962 would alter the nature of the US-Mexican relationship, creating an atmosphere of genuine cooperation that resulted in the resolution of a decades-long dispute and one of the crowning achievements of Mann's career. The first occurred in June, when Kennedy made an official visit to Mexico that proved to be a great success. "Mexico Acclaims Kennedy on Visit; 1,000,000 Cheer," announced the front page of the *New York Times* on 30 June. "Visit Unmarred by Any Signs of Hostility" was the *Washington Post*'s slightly less enthusiastic interpretation, although both papers described the vast cheering crowds that showered the Kennedys with confetti and the delighted president taking ninety minutes to travel the nine-mile route from the airport, admiring the posters featuring his own image that were "seemingly everywhere."[80] On 1 July, Kennedy wrote to his ambassador, congratulating him for "bringing our relations with Mexico to a point where a successful visit was possible." Mann's response was equally warm, informing the president that the welcome he had received was "unprecedented." Mann was not just attempting to flatter; years later he would recall: "I've never seen anybody make such an impression on the people of another country—anytime, anywhere."[81]

The most tangible result of Kennedy's visit was a joint communiqué issued with López Mateos that promised a "new era" of friendship. While the

President John F. Kennedy and First Lady Jacqueline Kennedy attend a luncheon at Hotel María Isabel during their visit to Mexico City, 30 June 1962. Thomas Mann is second from left. (Robert Knudsen, White House Photographs, John F. Kennedy Presidential Library and Museum, Boston.)

statement contained the expected declarations that both nations were committed to the Alliance for Progress and the principles of freedom and democracy, there were also pledges to address more practical matters. Two major disputes still existed between the nations, the Chamizal border question and a dispute over the salinity levels of the Colorado River, and the communiqué promised that solutions would be found to both. Utilizing the goodwill engendered by Kennedy's visit, Mann would spend the remainder of his time in Mexico trying to do just that.[82]

One other event in 1962 made Mann's task easier, the Cuban Missile Crisis. The drama of the thirteen-day showdown over the placement of Soviet missiles in Cuba served, according to Mann, to ease Mexican suspicions regarding American anticommunism. Once López Mateos and Tello were convinced that the crisis was a "bona fide thing, that we were in danger," Mann recalled, they were happy to support US actions. The crisis not only suggested that not all American concerns about communism were a result of national paranoia; it also "restored respect for the ability of the US to act in

President John F. Kennedy visits Columna de la Independencia, Mexico City, 30 June 1962. Thomas Mann and Mexican ambassador to the United States, Antonio Carrillo Flores, are to the president's right. (Robert Knudsen, White House Photographs, John F. Kennedy Presidential Library and Museum, Boston.)

a crisis." Furthermore, events in October also demonstrated the esteem in which Mann was held by Latin American experts in Washington. Edwin Martin, assistant secretary for inter-American affairs during the crisis, recalled: "ExCom had discussed at some length, drawing on his [Mann's] long experience in the region, the idea of sending him as a secret emissary to see Castro and try to persuade him that letting the Soviets set up missile bases in his country was a suicidal act." Ultimately, the idea was dropped, but the fact that Mann was considered a leading expert, possibly able to negotiate face-to-face with Castro, is not insignificant. Kennedy's younger staffers may have seen him as something of a relic, but, at higher levels, it appears that he was still held in notable esteem.[83]

Utilizing the cooperative atmosphere engendered by the Kennedy visit and the peaceful resolution of the missile crisis, Mann played a leading role in mediating the two major sources of conflict between Mexico and the United States. Regarding the first, the dumping of highly saline drainage into the Colorado River by American farmers, which breached a 1944 treaty and made the water practically unusable once it flowed into Mexico, Mann was able secure only a partial solution.[84] Believing that Washington was putting off a resolution and allowing the dispute to escalate into a crisis, Mann continually warned that Mexico had a strong legal case and that the entire situation was damaging the image of the United States, providing ammunition for "communists and opportunists" to foment unrest. It was time, he believed, to face the fact that the "salinity problem was not created by an act of God" and to take responsibility while an out-of-court solution was still possible.[85] No permanent agreement was reached during Mann's time in Mexico, but negotiations began at his prompting, and enough progress was made to forestall legal action. Much of his time and attention would instead be taken up by the second guarantee made by the joint communiqué of June 1962—to seek a resolution to the Chamizal border dispute. On this matter, he would achieve far greater results.[86]

The Chamizal border dispute was caused by a shifting of the path of the Rio Grande that by the end of the nineteenth century had added around 598 acres to the north bank near the El Paso–Ciudad Juarez border. The tract of land, known as *El Chamizal,* had been awarded to Mexico by a special commission in 1910, but the Taft administration refused to accept the validity of the ruling or cede any territory. When Mann arrived in Mexico, the Chamizal dispute was, in the words of Ed Martin, "one of the oldest unsettled matters in U.S. diplomatic history." It was also a problem that was familiar to Mann as, during his time in the Truman Administration, he had taken a keen interest in resolving the long-standing dispute, even going so far as to visit El Paso to explore possible solutions and gauge the feelings of local residents. When neither the US Boundary and Water Commission nor the Mexican government expressed any great enthusiasm for negotiations, the issue was dropped, but Mann had nonetheless gained a great deal of insight into the logistics that would be required for an agreement to be reached.

Thus, when Presidents Kennedy and López Mateos authorized Mann and Tello to begin seeking a permanent solution in June 1962, the two set about working "quietly and . . . without any publicity" to see whether such an agreement was possible.[87]

The story of the negotiating process that followed is long and convoluted, but the basic form of the agreement was presented to Mann by the State Department in August 1962, and involved rechanneling the Rio Grande to something close to its 1848 position. As part of the deal, the United States would gain a portion of the nearby Cordova Island, for which Mexico would receive compensation, although the cost of rechanneling the river and relocating citizens would be shared. Working from that initial proposal, most of the subsequent discussions were conducted between Mann and Tello. Described by Mann as "tortuous and difficult," the negotiations nonetheless soon yielded results. By February 1963 the ambassador and the foreign minister had agreed on exactly where the border should be, and the following month produced a joint statement that suggested a full agreement was nearly at hand. Discussions were nearly derailed on multiple occasions, but each time were wrenched back on track, largely due to the efforts of the two negotiators. Eventually, López Mateos appeared on television on 18 July 1963 to announce that an agreement had been reached. The broadcast was met with joy throughout Mexico, with politicians across the political spectrum expressing their delight, media outlets producing triumphal documentaries and publications, and the Catholic Church ordering every bell in Mexico City to be rung in celebration. After one last wrangle over the exact wording of the agreement, on 27 August 1963 Mann was issued full presidential authority to sign the initial convention on the Chamizal. Fittingly, it was he and Foreign Minister Tello who did so two days later.[88]

While many individuals were involved in the lengthy process, without Mann's presence as the lead negotiator for the United States, an agreement would not have been possible or at least would have been much longer in coming. Embarrassed by his nation's failure to accept the finding of the 1911 arbitration, Mann sought a fair and legal compromise, a process enabled by his solid and respectful working relationship with Tello. Possibly even more important than his relationship with Tello was his background as a border-dwelling Texan. His own experience of being raised in a border town gave him an inherent understanding of the feelings of those citizens who would be affected by the shifting of the Rio Grande and meant that he knew exactly

From left to right, Mexican senator Manuel Moreno Sánchez, Secretary of Foreign Affairs Manuel Tello Baurraud, and Thomas Mann, 25 May 1962. Mann and Tello's relationship was crucial in arriving at the Chamizal settlement. (Courtesy of the Texas Collection, Baylor University.)

whom to talk to, whom to convince, and whom to flatter in order to gain a groundswell of public support for the agreement. In July 1962 and February 1963, he visited El Paso, giving heartfelt presentations to the Chamber of Commerce and the International City Association in which he convincingly argued not only that his proposed agreement was the right thing to do but also that it would be in the long-term interests of the city to reach a solution. He also met with those residents who would be affected by the relocation, most of whom were Mexican Americans, many speaking little English. With a group of "two or three hundred" he discussed his proposal entirely in Spanish for over two hours, later noting the result: "We had more than 50 percent of the people with us . . . and in the town of El Paso itself, I think a much larger percentage." With the majority of El Paso in favor, Mann sought out Governor John Connally to secure his support before touring the major newspaper offices of Dallas, Houston, and Waco to bring them on board.

His status as the first Texan to serve as ambassador to Mexico undeniably made the process far smoother on both sides of the border. "Once Texas was convinced that this was the right thing to do," he later recalled, "there was no difficulty up here in the Senate."[89]

The settling of the Chamizal dispute stands as a testament to the success of Mann's period as US ambassador to Mexico. He and Tello achieved in one year what had previously seemed impossible for fifty. As 1963 drew to a close, relations between the United States and its closest southern neighbor were healthy, seemingly demonstrating the developmental and cooperative potential of President Kennedy's Alliance for Progress. The United States had recently agreed two $20 million loans, one for a low-cost housing project and another to enable Mexican banks to provide loans to farmers, a project Mann had been closely involved with. The United States had also provided nearly $1 billion worth of financing in public and private loans to stabilize the Mexican economy, and one State Department report estimated that annual trade and tourism resulted in a Mexican net gain of $500 million. The final details of the Chamizal agreement were almost complete, with four thousand people due to be relocated in a project that would cost almost $30 million, and the dispute over water salinity levels had descended from crisis levels to a constructive dialogue. Kennedy's personal popularity had also been demonstrated by his triumphal visit to Mexico City and the breakthrough that this had enabled in the Chamizal dispute. Nonetheless, the continued concern with potential Communist subversion that permeated Kennedy's administration was also reflected in the worries regarding the Mexican attitude toward Cuba, a diplomatic sore spot that would become increasingly troublesome in future years. In Mexico and beyond, US policy continued to be subject to the needs of the global Cold War, producing tensions and contradictions that threatened to undermine promising development efforts.[90]

By late 1963, such long-term problems were of little concern to Thomas Mann. Having experienced two presidential transitions, served as ambassador in two different countries, and helped push US policy to a place where commitment to Latin American development was a central tenet, he planned to retire. His tenure in Mexico had been broadly successful and would be a fitting end, so he believed, to a twenty-year career in government service. He had first sought to retire in 1962 but had been persuaded by Kennedy to stay and negotiate the Chamizal agreement. Having done so, he was looking forward to seeing out his remaining time in Mexico before entering 1964 as a private citizen with the Chamizal settlement a fitting denouement to a distinguished government career. Like so many others, however, his hopes and plans would be thrown into chaos by an assassin's bullet fired in Dallas on 22 November 1963 and then a phone call from Lyndon Johnson. The period of his greatest influence was yet to come.[91]

2

A New Deal for the New Frontier

From Kennedy to Johnson

On 22 November 1963, President John Fitzgerald Kennedy was murdered in Dallas, Texas, transforming the political landscape of the country in an instant. Vice President Lyndon Baines Johnson was traveling in the same ill-fated motorcade in his home state and was due to host the president and first lady at his Texas ranch before returning to Washington. Instead, a man who had been forced to watch from the political sidelines for the previous three years would be informed in a heavily guarded waiting room of the Parkland Memorial Hospital that he was now the president of the United States of America. While Johnson would soon be reassuring the nation that he sought continuity with his predecessor's policies and political agenda, the impact of such an abrupt and brutal change of leadership would nonetheless be widely felt. It was certainly significant for Thomas Mann, promptly recalled to Washington in December 1963 and appointed assistant secretary of state for inter-American affairs for the second time in his career, his plans for a quiet life interrupted because, as he put it: "Mr Johnson called me up and I didn't have much choice." The new president would provide his fellow Texan with more authority and power than ever before, but that power would come at a cost as Mann became caught in the political turmoil that followed Kennedy's assassination and embroiled in the contest to claim ownership of the JFK legacy.[1]

Johnson inherited a much-publicized development program that was falling far short of its ambitious targets and an isolated but belligerent and worrisome representative of global communism perched off the Florida coast, resulting in an approach to hemispheric affairs that struggled to balance idealistic visions of modernization with security-based fears. Johnson, a disciple of Franklin Roosevelt's and a man whose often-brash personal and political style contrasted starkly with that of his more polished predecessor, would struggle to convince many of Kennedy's former aides that he had anything to offer other than a dismantling of the more idealistic elements of Kennedy's policies. Early clashes with some of those Kennedy staffers would set much of the tone for the months that followed, and the degree to which Johnson and Mann maintained continuity with existing policy remains a point of debate among historians. Hence, this chapter is not an analysis of policy implementation in Latin America but a study of the transition of power from John Kennedy to Lyndon Johnson as it related to hemispheric affairs. The manner in which conceptions of inter-American policy developed throughout Kennedy's administration and how those conceptions affected interpretations of both Johnson's handling of the transition and his appointment of Mann as his key Latin American adviser are crucial to understanding subsequent events. Internal bureaucratic disputes, struggles with the press, and personal vendettas made for a turbulent period, the ripples from which would destabilize Johnson's presidency for years to come.[2]

Kennedy's Alliance

Despite the fanfare and bold transformative rhetoric accompanying its launch, the Alliance for Progress was a program beset by problems long before Lyndon Johnson entered the Oval Office; warning signs were visible before Kennedy had even delivered his inaugural address. The task force for Latin America established by the president-elect in 1960 spent much time considering various hemispheric problems and the challenges that the Alliance would face in trying to solve them, but significantly less thought was given to the practicalities of how such a program might be directed and implemented. Indeed, bureaucratic organization was a widespread issue in the early days of Kennedy's administration, with National Security Adviser McGeorge Bundy offering a variety of suggestions in May 1961 to address the "problem of management" that had led to press reports of "chaos in the White House." Bureaucratic squabbles and structural disorganization would hamper the program for much of its existence.[3]

From the start, it was never clear who took ultimate responsibility for the day-to-day running of the basic functions of the Alliance. Robert Woodward, who had replaced Mann in 1961 as head of the State Department's ARA, was responsible for coordinating relations with the rest of the hemisphere, theoretically including the Alliance for Progress. The Foreign Assistance Act of 1961, however, created a new department to oversee all US foreign aid programs—USAID. Given that the Alliance consisted largely of development aid, it also conceivably fell under the purview of USAID director Fowler Hamilton, particularly with regard to loan authorizations. Further complicating the picture was Kennedy's decision to name Teodoro Moscoso, a prominent Puerto Rican politician known for creating "Operation Bootstrap," as coordinator of the Alliance.[4] Moscoso may have been titular head of the program, but his relatively lowly status in relation to Woodward and Hamilton meant that he lacked the clout to stamp his authority on the foreign policy establishment effectively. The fundamental weakness of his position, as the historian Jeffrey Taffet has observed, was that he "could not compel other U.S. policymakers to do anything."[5]

Members of Kennedy's staff who had served on the Latin American task force but were not part of USAID or ARA often exacerbated the bureaucratic confusion, feeling that it was *they* who had formulated the president's approach to Latin America and that therefore *they* should play a primary role in implementing it. Among those who could be considered Kennedy's New Frontiersmen rather than part of the established foreign policy bureaucracy, there was a high concentration of idealists and true believers in the modernizing potential of the Alliance for Progress. Walt Rostow published his landmark work of modernization theory *The Stages of Economic Growth* in 1960 and was brought into the administration as deputy national security adviser the following January. The prominent Puerto Rican politicians Luis Muños Marín, Arturo Morales-Carrión, and Moscoso were all given influential positions by Kennedy, and, of his White House staff, it was Arthur Schlesinger Jr. and Richard Goodwin who would have the most regular involvement in implementing the Alliance.[6]

Schlesinger and Goodwin in particular viewed themselves as representatives of the president's true convictions, contending with a stuffy and out-of-touch State Department consisting mostly of leftovers from the Eisenhower era. A gifted historian, Schlesinger had previously advised Adlai Stevenson during his 1956 presidential campaign and left a professorship at Harvard University to join Kennedy's staff, having already won a Pulitzer Prize for his monograph *The Age of Jackson*. Goodwin had graduated from Harvard Law School and gained prominence clerking for Supreme Court justice Felix Frankfurter. Both men were talented, intelligent and prominent in Washington

Assistant Special Counsel to the President Richard Goodwin, 25 January 1961. (Abbie Rowe, White House Photographs, John F. Kennedy Presidential Library and Museum, Boston.)

President John F. Kennedy with Special Assistant to the President Arthur M. Schlesinger Jr., 26 July 1962. (Cecil Stoughton, White House Photographs, John F. Kennedy Presidential Library and Museum, Boston.)

social circles and believed that Kennedy's election heralded a liberal renaissance that would transform the execution of both domestic and foreign policy. Both were appointed as special assistants to the president and subsequently became key members of what McGeorge Bundy termed *the irregulars,* with wide-ranging responsibilities that included writing speeches, maintaining relations with extragovernment contacts, and drafting policy proposals.[7]

Predictably, the irregulars were not always welcomed with open arms by the foreign policy establishment. What for some was youthful vigor and enthusiasm was for others arrogance and inexperienced meddling. Hence, in June 1961, before the Alliance's charter had even been signed, President Kennedy received a lengthy memo from Schlesinger. Having spoken to Morales-Carrión about his recent appointment to the State Department, Schlesinger had apparently learned that the Foreign Service officers based in ARA were highly resentful of the interference of outsiders in their field. "Their attitudes are entrenched," Schlesinger declared, "[and are] predominantly out of sympathy with the *Alianza*." ARA contained men with "no joy, no purpose, no drive," Morales-Carrión had told him, and they openly discriminated against those whom they viewed as intruders. Schlesinger suggested that the president inform Woodward that he expected "ARA to overflow with affirmative commitment to the *Alianza*" and that any who disagreed should be moved to an alternative posting.[8]

In his memo, Schlesinger did not consider that the attitudes and behavior of himself, Goodwin, or Morales-Carrión might have contributed to the tension with ARA. He largely viewed the State Department as one of several obstacles to efficient policy making, noting in his diary that executive branch bureaucracy possessed "an infinite capacity to dilute, delay, obstruct, resist and sabotage presidential purposes." He was most likely referring to the hierarchical, military-style bureaucracy implemented by Dwight Eisenhower, which certainly possessed the capacity to smother creativity via a seemingly endless process of consultation and reporting. However, the most notoriously stifling element of that bureaucracy, the Operations Coordinating Board, had been abolished by Kennedy shortly after taking office, and other observers in fact found themselves complaining of a lack of structure and boundaries in the Kennedy White House. Bundy implored the president, "Close the back door to your office," while one congressman likened Goodwin's constant interference in Latin American policy to a "kid playing with fire" and accused him of attempting to run a "one-man State Department." In an effort to defuse tensions between the White House and Foggy Bottom, Kennedy appointed Goodwin to be Woodward's deputy in November 1961. According to Goodwin, this was to break the inertia of the State Department and provide the president with a direct line into ARA. While this may have been true in part, it was also designed to keep Goodwin on a tighter leash as it had not taken the two special assistants long to gain reputations as "crazy nuts on Latin America" who often stepped beyond the bounds of their authority.[9]

The divisions within the administration went beyond the formulation of policy in Washington, also stretching to Mexico City, where Thomas Mann resided in the US embassy. For some of Kennedy's New Frontiersmen, Mann was part of the bloc of out-of-touch Foreign Service officers who impeded true hemispheric progress. Deputy Assistant Secretary of State Arturo Morales-Carrión, for example, wrote an angry memo to his boss in April 1963 after he had read one of Mann's regular updates from Mexico City. Morales-Carrión believed that the reports contained an "undercurrent of self-righteousness," blamed Mexico for all problems between the nations, and failed to give enough weight to the history of US-Mexican interactions. Mann could undoubtedly be blunt on occasion and viewed the primary task of an ambassador as furthering the interests of the United States, but he was also well versed in Mexican history and had close relations with most of the senior members of the Mexican government. Considering his successes in resolving long-standing disputes with his Mexican counterparts, Morales-Carrión's criticisms seem at least somewhat exaggerated.[10]

Morales-Carrión's displeasure may have been related to Mann's perhaps inadvisable lack of interest in ingratiating himself with those Kennedy aides who had dismissed him as an irrelevance during the early days of the administration. Responding to suggestions that there were a disproportionate number of Texans in the Mexico City embassy, for instance, Mann made his feelings clear to Woodward. "This charge reminds me of a yarn about a Texas boy who came home from school in New York complaining to his father that Texans were considered uncultured and disliked," he wrote. "The father's advice was 'son, don't educate them; let them die in ignorance.'" Hence, when Richard Goodwin visited Mexico and wished to dine with some contacts Mann believed to be of the extreme left at the embassy, he was given short shrift. "Not in my house," he remarked before informing Goodwin that Mexico City had plenty of good restaurants.[11]

Back in Washington, an unimpressed Schlesinger and Goodwin began to take note of any evidence of Mann's apparent conservatism and lack of commitment to Alliance goals. In September 1962, for instance, Mann transmitted a lengthy criticism of the US Congress for attempting to enforce punitive actions in cases of expropriation of US investments, arguing that flexibility in such matters was preferable. The telegram had one sentence underlined by Schlesinger wherein Mann had favorably compared the use of economic leverage to that of military strength and was passed along to Goodwin. Another report in which Mann supported one of his embassy staff member's conclusions that a certain book, critical of aspects of US foreign policy, should not be distributed throughout the Americas as part of the programs of the US Information Agency (USIA) was similarly annotated and forwarded to Goodwin. Telegrams that did not support Schlesinger's view of Mann as ignorant, intolerant, and conservative were ignored. When Mann wrote in April 1962 that he was "concerned about the extent to which our visa procedures are alienating left-wing non-communists and liberal elements in Latin America" and "appalled" at how often visas were denied to left-leaning Mexicans, suggesting that the problem required "high-level attention," no notes were made, and the telegram sat buried in Schlesinger's files. While Mann remained in Mexico, this petty squabbling on both sides was relatively harmless, but it sowed the seeds for a much more damaging rift that would emerge more fully in time.[12]

While divisions within the executive branch in Washington hindered efforts to get the Alliance off the ground, in truth even the most organized and efficient bureaucracy would have found it impossible to fulfill all the promises made at Punta del Este. The language of the Alliance's founding spoke of wiping out disease, eliminating poverty, and eradicating social and economic injustice. By announcing that the program would have an initial ten-year life span, it was also implied that all this could be achieved within a decade, largely through grants, loans, and technical cooperation. Less clear was how the Alliance would further the cause of democracy, but this too was promised, along with the 2.5 percent per capita economic growth rate target that became an increasingly burdensome yardstick by which to measure progress. Increased economic production was a major challenge in itself, but the additional social and political targets demonstrated the scope of the ambitions established by the Alliance. As Chester Bowles, who briefly served as Kennedy's undersecretary of state, gloomily noted: "What we are asking is that the philosophy of Jefferson and the social reforms of FDR be telescoped into a few years in Latin America."[13]

Sure enough, attempts to foster social and political development would continually be undermined by the desire for stability and the need to avoid the embarrassment of another Cuba. As the Bay of Pigs fiasco so dramatically demonstrated, Cold War security concerns would be no less important under

Kennedy than they had been under his predecessor. Rapid political, social, or economic change could mean uncertainty easily exploited by extremists, and development would therefore have to be carefully balanced with stability and the prevention of Communist gains in the hemisphere. To do so, the United States had to maintain leverage by retaining a large degree of control over how Alliance funds were allocated and spent, severely undermining claims that it would be a truly multilateral undertaking. One obvious result was that Cuba was not part of the Alliance; indeed, covert programs such as Operation Mongoose, the CIA program of covert action in Cuba, repeatedly sought to eliminate or at least destabilize Castro's regime. In addition, aid was provided to such repressive but stable regimes as that of Luis Anastasio Somoza in Nicaragua, tarnishing the Alliance's commitment to democratic progress. The failure of the administration to overcome these contradictions was noted by Morales-Carrión in April 1962 when he argued that the majority of Latin Americans viewed the Alliance only as a US lending program, just on a greater scale than in previous years. Unable to successfully associate broader Alliance goals with disparate Latin American nationalism, the United States was viewed only as a banker, albeit an increasingly generous one. "We have yet to see a charismatic banker," Morales-Carrión observed drily.[14]

In order to generate momentum, the Alliance also required quick results, leading to a focus on short-term, high-visibility projects that could be presented as evidence of success. This problem was exacerbated by the need to go to Congress for foreign aid authorizations. The relevant committees included skeptics like Representative Otto Passman (D-LA), who once declared that his "only pleasure" in life was "to kick the shit out of the foreign aid program" and regularly used his position as chair of the Foreign Operations Subcommittee to do so. Hence, the need to have tangible results became ever more pressing. Economic growth rather than economic development became the priority. The kind of diversification and construction projects required for long-term change became harder to justify than short-term measures to try and reach the growth targets established in the Alliance charter.[15]

Even attempts to stimulate short-term growth were hampered by the predominance of the one-size-fits-all approach that governed many of the Alliance initiatives. Some of Walt Rostow's more ambitious ideas were mocked as unrealistic "bean soup" among certain colleagues, but his thoughts on modernization had nonetheless helped lay the foundations for the Alliance. His view of development posited that all nations were essentially on the same

economic path and that, broadly speaking, the same techniques could therefore be applied to speed them along. Combined with the common tendency
of many US policy makers to view Latin America as a relatively homogenous
region, this meant that little thought was given to country-specific development plans until individual nations submitted their own proposals, a process
that in some cases took years.[16]

The identification by Alliance planners of problems commonplace
throughout much of Latin America reflected a relatively superficial understanding of the challenges facing individual countries but was not wholly
inaccurate. Political instability was common, and some of the less turbulent
nations were effectively one-party states, such as Mexico or Bolivia, or dictatorships in all but name, such as Guatemala. While the late 1950s had seen
the emergence of successful democratic leaders like Rómulo Betancourt in
Venezuela and José Figueres in Costa Rica, such gains were always precarious; the period 1930–1965 saw more than a hundred illegal or unscheduled
changes of heads of state. Many countries failed to manage a single successful
constitutional transition of power in that period, and the first six years of the
Alliance alone saw the governments of eight nations overturned by force. For
a program that aimed to work with representatives of nineteen separate countries and establish plans for national development, this was not an encouraging record.[17]

Directly related to political instability in many Latin American countries was the struggle of governments to collect taxes effectively, resulting in
limited provisions for education and health care and widespread illiteracy.
The region as a whole in the 1960s was also experiencing a remarkable rate of
population growth, averaging 2.9 percent annually, compared to 1.4 percent
for industrialized nations. This growth rate also outstripped regions of comparable wealth and education levels, with Africa averaging 2.4 percent and
Southern Asia 2.5 percent. The speed of the population growth not only
meant that Latin America needed to achieve an economic growth rate of
5.4 percent to meet its per capita target but also hampered many Alliance
projects. For example, the 1960s saw more than 150,000 new hospital beds
created as a result of Alliance initiatives, but the ratio of beds per one thousand people fell from 3.2 to 3.[18]

While many of these problems were felt to varying degrees throughout
Latin America, the countries involved in the Alliance remained unique. Differences in history, geography, and culture abounded, as did varying political

systems, including issues of land distribution, taxation, and the racial and ethnic makeup of populations. Many countries may have shared similar problems, but potential solutions required detailed knowledge of regional, national, and local characteristics. This was distinctly lacking in early Alliance planning.

Unsurprisingly, it did not take long for Kennedy's Latin American policies to attract criticism. An editorial in *Vision* magazine marking the first year of the Alliance noted that "hyperbole has been the rule" but that there had been few concrete achievements. The *New York Times* was slightly more generous, pointing out that the program was being "smothered in pessimism" after too brief a period, but it also blamed this on the overly hyped launch of the program, which had raised "exaggerated hopes" as to what could be achieved in such a short space of time. The editorial in the *Times* seemed to confirm what Mann had warned of in the late 1950s. By promising so much, expectations had been raised both north and south of the Rio Grande; when those expectations were not met, disappointment was inevitable.[19]

Criticism of Kennedy's policies was not due wholly to overly ambitious targets as, even had hopes been set a little lower, the Alliance's record would have been disappointing. The lack of strong leadership in Washington resulted in delays of loans, and money that had been authorized by Congress was often not allocated to Alliance programs. Between March 1961 and January 1964, $828 million authorized by the legislative branch remained unutilized, contributing to Congress's decision to slash $1 billion from Kennedy's final foreign aid request. In 1962, the per capita GDP growth rate for the region was somewhere between 0.5 and 0.9 percent, nowhere near the target of 2.5 percent. Private US investment in Latin America—so important to the success of the Alliance yet regularly downplayed in administration rhetoric—had declined by $49 million during the first nine months of 1962. No matter how many roads or schools were built with Alliance funds, for Congress, for the press, and for the public, those figures were damning. For a politician as shrewd as John Kennedy, more of the same was intolerable, and, during the second half of his presidency, Latin American policy experienced a notable reorientation of priorities.[20]

Kennedy made his first major change in April 1962, replacing Woodward as head of ARA with Edwin Martin. Admitting that the Alliance had resided in a state of "creative chaos," the president relocated Martin from his position as assistant secretary of state for economic affairs and made him, in the words of Tad Szulc of the *New York Times,* "the closest thing to a 'boss' of Latin American policy the . . . administration has had." Martin was an experienced Foreign Service officer with a reputation as an efficient administrator, and his appointment was a clear signal from JFK that the Alliance needed more direction. His appointment also reflected the resurgent influence of the professional wing of the policy-making bureaucracy over the irregulars, reducing Goodwin's authority to the extent that he felt "forced" to transfer to the Peace Corps in early 1963.[21]

Martin's first priority was reinvigorating hemispheric private investment. Kennedy had long been aware that public funds alone would not be enough for the Alliance to be successful, but the administration had done little to court private enterprise. Where the Eisenhower administration had in many cases been too quick to support US corporate interests, consultations between the government and potential investors under Kennedy were often run by Goodwin, who had little enthusiasm for the task and did not disguise it well. This miscalculation on Kennedy's part was particularly damaging in an investment climate where memories of Castro's nationalization of the sugar industry in Cuba were still fresh and American businesses sought reassurances that their investments would have some measure of protection.[22]

The administration's apparent neglect of private industry was highlighted in February 1962 when a dispute over the nationalization of an IT&T affiliate in Brazil attracted congressional attention. Arguing that the State Department's conciliatory position would "stimulate expropriation in other countries by dissident groups," Senator Bourke Hickenlooper (R-IA) successfully attached an amendment to the 1962 Foreign Appropriations Act that required the suspension of all US aid if a nation illegally expropriated the property of North American investors. Although Arthur Schlesinger was dismayed, warning of a "neo-Republican" resurgence that would return to the "failed policies" of the Eisenhower era, even he admitted that the capacity of public funding alone to support development had been overemphasized.[23] Under Martin, Alliance rhetoric increasingly tried to balance the need for public funds with private, and, in his 1963 Message to Congress on Defense and Assistance Programs, Kennedy acknowledged a desperate need "to increase the role of private investment and other non-Federal resources in assisting developing nations." Efforts to bring the business community in from the cold reached a peak in September 1963 when the administration supported David Rockefeller's formation of the Business Group for Latin

America (BGLA). The BGLA brought together prominent investors with interests in Latin America to consult regularly with administration officials. Its endorsement recognized that business leaders had felt marginalized and excluded since Punta del Este and promised increased cooperation between the public and the private spheres.[24]

In addition to efforts to encourage potential investors, Martin's tenure also saw a more restrained tone enter public discussions of the Alliance's ability to foster political change in Latin America. Early Alliance rhetoric suggested that the Kennedy administration would show a strong preference for democratic nations, withholding recognition from any group that arrived in power by ousting an elected government. In October 1963, however, Martin published an article in the *New York Herald Tribune* under the headline "The Martin Doctrine." The piece was critical of "impatient idealists" and "defeatist cynics," who undermined the administration's hemispheric policies, but it also indicated a modification in attitudes toward the role of the military in Latin America. While making it clear that he was not "writing an apologia for coups," Martin provided examples of where he believed military governments had been successful and suggested that the United States would no longer automatically cut relations and aid following unconstitutional changes of government.[25]

Schlesinger was unimpressed, encouraging the president to announce publicly that "the Martin statement does not constitute a 'doctrine' . . . [or] 'official U.S. policy for Latin America'" and that "there has been no change in administration policy." Apparently, he was unaware that, days before its release, Martin's article had been circulated to all US embassies in Latin America, marked: "Cleared at highest levels . . . it constitutes U.S. policy vis a vis military governments in L.A."[26] The article also reflected the fact that, despite his rhetoric, Kennedy had long held a relatively pragmatic view regarding Latin American political development, and, in a press conference on 31 October, he tried to walk a delicate line somewhere between Schlesinger's and Martin's positions. While taking his aide's advice and denying that there had been any change in the US attitude regarding political violence, the president also confirmed that discussions were under way to resume relations with the government of the Dominican Republic, which had recently come to power via a coup. "We haven't got a consistent policy," he announced, "because the circumstances are sometimes inconsistent."[27]

The Martin Doctrine episode was just one indicator that the policies of the Kennedy administration were quite different in late 1963 than they had been in early 1961. Of the members of Kennedy's original task force on Latin America, only Moscoso continued to work directly on the Alliance for Progress. Lincoln Gordon was ambassador to Brazil, Goodwin was at the Peace Corps, and Rostow was in the Policy Planning Section of the State Department. Arthur Schlesinger remained as a special assistant, but his ability to keep the president focused on Latin American development was limited. It is not altogether surprising that Kennedy's policy priorities had shifted somewhat. Other distractions such as a civil rights bill, Soviet relations, escalating involvement in Southeast Asia, and an upcoming election served to draw his attention from the struggling Alliance. Targets had been set too high, promising too much, and by 1963 the program had lost a great deal of its momentum. Discussions within the State Department were soon taking place regarding the restructuring of the entire program into an open-ended, rather than a ten-year, commitment with smaller annual budgets targeted at long-term growth rather than unrealistic demands for immediate results.[28]

In the weeks before his death, Kennedy was not so pessimistic as to favor a complete restructuring of the Alliance, but he was seeking ways in which to improve the program's efficiency. In late October, for example, he was considering creating the position of undersecretary of state for inter-American affairs, a move that would have elevated the head of ARA above all other regional chiefs and into the number four position in the State Department. It was clear, however, that the optimism of the early days of the Alliance had given way to a more sober, security-oriented approach that emphasized flexibility in the political sphere and increased cooperation with American investors to fund economic development. In May 1963, the president had convened the "Kennedy Doctrine group" to draft a speech on hemispheric security, and, although he initially intended a stand-alone announcement, the major conclusions of the group's deliberations made it into one of his final addresses and indicated the greatest priority of inter-American policy. "We in this hemisphere," Kennedy informed a gathering of the Inter-American Press Association in Miami just days before his death, "must . . . use every resource at our command to prevent the establishment of another Cuba in this hemisphere."[29]

A Texan in the White House

At least one administration figure was notably absent from the debates surrounding the Alliance for Progress, Vice President Lyndon Baines Johnson.

For much of the 1950s, Johnson had been the most powerful man in Congress, the undisputed "master of the Senate" who could threaten, cajole, and bargain in order to pass legislation and who had transformed the position of majority leader from a poisoned chalice into a role of immense influence. George Smathers (D-FL), who served with both Johnson and Kennedy in the Senate, has recalled: "I know . . . a number of Republican Senators who thought more highly of Johnson than they did their own leadership. . . . [H]e was leader of the whole Senate, and the whole Senate knew it." In contrast, Smathers's memory of Kennedy was of "not an outstanding Senator": "On a scale of one to ten I'd have to give him about a six or a seven at most." Both Kennedy and Johnson had campaigned for the Democratic presidential nomination in 1960, and, when the younger man from Massachusetts won and offered LBJ the role of running mate, to the surprise of many the master of the Senate accepted.[30]

Perhaps Johnson thought he could mold the notoriously impotent vice-presidency into a more influential position, as he had with his Senate role; perhaps he realized it was the closest that a politician from the Hill Country of Texas would get to the office he truly desired in the America of 1960. Unfortunately for him, following Kennedy's victory in November, Johnson found his power to be no greater than the majority of his predecessors. Attempts to exert his influence in Congress were rebuffed, and the duties of his office often seemed demeaning. An article in *Newsweek* described him as "powerless as a freshman Senator and almost as obscure," and one Kennedy staffer noted that, "he could never recognize that he was no longer Senator from Texas, but Vice-President of the United States."[31]

While the president and his deputy enjoyed a certain degree of mutual respect, the same could not be said of Johnson's relationships with the majority of Kennedy's entourage. In the Camelot of Kennedy's White House, Johnson was a clumsy peasant, viewed with scorn by many of the president's erudite young staffers, who referred to him privately as "Uncle Cornpone," and with indifference by others. His isolation was further fueled by his own sensitivity and insecurities. A product of a tough upbringing in the pre–New Deal South, and educated at a teacher-training college in south Texas, Johnson was uncomfortable with and resentful of the *Harvards,* as he termed them, who seemed to surround the new president.[32] That tension was nothing, however, compared to the ill feeling between Johnson and Attorney General Robert Kennedy. Their personality clash and degree of mutual loathing was the stuff of Washington legend, with even Mann, never the sharpest observer of Washington's intrigues, noting that, without understanding the hatred between Johnson and Bobby Kennedy, "one could not understand anything about the 1960s."[33]

His towering reputation on the domestic scene would be borne out by his later legislative successes as president, but Johnson was less renowned for any expertise in foreign affairs. Unlike Kennedy's, his war record was thin, nor had he sat on the prominent Senate Foreign Relations Committee. As majority leader, moreover, he had thought it prudent to be broadly supportive of Eisenhower's foreign policy initiatives, which enabled him to maintain close contacts with the White House but limited his opportunities to establish independent positions on foreign affairs while fueling liberal suspicion of where his loyalties and convictions lay.

If Johnson considered himself well versed in relations with any region of the world, it would have been Latin America and more specifically Mexico. As the volume of mail dealing with border issues received by Johnson's office in the Senate Building attests, many Texans believed themselves experts on US-Mexican relations and made sure that their representatives were familiar with their views. Johnson's belief that this experience gave him greater understanding of the needs of his southern neighbors was mocked by some, such as Ralph Dungan, a staffer for both Kennedy and Johnson, who believed that LBJ "had kind of a romantic, Tex-Mex view of Latin America." Certainly, Johnson was more familiar with Mexico than with most other nations of the hemisphere, and his choice of language when discussing how best to deal with "Latins" could be coarse, but to dismiss his understanding of hemispheric affairs as Dungan did is to do him a disservice.[34]

While in the Senate, Johnson had responded to Richard Nixon's disastrous 1958 visit to Latin America by lamenting the "neglect of our close neighbors to the south" that had soured hemispheric relations. He subsequently threw his support behind the Eisenhower administration's new initiatives, making a speech on the Senate floor in favor of authorizing funds for the Act of Bogota, hosting Mexican president Adolfo López Mateos at his ranch in Texas, and calling on his fellow US citizens to "rededicate ourselves to the Good Neighbor policy." Despite possessing little influence as vice president, Johnson continued to keep himself abreast of events, using his relationship with Texas governor John Connally to ease the passing of the Chamizal border agreement, and making occasional speeches in support of Kennedy's

Latin American programs. On a more personal level, his experience teaching underprivileged Mexican children at a tiny school in Cotulla was one of his most commonly told stories, often used to help illustrate his commitment to the civil rights cause. Latin American policy was one field of foreign relations in which he could claim a certain degree of expertise, and, when Kennedy's assassination on 22 November 1963 elevated him to the presidency, it was one of the first arenas in which he would make his new influence felt.[35]

Considering the struggles of the Alliance for Progress, it is perhaps not surprising that President Johnson was unimpressed with the state of Latin American affairs, privately remarking just days after taking office that policy appeared to be run by "an alliance of misfits." The bureaucratic confusion that had so vexed his predecessor had not been fully resolved, and enthusiasm for the Alliance appeared to be waning among both the public and the legislative branch. Congress had made severe cuts to Kennedy's final foreign aid request, and press reports covering Latin American development regularly questioned the lack of results. After deciding that changes were required—if not in policy, then at least in personnel—on 2 December the new president met with National Security Adviser McGeorge Bundy and CIA director John McCone. It is notable that it was McCone and Bundy whom Johnson consulted, particularly as Bundy would certainly have qualified as one of Johnson's Harvards. Indeed, he had served as that institution's youngest ever dean of faculty and was described by the Kennedy aide Roger Hilsman as being "as close to . . . an aristocrat as America can produce." McCone was a wealthy Irish American Republican with a reputation as a fierce anti-Communist who had replaced Allen Dulles as intelligence chief following the debacle at the Bay of Pigs. Significantly for Johnson, neither was closely involved with the day-to-day implementation of the Alliance for Progress, and McCone in particular had not been part of Kennedy's inner circle. Schlesinger, Goodwin, and Moscoso were not invited.[36]

According to McCone's record of the meeting, Johnson opened by hinting that he would value suggestions as to how to remove the current attorney general from the cabinet before attacking the poor performance of the Alliance and requesting potential candidates to replace Moscoso as coordinator. McCone's impression was that major changes in the structure of policy making were likely to follow. The CIA director's response was to attempt to guide those changes, drafting a memo that would not have made pleasant reading for Moscoso or his staff.[37]

"My observation is that the policy formation and execution of the Alliance for Progress is deeply enmeshed in administrative problems between State and [US]AID and their respective missions," McCone began. "No new administrator—particularly a young man," he warned, "could be expected to take over the responsibilities of directing the program, overcome the obstacles that would confront him, and give the program the forward motion you desire." Moscoso should be replaced as coordinator, he suggested, and Johnson should appoint a new special assistant or deputy assistant secretary with great experience, stature within Latin America, and the confidence of Congress. For deputy coordinator, McCone suggested Ralph Dungan; for the new special assistant position, he believed former Treasury secretary Robert Anderson would be a good choice; and for coordinator of the Alliance for Progress, he endorsed Ambassador to Mexico Thomas Mann. When McCone and the president met again a week later, Johnson informed his intelligence chief that Anderson had shown little interest in a return to government but had vouched for Mann's credentials. His own inclination, Johnson said, was to concentrate power in one man who would be both the State Department's head of inter-American affairs and the coordinator of the Alliance for Progress, and he thought it should be Mann.[38]

It has been assumed by many, both at the time of the appointment and since, that Johnson's choice of Mann was based on cronyism. Mann, a fellow Texan, must have been an old friend and political ally of Johnson's, part of his powerful political machine, which included many prominent Texans in Washington.[39] In fact, there is little evidence to refute Mann's assertion that the two men barely knew each other and that their first conversation occurred in 1961. As Mann later noted: "The next time I had occasion to see him was when I was brought back from Mexico." In the records of his time in Washington during the Eisenhower administration, there is scant evidence to suggest that Mann had any kind of special connections in Congress. Furthermore, while Johnson supported his efforts in the Chamizal negotiations from afar, it does not appear that any close consultations took place between the two.[40]

Cronyism is not necessary to explain why Johnson was keen to recall Mann to Washington within the first month of his presidency, although clearly Mann's Texan background did him no harm. With Johnson now surrounded and served by the Harvards, appointing a plain-speaking Foreign Service officer raised on the border with Mexico and educated at a south Texas Baptist college held appeal in and of itself. Johnson may also have

President Lyndon Johnson meets with his "Mr. Latin America," Thomas Mann, in the White House, 7 May 1965. (Lyndon Baines Johnson Library photo by Yoichi Okamoto.)

remembered Mann campaigning for greater aid to Latin America yet warning about the consequences of a program on the scale of the Alliance for Progress, the disappointment and frustration that would follow the initial raising of hopes, and the folly of setting rigid economic targets. Mann had also made accurate predictions regarding the Bay of Pigs invasion, pointing out gaping holes in the plans when others were willing to hand all responsibility over to the CIA. Put simply, Mann possessed more experience in Latin American affairs than almost any other figure in government service, and, of almost four hundred Foreign Service officers based in Latin America under Kennedy, he was one of only seventeen the State Department classed as fluent in Spanish. He had a solid track record of achievement and a good reputation untarnished by any media criticism. "He's a coordinator," Johnson told the journalist Jerry Griffin, "a shy, quiet, progressive fellow." Clearly, LBJ thought he had found the man to bring some order and stability to his Latin American policy. As he put it, Mann would be his "Mr. Latin America."[41]

Despite his desire to retire from government service, expressed to Kennedy the previous year, Mann felt unable to refuse Johnson's request to return to Washington. Acceptance confirmed, Johnson issued a public letter to his new aide on 15 December 1963. "I have asked you," it read, "to undertake the coordination and direction of all policies and programs of the U.S. government, economic, social, and cultural, relating to Latin America." In doing so, Mann would be expected to "press to full realization the visions of President Roosevelt and President Kennedy of an American community of Nations moving forward together in progress and freedom." "Next to keeping the peace," Johnson told Mann and anyone else who cared to read. "No work is more important for our generation of Americans than our work in this hemisphere."[42]

Mann may not have been filled with enthusiasm at the prospect of a return to Washington, but Johnson's publication of the carefully worded letter was well judged. Several Mexican outlets reporting on Mann's departure reserved special praise for Johnson's words, particularly the references to Roosevelt and Kennedy. Mann's achievements were widely lauded, with *Excelsior* commenting that he had continually "shown his high regard for our country, his closeness to it and his affection, all of which go beyond the barriers of a cold and impersonal protocol." *Novedades* praised the wisdom of Johnson's decision: "No better move could have been made than to entrust this job to someone who, since he has lived and worked in Mexico, knows how these progressive programs can best be put into effect." Even a more sober assessment provided by Morris Rosenberg, the Associated Press bureau chief for Central America, noted: "Mann leaves here having won the respect of many Mexicans . . . [through] his personal dedication to achieving the return of the Chamizal tract alongside El Paso to Mexico, settling a century old dispute that had become a festering sore in U.S. Mexican relations." During his final press conference before departing on 19 December, Mann reemphasized his commitment to Mexico, informing reporters: "I consider it my second country, I was born on the border." He also promised that good relations would continue under President Johnson. His final engagement was a good-bye luncheon with his friend Foreign Minister Manuel Tello. Shortly after his departure, the headline of *El Universal* read: "Thomas C. Mann, Amigo Sincero de Mexico." His welcome in Washington would be nothing like as warm.[43]

The day after John Kennedy's funeral, President Johnson spoke at the White House to a gathering of ambassadors from Latin America. "We all know that there have been problems within the Alliance for Progress," he admitted, "but the accomplishments of the past 3 years have proven the soundness of our principles. The accomplishments of the years to come will vindicate our faith in the capacity of free men to meet the new challenges of a new day." The speech ended with a flourish, as Johnson promised that Kennedy would never be forgotten as the Alliance would serve as his "living memorial." Despite such public pledges, the hostility that many of Kennedy's staff felt toward the new president would not be assuaged by speeches.[44]

Ralph Dungan has recalled that resentment of Johnson was far reaching and that there "were certain people like Schlesinger, for instance, who declared war . . . the day that John F. went into the ground." For his part, Schlesinger believed that Kennedy's staff could be divided into two distinct factions, the "realists," who might mourn their fallen leader but valued their careers more, and the "loyalists," who were the true Kennedy believers and could never accept Johnson as their president. Richard Goodwin captured the feeling among the loyalists in his memoirs—"that the hardly won Kennedy renaissance, the liberal renewal, had been so abruptly, arbitrarily cut short; the fruits of progressive victory transferred to this 'conservative' Texan, this master political manipulator, peerless 'boss of the Senate,' personal protégé of Georgia's Richard Russell, whose values and convictions (if he had any) were remote from their own." Tapping into the myths that surrounded the Kennedy administration, Goodwin continued: "Not only had Camelot dissolved, but Mordred was in command." He also described how small groups of "Kennedy liberals" such as Schlesinger, J. K. Galbraith, and Labor Secretary Bill Wirtz discussed how Johnson could be denied nomination for a full presidential term.[45]

For some, these feelings would fade with time. Johnson's progressive domestic agenda, the Great Society, won the respect of many of his liberal critics, with Goodwin and Wirtz ultimately remaining in the administration for several years. Others, such as Schlesinger and the speechwriter Ted Sorenson, simply left government service as swiftly as they could. For a brief time, however, skirmishes were fought in a turbulent transition period during which political and personal grievances and ambitions led many to behave in ways they would come to regret. As Sorenson would later write (somewhat dramatically): "It was the worst of times for even the best of men." Latin American policy, and Mann's appointment in particular, provided a focal point for these battles.[46]

Given his previous problems with certain Kennedy aides, Mann had some idea of what might await him on his return from Mexico. Responding to a letter of congratulations from his former boss Spruille Braden, he confessed: "Not everybody is happy with my appointment and it means a great deal to me to have your friendship and moral support." Memories of the previous presidential transition, when he was treated as a conservative irrelevance, preyed on his mind, and he later recounted that he dreaded returning to Washington only "to debate with people about whether I was liberal or conservative or something else." Unfortunately for Mann, things were worse than probably even he had imagined. The sense of ownership regarding the Alliance among Schlesinger, Goodwin, and Robert Kennedy in particular extended to a belief, articulated by Schlesinger in his journal, that, "because of President Kennedy's intense personal concern with Latin America, no appointment should be made to the Latin American post without due consultation with his Latin American executors," by which he meant himself, Goodwin, and RFK. Aware that the new president was likely to make changes, in the days following Kennedy's death the group began to discuss their preferred appointments, which included Robert Kennedy and his brother-in-law Sargent Shriver, but rumors soon reached them of Johnson's preference for Mann.[47]

The thought of Mann, whom he had recently mocked as a conservative irrelevance, in charge of the Alliance for Progress was too much for Schlesinger to bear. Ralph Dungan had already written to Johnson to caution that some in Latin America would see Mann's appointment as a "turn to the right," but Schlesinger was determined to make the point explicit. Drafting a memo of his own, Schlesinger began by making it clear that, while he regarded Mann as a "noble and high-minded officer," he wished to "set down the reasons why this appointment would seem to me a mistake." He argued that Mann was "not only out of touch with the vital forces of contemporary Latin America" but also "actively opposed to them" and had "shown little patience with Mexican intellectuals." Mann's economic philosophies were conservative, according to Schlesinger, and this led him to be "deeply opposed to social reform governments." As evidence, he presented selected portions of Mann's messages from Mexico City, which he had been collecting, and concluded with a stern warning that Mann's views were "in sharp contrast with the basic premises of the Alliance."[48]

Schlesinger was too late; the same day he drafted his memo, Johnson's inherited press secretary, Pierre Salinger, announced Mann's appointment, followed the next day by the open letter. It did not go down well. "Johnson has won the first round," Schlesinger wrote to Robert Kennedy. "He has shown his power to move in a field of special concern to the Kennedys without consulting the Kennedys." To Goodwin he sent a copy of Salinger's announcement with a note attached that read simply: "R.I.P." Mann's appointment was taken by this group almost as a declaration of war, a statement by Johnson that he was preparing to dismantle JFK's legacy one piece at a time. "There is real gloom among the advocates of the Alliance for Progress," Goodwin wrote in his journal. "[Mann] has all the worst qualities coupled with a basic lack of belief in the Alliance."[49]

Schlesinger was not finished yet, however. He next approached Hubert Humphrey, one of the Senate's leading liberal voices, encouraging him to oppose Mann's appointment in Congress. Schlesinger was not subtle, and Mann was well aware of the efforts, although he later wryly reflected: "[Schlesinger was] up there lobbying on the Hill against my confirmation to a job I didn't want." The effort was also desperate. Not only was Humphrey an ally of Johnson's, later serving as his vice president, but few senators would have been foolish enough to risk LBJ's ire by attempting to block his first significant appointment. Humphrey turned Schlesinger down flat, and Mann's appointment was confirmed unanimously.[50]

Schlesinger was probably correct that, from a symbolic point of view, the selection of a Latin American coordinator with closer ties to John F. Kennedy would have made a clear statement of continuity, but what he failed to recognize was that Humphrey and many others did not share his level of concern regarding Mann's appointment and felt little need to oppose it. Many in the Senate in fact welcomed a move that might mean an end to the bureaucratic chaos of Kennedy's Alliance, as did others outside Capitol Hill such as the original task force member and ambassador to Brazil Lincoln Gordon. When Undersecretary of State George Ball was asked by a colleague if Mann's appointment was "as bad as I am told," he responded simply: "I have known Mann over a period of time and I think he will do a good job." The most prominent advocate of a progressive Latin American policy during the 1950s, Milton Eisenhower, also expressed his delight at the return of one "of our best Latin American experts" to Washington. There was little support for Schlesinger's position from the public either, other than very occasional letters to the president such as one from a concerned citizen unhappy owing to Mann's apparently well-known links with the Communist Party in East

Germany and his membership in "various fronts" for subversive activity. Unfortunately, the letter to the White House was scrawled in pencil, entirely in uppercase letters, and contained a stern reminder to the president: "A few weeks ago I informed you that I did not like your left-wing voting record, and that I was going to watch your activities."[51]

There is a temptation, then, to dismiss the hostility to Mann's appointment as a bureaucratic storm in a teacup. Johnson certainly attempted to do so, informing a journalist: "Schlesinger and Goodwin and some of these other fellows are not too happy about this, but you can understand that, if someone were brought in over you, you wouldn't be too happy either." Privately, however, Johnson was concerned. Having heard that the Democratic Party stalwart Averell Harriman agreed with Schlesinger's loyalists, he complained bitterly to his Senate ally William Fulbright: "What the hell do you do about an Undersecretary who goes to calling around people to lobby you?" The answer, Johnson thought, was to further strengthen Mann's position, naming him as a special assistant to the president a few days after the announcement of his other roles. Perhaps Johnson should have paid more attention to Dungan's and Schlesinger's warnings, but, given the limited nature of the criticism, his wariness of Harvards like Schlesinger, and his determination to get Latin American policy functioning more efficiently, this was always unlikely. Nonetheless, the hostility Mann was forced to deal with represented more than just territorial blustering. The resentment that Mann provoked was complex, encompassing as it did personal, political, and, to an extent, ideological concerns. The issues that arose exposed not only regional and generational divides but also conflicting ideas of what constituted a liberal approach to hemispheric affairs and a battle to claim the legacy and defend the reputation of John F. Kennedy. Understanding why Mann was able to provoke such hostility is vital to understanding the nature of inter-American policy in this period.[52]

First, it is clear that genuine grief at the loss of an inspirational leader and friend—and in some cases family member—helped provoke the resistance to what was seen as an attack on Kennedy's legacy. Men such as Schlesinger and Robert Kennedy were attempting to mourn while also dealing with the upheaval of a presidential transition. Genuine emotion coupled with a commitment to and belief in their vision of hemispheric affairs made the reaction to Mann's appointment more vitriolic than it might otherwise have been. After all, the appointment of Ed Martin, Mann's predecessor and another career diplomat, had raised little protest. With John Kennedy dead, his younger brother became the champion of his inner circle, yet it was his great enemy, an uncouth Texan with questionable liberal credentials, who now sat in the Oval Office. Under Martin, change had been gradual and still overseen by Kennedy. Mann, whom Robert Kennedy dismissed as "Barry Goldwater making a speech at the Economic Club," appeared to be Johnson's creature, another Texan and another outsider who would never understand Camelot.[53]

Emotional considerations were, of course, mixed with basic political concerns. The influence of Schlesinger, Goodwin, Moscoso, and Morales-Carrión had already begun to wane in the final months of the Kennedy administration, and Mann's appointment represented the final nail in their collective coffin. For the previous three years, Robert Kennedy's responsibilities and influence had also gone far beyond those of a typical attorney general, but that too would be coming to an end. Through Mann's appointment, the delicate balance of influence that had been shifting during Kennedy's Alliance for Progress would swing decisively toward the professional State Department wing of policy making. Mann had not been a vocal Alliance supporter—he had indeed predicted the problems of such a program—and his appointment was a direct threat to the more unconventional policy-making apparatus that had existed under Kennedy.

Mann would later reflect that the dispute over his appointment represented "a struggle for power between two factions of the Democratic Party, the conservative and the liberal." While true that the brief fight for control of Latin American policy reflected ideological concerns, it was more complex than simply conservative versus liberal. Indeed, Mann would also acknowledge: "I don't know what those words—conservative and liberal—mean; those are two I can't define anymore." Regional differences and corresponding prejudices complicated matters, with a clear divide between Northeast and Southwest sensibilities at play, but both sides essentially conceived of themselves as liberal. The difference was that Mann's and Johnson's form of liberalism was grounded in the New Deal and the Good Neighbor policy, not the liberal internationalism and belief in modernization theory from which the Alliance for Progress had emerged.[54]

Johnson and Mann had both entered Washington politics in the era of Franklin Roosevelt. Johnson was as close to Roosevelt as a junior congressman could ever hope to be, and he and Mann both witnessed the disastrous effects of the Great Depression on their beloved Texas and how New Deal programs had alleviated the worst of them. More significantly for Mann, he began his long association with Latin America in the era of FDR's Good Neighbor policy, which promised nonintervention in political affairs and increased economic cooperation throughout the hemisphere. For both men, FDR would be a constant touchstone in speeches and statements, with commitment to being a good neighbor almost always accompanying the expected professions of dedication to the Alliance for Progress.

By the time Mann joined Johnson's policy-making team, his views on inter-American affairs were well established, but, as his past record demonstrated, they were too complex to be described simply as conservative. Regarding political development, Mann was very much of the Good Neighbor era, favoring democracy, but extremely wary of the unforeseen consequences that accompanied intervention in Latin American domestic politics. Little in the first years of the Alliance would have convinced him that anyone in Washington had figured out how to further the cause of democracy throughout the hemisphere. In terms of economic policy, Mann reflected New Deal–era politics in his commitment to serving as an intermediary between national governments and private industry and encouraging cooperative ventures between them both.[55] However, he had also demonstrated that his thinking on economic matters had progressed beyond both the Good Neighbor era and Eisenhower administration free market orthodoxy in his encouragement of increased development aid, tax reform, and international agreements to stabilize the prices of commodities vital to Latin American exports. Indeed, National Security Adviser McGeorge Bundy described Mann's views as "very Fabian," implying a form of cautious, moderate socialism that suggests a very different figure to the one reviled by some Kennedy loyalists. Mann would certainly not have thought of himself as a socialist of any stripe, but, considering that the guiding principles of the Fabian Society include "the value of collective action and public service . . . sustainable development [and] multilateral international cooperation," Bundy may not have been completely wide of the mark.[56]

Despite an occasional tendency to dismiss the most liberal wing of his party as "bomb throwers," Lyndon Johnson would not have considered himself a conservative either. He had begun his political career as a New Dealer, serving as the nation's youngest director of a National Youth Administration branch before dedicating many of his early years in Congress to an ultimately successful campaign on behalf of rural electrification programs for Texas. As president, his great ambition was to fulfill the promise of Franklin Roosevelt's New Deal by creating a more equitable country via his Great Society programs. While foreign affairs had not been his primary concern prior to the presidency, he had supported the Good Neighbor policy and was critical of the Eisenhower administration's reluctance to assist Latin American development, commenting that post–World War II levels of economic assistance did not constitute "a record of which we can be proud." Like Mann, he had supported the Act of Bogota, helping guide Eisenhower's funding requests through the Senate, and believed that, through technical assistance programs, the encouragement of private investment, and the judicious use of public funds, the United States could aid in Latin American development.[57]

Where Johnson and Mann sought to build on past achievements, Kennedy's Latin American task force had instead emphasized that the Alliance for Progress was a bold new step in hemispheric relations, dismissing the Eisenhower years as a period of stagnation that had failed to be redeemed by some last gasp olive branches like the Act of Bogota. If Arthur Schlesinger was not in favor of a particular aspect of administration policy, he would warn that it was reminiscent of the failed methods of the 1950s and suggest that, if economic policy reverted to that of the Eisenhower era, "we might as well kiss the Alliance—and the hemisphere—goodbye." When a March 1962 piece in the *New York Times* suggested that Dwight Eisenhower had laid the foundations for the Alliance for Progress and Kennedy had simply named it, Richard Goodwin responded furiously: "For the first seven years of the previous administration there was no policy toward Latin America."[58]

The liberal internationalist worldview that drove the creation of the Alliance clearly had roots in the past, including Woodrow Wilson's post–World War I efforts to reshape the global order and the more successful institution building that followed World War II, and is part of a longer narrative of US international engagement and democracy promotion.[59] Yet the Kennedy administration's determination to frame policy developments as a clean break with the past appears to have elevated predictable friction between new arrivals and old hands into an exaggerated clash of worldviews. While it is of course necessary to distinguish between the reality of policy making and the administration's "pay any price, bear any burden" rhetoric, for men such as Schlesinger and Goodwin, Kennedy's presidential victory marked the beginning of a new era of liberal internationalism, and they fully agreed with their leader that the "torch [had] been passed to a new generation." They were also seemingly unable or unwilling to acknowledge the extent to which Kennedy's priorities shifted during his three years in office and that efforts were already under way to adjust the organization of Latin American policy. Had they done so, they may have recognized that their differences with Mann and Johnson were outweighed by their similarities. Fundamentally, they all believed that the US government should be helping create a prosperous, safe, and democratic Latin America through aiding in economic development. Certainly, Mann's and Schlesinger's views differed on issues of democracy promotion and the prominence of private investment, and Mann possessed a less ambitious but perhaps more realistic conception of the limits of American power. Still, compared to the standpoint of men like George Humphrey and John Foster Dulles who had dominated policy for so long in the Eisenhower era, their views were practically harmonious. In their conflation of Eisenhower-era fiscal conservatives and New Deal liberals, the stance of some of the Kennedy loyalists was that not to embrace the Alliance for Progress fully was not to believe in progress at all, and hence the appointment of Mann marked the program's death.[60]

As had been the case in 1961, an opportunity was missed to ally Mann's more cautious and pragmatic nature with the ideas, ideals, and enthusiasm of Schlesinger, Goodwin, and Moscoso. Mann was not blameless in this process, doing little to reach out to the other side or convince them of his intentions.[61] Instead, personal, political, and ideological clashes transformed his appointment into a lightning rod for the brewing discontent over the formulation of Latin American policy. Consequently, any changes implemented by Mann and Johnson in the months that followed could be interpreted within the context of these disputes, easily criticized as contrary to what Kennedy would have intended. In truth, the behavior of both sides would serve to exacerbate the situation at various points, but the hostility of such an influential group of Kennedy associates would certainly make a difficult job all the harder as Mann and Johnson sought to establish control of Latin American policy.

Mr. Latin America

Just as John Kennedy had been toying with the idea of creating a more powerful State Department position to oversee Latin America, Lyndon Johnson was adamant that Mann's influence over policy making was to be wide-ranging. While Mann was still in Mexico, Johnson had impressed on him via telephone that he wanted "one man for the entire operation" and that Mann should "lay it out the way you want to see it done." In response, Mann immediately sketched out some notes regarding the biggest challenges he expected to face. "Conditions in Latin America [are] likely to get worse before they get better," he noted gloomily. But the real obstacle would be "telling the American people the truth without tarnishing the image of [the] Alliance in Latin America." The other major task he foresaw would be bringing some order, coordination, and a clear hierarchy to the formulation and implementation of policy. The first months of his tenure as Johnson's Mr. Latin America would see him attempt to address both these problems. His efforts to impose order would result in a bureaucratic reshuffling of both State and USAID, yielding a degree of success, but the problem of playing down the expectations of the public while not losing what little enthusiasm remained for Alliance programs would tarnish his reputation almost beyond repair.[62]

In a conversation with John Bullet of the Treasury Department in January 1964, the new assistant secretary for inter-American affairs and coordinator of the Alliance for Progress made it clear that he intended to follow his president's orders and exercise far more direct control over Latin American policy than any of his predecessors. USAID dealt with the whole world, Mann remarked, but he would control loans for Latin America, cut the "red tape," and "eliminate these endless debates with 14 people with vetoes." His task was made far easier by the changes in administration personnel that had occurred since the death of President Kennedy, most notably the departures of Schlesinger and Moscoso from government service. Moscoso had chosen to return to Puerto Rico after he had been replaced as coordinator of the Alliance, while Schlesinger had been asked by Johnson to remain in his role as special assistant to the president but felt unable to do so, departing in January 1964. Goodwin remained in the White House, but his position under Johnson would be primarily that of a speechwriter, with greater focus on domestic than foreign affairs. National Security Adviser McGeorge Bundy would now play a more prominent role in inter-American issues than he had previously, and Mann would deal primarily with him, his assistant Gordon Chase, and Ralph Dungan, whom Johnson had convinced to remain in the White House. While Mann would occasionally quarrel with all of them, only Dungan had voiced any objections to his appointment, and even then he had been far less vociferous in doing so than Schlesinger. Mann's immediate superior was Dean Rusk, but the secretary of state took little interest in Latin America, with the exception of Cuba, and largely left Mann to run ARA as he saw fit.[63]

Mann's position was also strengthened by Johnson's very public backing. At the press conference announcing Mann's appointment, Pierre Salinger had stated that the new assistant secretary would be given an "extraordinarily free hand to shake up Latin American operations," and so it transpired. According to Senate Foreign Relations Committee chief of staff Pat Holt, Johnson "made it known far and wide that when Mann said something it was the president talking, and he didn't want Mann taking any guff from the rest of the bureaucracy." With Johnson's backing, Mann was able to force his way through what one reporter evocatively described as the "marshmallow curtain" of Alliance bureaucracy to drastically reshape the working relationship between State and USAID. In what Mann termed "back-to-back" organization, the execution of Latin American policy was rearranged into nine geographic departments within which both State and USAID employees would work together under one director with responsibility for a small group of countries. The telegram to diplomatic posts informing ambassadors of the changes announced that this would "bring the operations of the two organizations closer together for the purposes of centralizing responsibility, . . . accelerat[ing] actions on Alliance programs . . . [and] providing for increased decision making authority."[64]

The reorganization, which came into effect on 16 March, reflected not only Mann's dual role as coordinator of a major aid program and head of inter-American policy but also his distaste for broad theories that were not based on specialized knowledge. By combining USAID and State employees into one bureau dealing with a handful of nations rather than an entire hemisphere, Mann hoped that the individual needs of disparate nations could be met more effectively and that further bickering between different offices could be prevented. Explaining his reorganization process to the Chambers of Commerce annual meeting in September, Mann pointed out that previously "rivalries developed when there should have been teamwork" but that since the changes the improvement in coordination had "exceeded our expectations." Specialized country knowledge, awareness of the long-term goals of the Alliance, and speed of decision making had all improved, he announced, with the result that, in the first six months of 1964, more money had been approved for Latin American projects than in the whole of the previous year. William Rogers, a former deputy to Moscoso, agreed, noting: "Clearance time within the organization was reduced, and older attitudes of competition between Foreign Service officers and [US]AID were softened. Technical issues were resolved at a lower level."[65]

Mann's reorganization was not welcomed in all quarters, however, and, for the first time in his career, he began to receive criticism from prominent sections of the press. Tad Szulc, a resident Latin American expert for the *New York Times* best known for his exposés of the Bay of Pigs operation, wrote of Mann's back-to-back scheme: "The plan has set off considerable criticism among officials of the State Department and the [US] Agency for International Development at a time when morale among officials concerned with Latin America is markedly sagging." Such criticism and issues of morale stemmed less from Mann's bureaucratic maneuverings, however, and more from his attempts to inject a sense of realism into conceptions of what the Alliance could hope to achieve. On his departure from ARA, Ed Martin had informed his successor that probably the greatest challenge he would face would be to convince the nation that engagement with Latin America was "a long historical process in which miracles don't happen," one "requiring great patience with slow progress and acceptance of occasional defeat as inevitable." The soaring rhetoric, usually penned by Sorenson or Goodwin, with which John Kennedy had launched the Alliance made this a tricky proposition. The suspicion and hostility with which Mann was viewed in some quarters served only to increase the delicacy with which he would have to tread, but nonetheless the new Latin American chief set about trying to place expectations on a more reasonable level.[66]

In a conversation with Johnson's aide George Reedy, Mann laid out the conundrum he believed he faced. "What the Latin Americans need is spirit, optimism and hope, and what the Americans need is more realism," he observed. "We have to find a good middle ground but I don't think there is one." He decided that the best option would be to take a line that emphasized the achievements of the Alliance so far while also highlighting the great challenges that remained. Shortly before his death, Kennedy had authorized the creation of the Inter-American Committee on the Alliance for Progress (CIAP), a multilateral body that would, he had believed, go some way to convincing Latin America that the Alliance was a communal effort rather than a US lending program. Mann hoped that, by emphasizing developments like CIAP and suggesting what could be achieved in the long term through a

C40-1-64 [January 23, 1964]
Pres. Johnson with OAS Group

President Johnson and his new assistant secretary of state meet with representatives of the Organization of American States and Secretary of State Dean Rusk at the White House, 23 January 1964. (White House Photo Office Collection, LBJ Presidential Library.)

truly multilateral program, it would be possible to "come down a few octaves from the line we have been taking, that everything will be solved right away," without giving the impression that the Alliance was being abandoned. Unfortunately for Mann, his efforts would culminate in serious damage to his relationship with the press and the creation of the notorious Mann Doctrine.[67]

The criticism that Mann had received over his bureaucratic reorganization reflected the fact that his relationship with members of the press who had been vocal supporters of the Alliance had been troubled from the moment he returned from Mexico. In particular, he felt that Tad Szulc and Henry Raymont of the *New York Times* were overly hostile and placed too much weight on the word of disgruntled Kennedy loyalists. Johnson, ever sensitive to criticism, was concerned. Desperate for approval from the liberal press, in February he asked Mann to reach out to the *Times,* or as he put it: "Tell those guys that State leaks to—Szulc and Raymont . . . [to] give us a chance to work on this." "What you picked up is pretty bad," he reminded Mann, who should tell them that he needed "time and help." Mann was not enthusiastic about the prospect, believing that Szulc and Raymont had bought into the rhetoric of the Kennedy administration with little concept of the reality of making the Alliance work. "It is difficult to handle crusaders," he complained.[68]

Mann and Johnson both hoped that the upcoming celebrations to mark the third anniversary of the Alliance would provide an opportunity to reaffirm their commitment to Latin America and placate the "crusaders" in the process. The ceremonies would include the official launch of CIAP and an address by Johnson to be delivered at the headquarters of the OAS to an audience of the hemisphere's leading diplomats. Almost as an afterthought, Mann also planned to use the opportunity to organize an off-the-record gathering of US ambassadors while they were assembled in Washington to "review trends and developments" and discuss the future of Latin American policy. The first part of the plan, Johnson's speech and the CIAP launch, was a qualified success. Szulc's reporting of the event contained some praise for Johnson's address but also noted that the president "did not quite accomplish" his goal of allaying the fear that "Latin America no longer commands the political attention it did during the Kennedy administration." The real problems began the following day, 18 March, when Mann spoke to US officials serving in Latin America and his worries regarding leaks were confirmed.[69]

The 19 March edition of the *New York Times* led with a story by Szulc, "U.S. May Abandon Efforts to Deter Latin Dictators," that claimed to know the content of Mann's speech and coined the phrase *the Mann Doctrine*. According to the article, Mann had disparaged attempts to separate "good guys and bad guys" in Latin America, instead arguing that the United States should be focusing mainly on economic progress. Szulc reported that Mann announced four main goals for US policy—"economic growth . . . , the protection of $9 billion in United States investment there, non-intervention in the internal political affairs of the hemisphere's republics, and opposition to Communism"—making no mention of democratic development. Mann had also apparently claimed to see little difference between the democrats and the dictators of the region and found it difficult to distinguish politically between President López Mateos of Mexico and Alfredo Stroessner, the dictator of Paraguay. According to Szulc, Senators Wayne Morse and Hubert Humphrey had also spoken to the gathered ambassadors and were dismayed at the potential reversion of Kennedy's policies. "In his entire presentation," the article concluded, "Mr. Mann made no mention of the Alliance for Progress."[70]

Mann was firefighting immediately, phoning Johnson and Bundy to protest: "This is a gross distortion of what I said, . . . that we were in favor of democracy." He also blamed USAID for leaking inaccuracies. Mann was furious, complaining that "it's a matter of semantics whether we go around slapping dictators," and pointing out the hypocrisy of the press as Kennedy had maintained "relations with every dictator in the hemisphere." He was offered some consolation by two of the senators to have spoken at the same event, Ernest Gruening and Wayne Morse. Despite the reports of Morse's dismay at Mann's comments, the senator dismissed the article, commenting that he himself had been misquoted "too many times to count." For his part, Gruening concurred with Mann's belief that "someone is driving an axe," remarking: "Szulc has a definite bias and is very sentimental on the subject."[71]

Mann's sense of injustice was undoubtedly fueled further by the lack of outcry when his predecessor, Ed Martin, had published his own doctrine regarding the possible benefits of military governments in Latin America. On that occasion, the only mention in the *New York Times* of the Martin Doctrine article occurred a week after its publication, buried on page 28 as part of an editorial on how Latin American policy affected US electoral politics. While Martin's comments were called "ill-timed and indiscreet," readers were assured that "the important thing to say—and Secretary Rusk and President Kennedy did say it—is that the United States strongly condemns all military coups in Latin America." The press did not let Mann off the hook so easily, seizing on his comments far more aggressively than they had the Martin Doctrine. Szulc's follow-up article of 20 March commented that, although the State Department had issued a statement that "the United States' devotion to the principles of democracy is a historical fact," Mann's comments signified "a gradual change of emphasis, leading to a basic modification of the entire United States philosophy of dictatorships." Drew Pearson in the *Washington Post* went even further, claiming that the Mann Doctrine "decreed on behalf of a president from Texas that henceforward we were going to recognize Latin dictators" and that "it remains a fact that in Latin America the Texas brand hurts."[72]

Not all outlets were so critical, with *Newsday,* for example, calling Mann's comments "a welcome reappraisal" of the unrealistic idealism of the Alliance for Progress. Those were the exceptions, however, with most coverage siding with the assertion by the *Times* that Mann was leading Latin American policy away from the path that Kennedy had intended. Another point of general agreement was that the leaking of the speech, accurate or not, demonstrated the opposition that still existed to Mann within the executive branch bureaucracy. The *Miami Herald* quoted one particularly ominous official as saying: "Mann got the knife—and when the shiv is stuck in, it's awfully hard to pull out."[73]

Mann was certainly wounded and struggled to mitigate the wider damage of the reporting. One press contact informed him that, even if the coverage was distorted, the fallout would "raise hell in Latin America." With this in mind, Mann contacted Szulc's boss at the *New York Times,* James Reston, who offered assurances that his paper was not "in the business of getting anybody" and had no vendetta against him. Mann allowed his frustrations to boil over during the course of the conversation, complaining bitterly: "The attacks started in a certain circle here while I was still packing in Mexico." He further noted that the attacks were founded "on a personality basis, not on the basis of issues." If the *Times* was out for blood, Mann let them know that it had succeeded. "The boys who are writing the stories . . . [made] no effort to find out what I think," he told Reston. Instead, they went straight to employees who they knew would agree with them. Reston promised he would look into the situation and hung up. Little came of the conversation, although it appears to have convinced Mann that it was specific reporters, not the entirety of the *Times* staff, who were hostile. When FDR's former assistant secretary of war John McCloy telephoned him in early April, offering to use his press contacts to help calm the situation, Mann assured him that it was only Szulc and Raymont who had their "knives out," that Reston was looking into it, and that he would prefer to leave it at that.[74]

The whole episode left Mann—whom Bundy described as possessing a "temperamental distaste for public relations"—even more guarded with the press than he had been before. Never one to court publicity or attempt to utilize the media to his advantage, he became wary of public statements. Indeed, Gordon Chase commented to Bundy later that year that they would need to encourage Mann to give more press briefings as he had been "excessively quiet" of late. Reston may have convinced Mann that any vendetta was limited to a few individuals, but the *"New York Times* twins" were certainly not forgiven. Were he not in government with an election approaching, Mann assured his president in May, he would "answer them in proper Texas style," but political considerations meant that he was not in a position to "get into a donnybrook now." Johnson, another Texan who endured a fractious relationship with what he considered the Northeast-dominated media, was broadly sympathetic to Mann's insistence that "they twist what you tell them" and that it was better to remain aloof. Others, he was convinced, were not so reticent. When Johnson asked him where "the twins" got their information, Mann replied that it was probably Schlesinger and Moscoso.[75]

The whole Mann Doctrine episode would deeply affect the rest of Mann's career and assessments of the Johnson period more widely, but it is still unclear exactly how accurate Szulc's reporting was. Even at the time, opinions varied. Chase thought the story to be fairly accurate, William Rogers thought it "moderately garbled," and of course Mann swore it to be a "gross distortion." The truth most likely lies somewhere in between. After spending so long in the field, including three successful years in Mexico, Mann is unlikely to have claimed to see no difference between López Mateos and Stroessner, at least in the context Szulc's story suggested. However, his belief in the importance of nonintervention and the need to increase the level of private investment in the region, along with his desire to inject more realism into Latin American policy, almost certainly resulted in a speech quite different than those heard in previous years. The rhetoric of the Kennedy administration had created different expectations as to what an administration official should say, even if it did not reflect what he actually intended to do. Mann's blunt assessments of what was required in order to make policy more effective played straight into the hands of his critics, who were all too willing to paint him as a relic of the past, supporting dictators and opposing development.[76]

The Mann Doctrine episode harmed Mann's relationship with the press, but it also did him no favors within the administration. Although he largely retained the support of the president, on 25 March Mann received a memo from Bundy, approved by Johnson, explaining that any substantial speeches he drafted in the future needed to be cleared through the national security adviser's office. In increasing his own influence within the administration, Bundy was not averse to reminding Johnson of "Tom's sometimes unfortunate public image," and his relationship with Mann would remain uneasy until they both left government service in 1966.[77]

Assessing the Transition

Lyndon Johnson's leadership of the nation during the traumatic transition period that followed Kennedy's death, his emphasis on continuity, and his respect for his predecessor's legacy have been widely and rightly praised. His handling of Latin American policy—one area in which he sought to introduce change—has not received such positive assessments. Indeed, the Mann Doctrine and the subsequent fallout provide ample evidence for those who argue that there was a fundamental shift in approach following Johnson's ascension to the presidency.[78] Mann controlled all the key levers of power involved in shaping Latin American policy, and his early attempts to dampen expectations suggested a much less dynamic outlook than that which prevailed under John Kennedy. Certainly, a comparison of Latin American policy in the first months of the Kennedy administration with that in the first months of Johnson's presidency would likely lend itself to the argument that there was a major upheaval. However, it is clear that policy in the final months of the Kennedy administration had changed a great deal from what it was when the Alliance was launched in 1961. As Kennedy had with Eisenhower, Johnson largely continued down a path established by the latter part of his predecessor's term of office, a path that was far less wedded to the idealistic rhetoric of the Alliance than some of the Kennedy loyalists were willing to admit. The most common criticisms of the Johnson-Mann approach to hemispheric policy—the lack of active democracy promotion, the placing of Cold War security concerns over the interests of Latin American development, and the increased emphasis on private investment— were all part of a process that began well before Lyndon Johnson entered the Oval Office.

On being replaced by Tom Mann, for instance, Ed Martin had admitted to his successor that no one in the administration really had any idea how to foster political development and assist the growth of Latin American democracy. Where initially the stated Kennedy policy had been to use the withholding of recognition as a tool to discourage unconstitutional changes of government, Martin admitted to Mann that by 1963 this had been replaced by a "sensible, pragmatic, middle of the road course with respect to military coups, one which takes account of Latin American history and attempts to move them forward from where they are, rather than from where one might like them to be." In Guatemala, for example, a military government that had come to power through a coup was afforded swift recognition for the stated reason that it had pledged to fulfill Guatemala's international obligations. An additional but unpublicized factor was that before the coup it had appeared likely that Juan José Arévalo, a former president and an associate of Jacobo

Árbenz's, would win the upcoming elections. To spare Kennedy the embarrassment of another Árbenz situation, the military rule of Colonel Enrique Peralta had only to wait a matter of days before being granted recognition as the legitimate government of Guatemala.[79]

The number of coups that occurred during Kennedy's administration also seemed to suggest that the policy of withholding recognition was not having the desired impact. After military officers seized power in Honduras in October 1963 and relations were suspended, the new government waved off the departing ambassador with, "You'll be back in six months." "And we *were* back, of course," he later recalled, "and nothing much was accomplished." The decision had been taken to restore relations with Honduras and the Dominican Republic, which had recently suffered a similar takeover, by November 1963, but not until Johnson was in office would this be publicly confirmed. The case-by-case approach to recognition that Mann advocated—which he insisted had been the main point of his Mann Doctrine speech—was largely a continuation of the policies that he inherited.[80]

That stability and pragmatism trumped idealism is not in itself surprising. For all its grand rhetoric, the Alliance had always been designed as a method of securing Latin America during the Cold War, preventing the spread of either global or indigenous Communist movements. Nowhere was this clearer than in the scope and nature of military assistance that the Kennedy administration provided throughout the region. Although the United States had long provided funds for the armed forces of most Latin American nations, under Kennedy this policy became almost entirely focused on internal security. Counterinsurgency training was provided for officers at the School of the Americas in the Panama Canal Zone, and regular attempts were made to steer Latin American purchases away from equipment or supplies to guard against external threats such as ships or long range artillery and toward those that would help maintain internal security such as small arms and light vehicles.[81] Military assistance was viewed as entirely complementary to the Alliance, supporting internal stability and security while Alliance programs looked to other aspects of national development. By the time LBJ took office, Congress had approved over $1 billion a year in military aid to Latin America, prompting the new president to request a State Department report on the uses of military funds. The response was almost identical to the conclusions of the previous administration: continue to focus efforts on counterinsurgency and internal security.[82]

The Kennedy administration had also been well aware that private investment was vital for the success of the Alliance for Progress yet had continually failed to encourage increased flows of private capital into the region. The moves to acknowledge the need for private investment more openly that occurred in 1963 had served to slow the decline in US investment in Latin America but not arrest the slump entirely. When Johnson later told a gathering of CIAP representatives that "you could take all the gold in Fort Knox and it would just go down the drain in Latin America" unless private inves-'tors were confident of being given fair opportunities, he was only acknowledging what Kennedy had come to realize. That Johnson and Mann fared better than their predecessors, with $26 million in new investment in the first three months of 1964, was less a major change in policy and more an improvement in implementation. Nor did it mean that private investment took the place of public financing. The United States consistently provided more loans and grants to Latin America under Johnson than it had under Kennedy, averaging around $100 million a year more.[83]

In policy terms, the period following President Kennedy's death witnessed more continuity than it did change. However, it is also impossible to ignore the significance of the fact that many observers perceived things to have changed. With the majority of the initial Alliance planners no longer in positions of authority, and with Johnson's decision to turn hemispheric policy over to a quiet, practical Texan who lacked the charisma of the Kennedy loyalists, it was easy to make the argument that the events of November 1963 led to the loss of most of the Alliance's spiritual élan. Despite the fact that a reorientation of priorities was well under way during the Kennedy presidency, and despite the fact that Kennedy was ready to replace Moscoso and appoint a powerful Latin American chief through a State Department reorganization, it was Johnson to whom the responsibility of making those changes a reality eventually fell. Hence, the personal, political, and ideological resentments that fueled the opposition to Mann's appointment were given added weight and substance and found a receptive audience among several journalists frustrated by the squandered promise of the Alliance for Progress.

Mann and Johnson were far from blameless in this process. The speed with which Johnson made his changes may have been reasonable from a practical standpoint, but it fueled suspicion that he was making a statement of intent regarding his predecessor's legacy. Similarly, Mann should have been aware that he had to tread lightly and couched some of the harder truths he felt needed to be told regarding Latin American policy in the more optimistic language of the Alliance. As it was, the Mann Doctrine confirmed the worst fears of those who were all too ready to condemn him as a reactionary relic. As a result, subsequent years would see Johnson and Mann fighting an uphill battle to convince large sections of the press, public, and Congress that they sought anything other than a reversion to the domination, intervention, and exploitation that had so often marked their country's relations with its southern neighbors.

3

The Good Neighbor Returns?

Panama, Brazil, and the Alliance for Progress

Following a difficult and emotionally charged transition of power in the wake of John F. Kennedy's death, the Johnson administration would also face a challenging first year in its attempts to implement its Latin American policy. The nature of the transition and the reaction to Thomas Mann's new role in the administration had placed inter-American affairs under the microscope, a situation the new president felt owed as much to his upbringing as it did to any policy developments. "There is a question whether or not there's bigotry in the North against a Southerner on questions that involve his ability to handle foreign relations," Johnson complained to his aide George Reedy. As he pointed out: "[Political cartoonists] always put a string bow tie on me. . . . I never wore one in my life." His decision to host his first major international summit, the visit of German chancellor Ludwig Erhard, at his Texas ranch did little to adjust this perception; nor did Mann's appointment, with the press taking note of Johnson's choice of a fellow Texan to oversee Latin American policy. The *Washington Post*, for example, noted disapprovingly: "Texas, in the opinion of many Latins, connotes big oil, brash bulldozing tactics, and the unforgiven Texas war against Mexico."[1]

While 1964 would witness no trauma on the scale of the Cuban Missile Crisis, a series of challenges would test the two Texans' ability to manage hemispheric affairs and ensure that the region remained in the public eye. Eschewing a fundamental reassessment of the Alliance for Progress, Johnson and Mann would instead attempt to get the program functioning more efficiently, reassure hemispheric allies and skeptics in the media that the program had not died with Kennedy, and negotiate any crises that could threaten a Democratic victory in the upcoming presidential election. The manner in which this was achieved would demonstrate a far greater degree of continuity with recent policy than many of Johnson's critics were willing to admit, but it also reflected the transition from the dominance of the New Frontiersmen to Mann's leadership. By December, the Alliance would be showing some statistical improvements and boasting an impressive list of achievements, while crises in Panama and Brazil would be navigated with minimal harm to the administration. Johnson and Mann would also develop a close working relationship and level of trust that remained in place until Mann's departure from government service in 1966, in part reflecting the president's satisfaction with his handling of preelection hemispheric affairs. Although 1964 would be in many ways a bruising year, by the end of it there would be some cause for optimism that the prospects of the Alliance for Progress, and Mann's reputation with it, were improving, but there would also be warning signs of greater problems yet to come.

Crisis Diplomacy: Panama

1964 was just a week old when a crisis that would sorely test Johnson and Mann's diplomatic abilities erupted in a region of vast strategic importance, the Panama Canal Zone. As a student protest swiftly escalated into a major diplomatic confrontation and a break in relations, media outlets around the world would closely follow this "first major foreign affairs test of the Johnson administration." Coverage throughout much of Latin America was sympathetic to Panamanian grievances and wary of any overt exercise of power by Washington, while media outlets in China, the Soviet Union, and Cuba would be full of charges of US "imperialism and aggression." For Johnson, the Panama crisis would provide an opportunity to dispel doubts over his ability to handle foreign affairs, and it would be Mann's first chance to prove that his president had not erred in recalling him from Mexico. Despite setbacks and criticism along the way, the skill and flexibility with which Johnson and Mann would steer the crisis to a satisfactory conclusion would be impressive, providing an early riposte to claims that the new administration ushered in a period of rigid and reactionary responses to hemispheric challenges.[2]

Holding a unique place in American foreign relations, the intimate and uneasy ties between the United States and Panama can be traced to the start of the twentieth century when President Theodore Roosevelt harnessed the nationalism of the Panamanian people, at that time officially a part of Colombia, to secure access to a site for a transoceanic canal. Encouraging a declaration of independence in November 1903, Roosevelt used American warships to ensure that Colombia, whose congress had recently rejected a proposed canal treaty, would not attempt to reclaim its lost territory by force, before negotiating a new treaty with Panama that same month on terms far more generous to the United States. He would later claim that he had behaved "in absolute accord with the highest standards of international morality."[3] The rapidly agreed Hay-Bunau-Varilla Treaty of November 1903 secured the "use, occupation, and control" of an area extending five miles on either side of the proposed canal route and allowed for the future occupation of "any other lands and waters" that might be necessary for the smooth operation of the canal. The use of this land was granted "in perpetuity," and, although the Canal Zone would not technically be sovereign US soil, its occupier would have all the rights it "would possess and exercise if it were the sovereign of the territory." In return, Panama would receive a one-off payment of $10 million, an annual fee of $250,000, and a guarantee that the United States would "maintain the independence of the Republic of Panama."[4]

Fifty years later, the Canal Zone was a curious oddity. Wrapped around the 48-mile-long waterway were 553 square miles of US military bases and homes for the mostly North American zone employees, many of which were the epitome of white-picket-fence and manicured-lawn 1950s Americana. The zone physically divided a nation that, while literate and stable by Central American standards, enjoyed nothing like the wealth afforded to the "Zonians." Panama received only a fraction of the profits from the canal, and resentment was further stoked by discriminatory practices within the zone, notably the disparity in wages between Panamanians and North Americans.[5]

Economic discrimination was compounded by a symbolic insult that led to major riots in November 1959—the Zonians' refusal to fly the Panamanian flag. President Dwight Eisenhower's response was to acknowledge publicly Panama's "titular sovereignty" in the zone and announce that the Panamanian flag would be flown alongside the Stars and Stripes at select locations. Congressman Daniel Flood (D-Penn) called the actions "Munich in spades" and demanded that the president be impeached, a reaction that earned him the designation "Panama's enemy number one" within the Panamanian National Assembly.[6] Unfortunately for Panama, Flood represented only an extreme example of what most Americans—and particularly Zonians—believed. As

Richard Scammon, director of the Commerce Department's Bureau of the Census, would later tell Lyndon Johnson, the willingness of the American public to placate foreign nations did "not extend to getting pushed around by a small country about an area which every grade school history book features with an American flag, a snapshot of Teddy Roosevelt, and an image of gallant engineers overcoming the mosquito."[7]

For Eisenhower and his successor, John F. Kennedy, Panamanian complaints were a regular source of irritation. Tensions were generally not eased by the Panamanian ruling oligarchy, described as "perhaps the most socially irresponsible [elite] in Latin America" by one scholar of the nation's political scene. Unwilling to implement reforms that might undermine its authority, during the 1950s and 1960s the oligarchy sought instead to harness burgeoning nationalist feeling through regular criticism of the United States. In an attempt to draw attention away from the canal issue, Kennedy would increase the scale of US aid to Panama, but protests continued, and, in late 1962, he agreed to more sites where the Panamanian flag could fly as well as issuing a joint communiqué with Panamanian president Roberto Chiari announcing that a bilateral commission would examine all sources of tension between the nations.[8]

In May 1963, US ambassador to Panama Joseph Farland recommended that, in light of growing tensions and the inadequacy of periodic symbolic concessions, the United States should announce its willingness to negotiate an entirely new canal treaty. This advice was so unwelcome in Washington that Farland was removed from his position the following August. The joint commission achieved nothing, and the State Department decided instead that the best course of action would be to "give a liberal interpretation to existing treaties in order to place United States–Panamanian relations on a more mutually satisfactory basis." In effect, this meant more of the same; Washington would offer minor concessions to pull the sting from the "ultranationalistic sentiment" that threatened peaceful operation of the canal.[9]

The shortcomings of this approach were soon starkly exposed when, on 7 January 1964, American students at the Balboa High School in the Canal Zone raised the Stars and Stripes, ignoring a decision of the previous year that it would be flown side by side with the Panamanian flag at civilian institutions. In response, a group of Panamanian students marched into the zone on 9 January and attempted to raise their own flag. When Canal Zone police intervened, riots broke out that would last for days. Unable to defuse the situation, the zone police called in the US Army, and, by 13 January, 4 American soldiers were dead, 85 North Americans were injured, 24 Panamanians had lost their lives, and a further 200 had been wounded. The confrontations sparked a furious reaction from the Panamanian government. In a message to Dean Rusk, Foreign Minister Galileo Solís registered a "formal protest over the acts of ruthless aggression" and placed the entire blame on "the uncontrollable aggressive acts of the American armed forces." As a result, he concluded: "The Government of Panama considers that its diplomatic relations with your distinguished government are broken."[10]

The initial response in Washington was confusion. Panicked situation reports from military sources in the zone passed on rumors of armed mobs roaming the streets and American citizens being lynched. Mann immediately instructed the embassy to burn classified codes and documents and ordered that no flags should be flown "at any place" in the zone. At a meeting with the president on 10 January, he noted that the Panamanian government appeared to be doing little to curb the violence. After CIA director John McCone opined, with little evidence, that Communist agitators had seized control of the flag issue to spark the riots, Johnson ignored the traditional diplomatic channels and demanded to talk to President Chiari on the telephone. Speaking through an interpreter, he deplored the current violence and warned that it could be exploited by extremists. Chiari responded that only "a complete revision of all treaties" could resolve the impasse, reminding Johnson that, since Kennedy had promised a joint commission, "not a thing has been done to alleviate the situation." Partially mollified, Johnson responded that "violence is never any way to settle anything" but promised Chiari: "The most respected people I have . . . [will be] in the plane in 30 minutes." Sure enough, that afternoon Thomas Mann and Deputy Secretary of Defense Cyrus Vance were on their way to Panama.[11]

Arriving in Panama City on the afternoon of 10 January, Mann expressed his and his president's "deep regret" at the current disorder. The only way forward, he stated, would be the path of "peace and understanding, not that of violence." His immediate objectives were to avoid an embarrassing mutual withdrawal of embassy staff and to begin discussions with Chiari on how to stop the current violence and prevent future outbreaks. He and Vance also needed to control the Zonians, whose flouting of Kennedy's pledges had torpedoed the State Department's attempts at defusing Panamanian nationalism. The latter task proved the easier. With many Zonians shocked by the anger of the Panamanian reaction, they cooperated with an order from Mann and Vance to fly the flags of both nations side by side at as many locations in the Canal Zone as possible. They were also given little choice, with Rusk reminding Mann: "We cannot accept defiance of US govt [*sic*] by its own citizens on a matter of international agreement. . . . [I]t must be made clear that discipline on such matters is a condition of continued Canal Zone employment for Americans."[12]

Building bridges with Roberto Chiari would prove to be far more challenging, with Mann soon convinced that the Panamanian president was milking the disturbances for all they were worth. "We were met at the airport and conducted to the palace in cloak and dagger fashion," he reported to Washington the next day, "and much of the conversation was conducted with the background of 600 Panamanians outside chanting 'out with the Gringos.'" Mann noted in his report that some of the protesting he witnessed felt "staged," and he would repeat this claim in an interview several years later, noting that his delegation was driven on a circuitous route through various checkpoints before arriving at a presidential palace surrounded by boisterous crowds. "We were asked to sit down by a large plate glass window which opened out into the square. People . . . began to throw rocks and yell and scream at the plate glass window so that we had difficulty in talking above the noise. I thought it was rather strange that we would sit there by the noise and by the window instead of a place where we could have talked more quietly."[13]

Chiari likely was exploiting the protests for maximum impact. Having placed renegotiation of the 1903 treaty at the heart of resolving the differences with Washington, he desperately needed some significant concessions to demonstrate to his people that he had not been forced into a humiliating climbdown. Hence, his opening position during his initial meeting with Mann was to indicate that, unless the United States could promise a full revision of the canal treaty, he would go ahead with the break in relations, leaving the problem of whether to resume them to whomever succeeded him in the election scheduled for the coming May.[14]

Mann was not lacking in sympathy for the Panamanian position, informing Washington that, while subsequent protests may have been managed, there was no evidence that the initial riots were premeditated. Some Communists may have been involved in the disturbances, he admitted, but the Panamanian people had enough genuine grievances that this was "not necessary . . . to explain this outburst of anti-US feeling." He was less impressed with Chiari's manipulation of public anger, however, agreeing with Johnson that "we cannot negotiate under the pressure of violence." Hence, Mann's response to Chiari's demands was to inform the president that, once the riots had been calmed and relations normalized, talks could begin. If Chiari wished to break relations, "this was something we could live with," but it would gain his country nothing.[15]

Over subsequent days, Mann became only more convinced that, while the riots had erupted spontaneously, the conservative oligarchy was playing the dangerous game of trying to harness public anger in order to gain significant concessions from the United States. In a telegram to Rusk and Defense Secretary Robert McNamara, he explained that, despite the ruling elite controlling almost all media outlets, "highly inflammatory" reports continued to provoke further violence, and he had seen "no sustained effort . . . to get Panamanian people to remain calm and refrain from participating in mob violence." Unwilling and unable to promise treaty revisions, he met briefly with the hastily convened OAS Inter-American Peace Committee (IAPC) to offer the full cooperation of his government before heading out to meet with Chiari, where he made a final effort to prevent the formal breaking of relations. The United States was willing to discuss anything and everything, he promised Chiari in Spanish, as long as there were no preconditions, such as a promise to negotiate new treaties. Chiari responded that such a promise was the only way to resume relations and called for the official withdrawal of US diplomats from the embassy. Switching to English for the benefit of Vance and Ralph Dungan, who were also present, Mann warned that, the longer violence continued, the greater the influence of the extremists would become. The United States would keep the Zonians in line, but, if there were further Panamanian incursions into the zone, there would be repercussions. Chiari agreed, and, on that unpromising note, the United States delegation returned to Washington.[16]

Arriving back in the United States, Mann went immediately to the White House to report to Johnson and his senior foreign policy team. He advised maintaining the stance of no negotiations "under duress" but also expressed frustration at past and present US policy. The Zonians were a major part of the problem, he pointed out, totally unadjusted to the nation in which they lived, and hostile to native Panamanians. More pertinently, the current treaties with Panama were unfair, he argued, suggesting that, if the OAS could repair the broken relations, then wide-ranging negotiations with no preconditions should begin. Just as he had during his successful negotiation of the Chamizal border dispute with Mexico, Mann recognized that clinging to outdated and unfair agreements was of little benefit, damaging the reputation of the United States and providing a focal point for instability. Echoing Ambassador Farland's suggestion of the previous year, he endorsed a new Panama Canal treaty, although this time the advice would be more warmly received.[17]

Mann's presentation swayed Johnson toward a position of conciliation, but in an election year the president remained wary of appearing to be giving in to Panamanian pressure for treaty revision. When Mann and Vance had departed Panama City, they had left behind Ed Martin, Mann's predecessor in ARA, as the US representative. Mann wanted Martin to negotiate an agreement through the IAPC and assured Johnson that under no circumstances would Martin make an open commitment to treaty revision. Johnson was adamant that he would not give the impression that foreign nations could "burn the USIS [i.e., USIA] and kill soldiers and we will come running," but, if Rusk and McNamara were in agreement, Martin could begin discussions.[18]

This reticence was somewhat understandable. The Panama crisis was a first test in foreign affairs, and Johnson was keenly aware that the press would be observing his performance closely. Determined to appear strong and decisive but also fair, he was still operating under the same domestic pressures that had hampered his predecessors. Congressman Flood, for example, believed Panamanian demands to be "part of the audacious, cunning, and far reaching strategy of the Soviets" and urged him to expand the Canal Zone by force. Flood's was the loudest but far from the only voice to raise concerns, with more levelheaded politicians and Johnson allies in the Senate also demanding a firm response. His old mentor Richard Russell (D-GA) informed the president that he was opposed to any concessions over a canal built by "American ingenuity and blood, sweat, and sacrifices," and Everett Dirksen (R-IL) blustered: "We are in the amazing position of having a country with one-third the population of Chicago kick us around. If we crumble in Panama, the reverberations of our actions will be felt around the world." With senior figures from both sides of the aisle endorsing a show of strength—and in an election year no less—the president felt he had little room to maneuver.[19]

To Johnson's great relief, then, his decision to remain firm while dangling the possibility of future treaty revisions was initially met with widespread approval from the press. Most criticism was in fact reserved for the behavior of the Zonians, and numerous editorials favored entering treaty negotiations once order was restored. On 23 January, Johnson announced that, while "violence is never justified and is never a basis for talks," he was prepared to resume "peaceful discussions" with no "preconceptions of what they will produce" and hoped "that Panama can take the same approach." He appeared to have judged the public mood accurately, with State Department reports noting that his statement had received widespread editorial support, with most debate reserved for what concessions would be considered reasonable.[20]

Johnson was not the only president with domestic pressures to consider, however. Riding on a wave of nationalist feeling, Chiari had sworn to the Panamanian people that there would be no diplomatic relations with the United States until a new treaty was promised. "I will not deviate one instant from that position," he vowed. Mann had little patience for what he saw as political grandstanding, telling BGLA chair David Rockefeller that Chiari was "riding this public tiger and sort of likes it." Nonetheless, both he and Martin worried about Chiari's future and believed that the president's more extreme pronouncements were a result of pressure from the radical elements of the Panamanian public and government. Chiari could be difficult, but he was a known quantity who could be bargained with. If he was overthrown, Mann feared a resulting struggle for power between the extreme right and the extreme left could lead to an ultranationalistic and potentially Communist regime in an area of vital strategic interest to the United States.[21]

Lending credence to Mann's fears were rumors of a potential coup led by former president Arnulfo Arias. On 14 January, Martin informed Mann that Arias had sounded out Robert Walker, the chief of Canal Zone security, regarding the attitude of the United States toward such an eventuality. Unfortunately for Arias, Mann considered him to be "two-faced, unpredictable, anachronistic, and racist." Martin was told: "We do not wish in any way to lead Arias to believe that he has United States support." Walker was instructed to ignore the former president's advances. As the stalemate dragged on, Mann reminded Martin in February: "We would prefer to see Chiari continue in office because of inevitable risks for us inherent in any political upheaval, and probability that United States will be blamed for causing Chiari's downfall."[22]

Mann and others update President Johnson on the situation in Panama, 29 January 1964. *Left to right:* Ralph Dungan, Secretary of State George Ball, Cyrus Vance, Thomas Mann, Ambassador Ellsworth Bunker, President Johnson (back to camera). (Lyndon Baines Johnson Library photo by Yoichi Okamoto.)

By late January, the situation appeared deadlocked. Mann had sold Johnson on negotiating a new treaty, but the president refused to admit as much publicly until Chiari restored relations. Chiari, on the other side of the equation, had backed himself into a corner by declaring that there would be no relations until a new treaty was promised. Dean Rusk assured nervous senators that the situation was simply choreographed diplomatic procedure, "a kind of minuet," but in reality both partners were temporarily unwilling to dance. A seemingly endless series of talks followed, first in Panama, then in the United States, but rarely did they offer genuine hope of a resolution. In late January, Martin believed that he had formulated a statement with the Panamanians that could be satisfactory for both sides, saving face while also providing a basis for the resumption of diplomatic relations. The agreement collapsed when the Panamanians wanted a commitment to *negotiate* while Johnson would allow only the use of the word *discuss*. Mann was willing to go so far as to promise *revisions,* but Johnson would have none of it, and the IAPC gave up in disgust, issuing a statement that effectively declared, according to Mann, "a plague on both your houses." Exasperated, Mann looked for alternative solutions, including offering a new contract for a potential sea-level canal. He envisaged the new canal contract as both carrot and stick in the negotiations; it could be used as an incentive to placate angry Panamanians, but the possibility that the United States would negotiate the contract with one of Panama's neighbors was also a threat that carried real weight. On 21 January, he asked the Johnson aide Bill Moyers whether they should present it to the president as a serious plank in their negotiation strategy. "Let's do it," Moyers responded.[23]

Recognizing the potential leverage provided by the sea-level-canal issue, Johnson incorporated the strategy into his overall approach, openly exploring the possibility of building a new waterway in another Central American country, largely in an effort to weaken Panamanian resolve. Mann's advocacy of the strategy did not, however, detract from his genuine commitment to securing a long-term solution to the dispute over the existing waterway, but, on 29 January, the process hit a new low when Panama invoked the Rio Treaty, effectively declaring that US actions had constituted an armed attack on a sovereign nation. A frustrated Ralph Dungan told Mann that he was placing too much faith in the leverage provided by the sea-level canal and suggested that improved economic aid could instead buy the United States twenty more years under the current treaty. He urged Mann to draft a statement for the president that included some "sweet music," promising economic development for the Panamanian people. Convinced that a fundamental renegotiation of the bilateral relationship was essential, Mann cut him down immediately. The issue is not levels of aid, he snapped: "The issue is sovereignty and perpetuity. . . . [W]e can't buy them off and think we have worked our way out of basic issues." Unfortunately, resolving those basic issues remained frustratingly complex, and the deadlock continued into March, with twenty-eight different proposals failing to satisfy either the Americans, the Panamanians, or both.[24]

The breakthrough eventually came when, feeling that he had displayed the necessary toughness without appearing unreasonable but also beginning to worry about Chiari's ability to remain in power until the May elections, Johnson decided that the time had come to be magnanimous. In a statement to the press on 21 March, he described the current impasse as "a source of deep regret," acknowledged Panamanian support during World War II, and accepted that demands for a new treaty stemmed not "from malice or hatred of America" but from a "deeply felt sense of the honest and fair needs of

Panama." The sooner relations were restored, he noted, the sooner both nations could tackle the real enemies of the hemisphere, "hunger and ignorance, disease and injustice." With Panamanian resolve already wavering, Johnson's statement was just enough to allow US ambassador to the OAS Ellsworth Bunker and Miguel Moreno, his Panamanian counterpart, to draft a new statement that would be acceptable to both sides, settling on the word *agreement*. Relations would soon be restored, but not without one last piece of stage management on Johnson's part.[25]

On 3 April, the president held a rare meeting of the NSC and invited key congressional leaders to attend.[26] Announcing a breakthrough in the impasse, he informed the gathering that he would be sending former secretary of the treasury Robert Anderson to discuss all issues with Panama and was appointing the Peace Corps official Jack Vaughn as the new US ambassador there. There would be no preconditions on negotiations, he promised, reminding his audience that this had been "our first and last position." Finally, unable to resist one last flourish, he picked up the telephone and called Roberto Chiari. Promising that Anderson would have "full power to listen to all differences between the two nations, without limitation," he assured Chiari of his belief that their nations would reach "a fair and just agreement." "That's the way to do it," responded Chiari in English, and relations were duly restored. Johnson's somewhat self-indulgent display had the desired effect, with even the professional skeptic Wayne Morse writing in his newsletter of the "thrilling experience" of being present for the "historic telephonic conference" during which LBJ had reestablished relations with Panama.[27]

Following the April resumption of relations, Mann's focus turned inward, toward convincing skeptical members of the administration to support the negotiation of a new canal treaty rather than simply adapting the original, 1903 one. Although he had expressed doubts to Johnson about his ability to convince the administration hawks of the plan's viability, Mann ultimately succeeded, and, on 18 December 1964, the president was able to make one more significant statement on Panama. Reminding the nation of the tough stand he had taken during the first days of the crisis, Johnson noted that the United States "never made concessions to force" but also "always supported fair play and full respect for the rights of others." With that in mind, he announced, negotiations would begin on an entirely new Panama Canal treaty. Although for Congressman Flood this marked the victory of the "Bolshevik Revolution of 1917 and the international communist conspiracy," for Johnson and Mann it represented a satisfying conclusion to their first major Latin American policy challenge.[28]

A dispute with a tiny Central American nation was not the most auspicious start to the new administration's management of hemispheric policy. Johnson had found himself negotiating the fine line between appearing a weak and indecisive negotiator and coming off as a bullying imperialist clinging to the gains of an era long since passed. With that in mind, his and Mann's handling of the initial riots and the subsequent diplomatic wrangling was relatively impressive. Mann displayed a clear understanding of the political realities of Panamanian society, recognizing that Chiari's grandstanding was designed to maintain his domestic position, and dismissing Communist influence as negligible. He also convinced Johnson that Panamanian claims were legitimate and that, once relations were restored, negotiations should proceed on a more acceptable treaty. For his part, the president unsurprisingly never lost sight of the domestic pressures that limited his freedom of action, never relinquishing his stance that there could be no negotiations under the threat of violence. Nonetheless, Johnson did recognize when the time had come to use more conciliatory language and open the path to restoring relations, then proceeding to authorize wide-ranging talks that would result in, albeit more than ten years later, a new Panama Canal treaty. In doing so, he tackled a long-standing international dispute that was not of his own making. As Ralph Dungan would later concede: "[The Panama Canal crisis was] not at all attributable to Johnson, and indeed if anything that can be laid at the feet of the Kennedy Administration for not having . . . square[d] that business away."[29]

The crisis also saw Mann and Johnson establish a level of trust that would remain until Mann's departure from government service in 1966. Mann swiftly became accustomed to Johnson's tendency to veer from harsh criticism to fulsome praise without taking either too seriously.[30] He also learned how to coax his president into fulfilling unappealing duties and phrase his requests in a way that appealed to Johnson's sensibilities. When LBJ at one point moaned that meeting the IAPC would be "just a waste of time," Mann agreed but pointed out that not to do so would "create a big problem." Just "give them a pat on the back," Mann soothed, and Johnson went ahead with the meeting. Most importantly for their developing relationship, Mann's judgment on Panama proved to be correct. Communist influence was minimal to nonexistent, the potential sea-level canal proved to be effective as carrot and stick, and the promise of a new treaty after a period of cool restraint allowed Johnson to appear both strong and reasonable. As the historian Walter LaFeber has acknowledged: "Mann understood that a new treaty would cost the United States little, while it would effectively neutralize more radical Panamanians." He therefore advised his president accordingly. Johnson could feel not only that he had made a wise choice in bringing Mann back from Mexico but also that his administration "had passed [its] first test in Latin America."[31]

While Johnson's handling of the Panama crisis was largely successful, there were troubling signs that all was not well with the administration's hemispheric policy. Although the crisis was eventually resolved through diplomatic means, there is evidence that the potential use of force was never far from the minds of US policy makers. In a telephone conversation with Vance regarding the possibility of Chiari's overthrow, Mann commented that the best US response regarding a potential power struggle would be to "let them fight it out themselves." However, if a Communist takeover ever appeared likely, he believed Johnson might be required to send in troops. McNamara concurred and drew up a detailed contingency plan for military intervention based on a scenario in which Communist forces seized power from Chiari. Such contingency planning was relatively common, particularly for a region as strategically crucial as the Canal Zone. Nonetheless, it is clear that, as had been the case under Eisenhower and Kennedy, the fear of communism spreading in Latin America was never far from the minds of Johnson's policy-making team, which was ready and willing to back up diplomatic and economic efforts with military force in the face of a real or perceived Communist threat.[32]

The crisis also revealed that the internal bickering that had plagued the Kennedy administration's Latin American efforts had not entirely subsided. In particular, Mann and Dungan had a number of disputes and terse exchanges, with Mann believing that Dungan was using his position in the White House to undermine State Department policy. Their differences helped create the false impression among a number of observers that Mann was advocating a "tougher line" than Dungan's more conciliatory position, despite Mann's commitment to a new treaty. By June, the disputes between the two had reached a point where McGeorge Bundy informed Johnson: "As long as Tom Mann is No. 1 on Latin America, it simply will not be practicable for

Ralph to play the role . . . which he had in the last administration." Dungan would be appointed ambassador to Chile in December, but for several months his relationship with Mann would remain uneasy.[33]

Finally, despite the generally positive press coverage, there were signs of Mann's problems with the media that would fully emerge with the Mann Doctrine controversy in March. One particularly critical article published in the *New York Times,* for instance, led Mann to complain bitterly to Johnson: "No matter who we're fighting, they're on the other side." The disputes over the language used in the multiple failed proposals also led the press to question whether the administration possessed a consistent policy. When Mann appeared to have prematurely endorsed one particular wording, it was widely reported that he and Johnson were at loggerheads over what would constitute a reasonable agreement. The *Washington Evening Star,* for example, stated: "A blanket of rumors and counter-rumors today covers the relationship between President Johnson and . . . Thomas C. Mann." Although relatively innocuous, these reports reflected the struggle that Mann and Johnson were undergoing in getting the press on their side and presaged the furor that would occur after Mann's speech on 18 March. Mann would still be attempting to fight the fires caused by Tad Szulc's Mann Doctrine article when the hemisphere would be rocked by yet another major crisis, this time in Brazil.[34]

The Brazil Coup

By geography alone Brazil was of significant strategic importance to US policy makers during the Cold War, its vast borders abutting almost every other nation in the Southern Cone. John Kennedy made this point clear to former Brazilian president Juscelino Kubitschek in 1962, remarking: "Cuba doesn't bother me much, it is a small island; but Brazil . . . is a continent. Communism in Brazil would endanger the security of the western world." His concerns focused on President João Goulart, who had risen from vice president when his predecessor, Jânio Quadros, had ill-advisedly submitted his resignation in a misguided attempt to strengthen his position with the Brazilian National Congress. A CIA report from July 1963 described Goulart as an opportunist, possibly waiting for an opening to impose a "Perón-type" regime, and observed that growing hostility from the Brazilian right meant that "Goulart would be in great danger of a military coup effort if he engaged in patently unconstitutional action." Less than a year later, these observations proved prophetic. Accused of attempting to ride roughshod over the National Congress and entrench himself in power, Goulart would find himself ousted by a coalition of his military and political rivals with few tears shed in Washington over his downfall.[35]

Goulart's fate would prove to be both blessing and curse for Johnson and Mann. No CIA operation of the type employed against Árbenz in the 1950s would be required to remove a leader considered a serious threat to hemispheric security, and the resultant economic stability the military government provided gave a welcome boost to the disappointing growth statistics of the Alliance. The cost of those developments, however, was the establishment of a repressive military regime in Latin America's largest nation, confirming the worst fears of many critics that the administration was abandoning democracy in the hemisphere. For some observers, at the time and since, Johnson's support of the military government was evidence of the Mann Doctrine in action, demonstrating a renewed commitment to private economic interests and anticommunism at the expense of the Alliance's reformist goals.[36] While the administration's response would be in line with Mann's advocacy of judging new governments on a case-by-case basis, the coup itself was driven by domestic Brazilian factors, and the US policies that helped encourage the plotters were deeply enmeshed with the early days of the Alliance for Progress. While the administration's subsequent support for an increasingly repressive regime as security concerns outweighed more idealistic considerations was hardly admirable, it would demonstrate a high degree of consistency in US priorities rather than any new approach or doctrine.[37]

Developments in Brazil had been a cause for concern throughout much of John F. Kennedy's term of office. As president, Goulart enacted a moderate program of land and tax reform but also displayed little enthusiasm for the Alliance, legalized the Brazilian Communist Party, and established a foreign policy demonstrably independent from US influence. In response, CIA funding was provided to anti-Goulart candidates in gubernatorial and congressional elections, and, in 1963, the "islands of administrative sanity" policy was introduced whereby Alliance funds would circumvent the central government in Brasilia and be given directly to state governors who demonstrated more favorable attitudes toward the United States. By the time Johnson entered office, US hostility to Goulart's presidency was firmly established.[38]

The most influential figure regarding US policy toward Brazil was Ambassador Lincoln Gordon. A former professor of international economics at Harvard University, Gordon was part of the task force that had planned the Alliance for Progress and had turned down an offer from Kennedy to head ARA, preferring an ambassadorial role. His links to the Alliance and progressive reputation appealed to Johnson, keen as he was to appear to be maintaining continuity with his predecessor's policies. Further enhancing the ambassador's standing in Johnson's eyes was that he was not part of the hostile group of Kennedy loyalists, with Schlesinger, for example, referring disparagingly to Gordon as "that embodiment of the conventional wisdom." Gordon was not universally liked in Brazil either, where some colleagues found him austere, judgmental, and condescending.[39]

Nonetheless, Gordon's input had been influential in establishing both the Alliance and Kennedy's islands of administrative sanity policy, and he would continue to guide Washington's approach to Brazil during the subsequent administration, inundating Mann and Johnson with his doubts regarding Goulart's intentions, portraying him as "childish and erratic" and a "personable demagogue." From an early stage of his ambassadorship, Gordon had been advocating the cultivation of closer ties with the Brazilian military and during the first month of Johnson's presidency was preparing contingency plans suggesting potential economic reprisals in case of a "sharp leftward turn in Brazilian economic policies." He was soon informing Washington of rumors that "Jango," the common nickname for Goulart, was planning a "provocation" that would allow him to assume wide-reaching powers.[40]

Mann shared many of Gordon's concerns, informing Johnson in February 1964 that "Brazil is sick, [and] Goulart is irresponsible," and endorsing the continuation of Kennedy's economic policies. Utilizing the power over loan authorizations that his recent bureaucratic reorganization had provided him, he continued to divert Alliance funds away from Goulart's control, citing his failure to arrest Brazil's runaway inflation. Under Kennedy, the Alliance had provided around $750 million in aid, yet it was estimated that the cost of living for the average Brazilian had increased in 1963 almost 80 percent on the previous year. In such an economic climate, rumors of coups were rife, and, in early March, Gordon informed Washington that, sooner or later, turning to the Brazilian military might be a viable option. "Traditionally [the] Brazilian military . . . have been a stabilizing and moderating factor in [the] Brazilian political scene," he observed, predicting that, if a "reaction to

[a] left-wing coup attempt led to [a] temporary military takeover, they would be quick to restore constitutional institutions and return power to civilian hands."[41] Gordon's views may have had some tenuous grounding in history, but the fact that he was seriously contemplating the benefits of a military seizure of government suggests just how unstable and dangerous he felt the Brazilian political situation had become.[42]

The crisis that would topple João Goulart and result in the military rule of Brazil began to gather momentum throughout the early spring of 1964. On 10 March, the *New York Times* reported that Goulart was planning seizures of private property, and these fears were soon realized when Brazilian petroleum production was nationalized under the umbrella of Petrobras, followed by a warning from the president that, if Congress was unwilling to cooperate with his measures, he would find a way to dramatically reduce its power. While visiting Washington on 18 March, Gordon received messages from his embassy indicating that Goulart's actions had pushed the Brazilian political scene to the breaking point. Most of the Brazilian Congress believed Goulart to have revealed his "Golpista intentions," one telegram commented, and the only alternatives were now "Cubanization or impeachment." Organized opposition to the president then emerged on 19 March when the conservative governor of Guanabara State, Carlos Lacerda, asked his fellow governors to join him in "democratic union against usurpation and demagoguery" and accused Goulart of secretly receiving support from the Soviet Union.[43]

Gordon rushed back to Brazil in time to witness almost 200,000 people take to the streets of São Paolo in opposition to Goulart's perceived attacks on Congress. Impressed by the scale and democratic nature of the protests, he nonetheless noted the "indifference, perhaps even hostility, of much of [the] lower class" and reflected that "polarization of public opinion has gone far."[44] Any doubts he may have had about the nature of the opposition paled, however, in comparison to his worries regarding Goulart's economic plans. The day after the rally, 25 March, he reported rumors that Goulart planned to abandon the struggling debt-restructuring program, nationalize all industry, and appoint Leonel Brizola, his controversial political ally and brother-in-law, to a senior cabinet position.[45] Goulart then angered senior military figures by pardoning a group of navy sailors who had revolted over their working conditions while pledging support for the embattled president. The pardons were described by Gordon as "body blows to the morale of the officer corps of all three services," and the ambassador decided that the time had come to lay his cards on the table.[46]

"My considered conclusion is that Goulart is now definitely engaged on [a] campaign to seize dictatorial power, [and] accepting the active collaboration of the Brazilian Communist party," Gordon informed Washington in a lengthy and influential telegram on 27 March. "If he were to succeed," he warned, "it is more than likely that Brazil would come under full communist control." He argued that the US government should lend its support to the opposition coalition of military and political figures coalescing around the army general Humberto Castelo Branco, be prepared for "prompt US recognition [of] our side" if a civil war erupted, and even consider the possibility of overt military intervention. One phrase in particular was perfectly chosen to grab Lyndon Johnson's attention. If Goulart succeeded in his "desperate lunge for totalitarian power," the telegram warned, Brazil could become not just another Cuba but the "China of the 1960s." For a politician as sensitive to domestic criticism as Johnson, the threat of suffering the same fate as Harry Truman, who had been lambasted for losing a major nation to communism, was an exquisitely judged barb.[47]

On 31 March, the *New York Times* ran the headline "Brazil at the Brink Again." The article claimed that "Brazilian affairs have been deteriorating for a few years," that inflation was rising at "7 or 8 per cent a month," and that the political situation was "close to chaos." That same day, the tensions that had been building for months culminated in a coup that would see Goulart, described in the *Times* as a "curious combination of stubbornness and weakness," deposed and exiled.[48]

Attitudes in Washington since Gordon's forceful telegram had been mixed. State Department, NSC, CIA, and military officials all shared Gordon's concern at Goulart's policies yet were undecided as to what could be done from Washington. An appeal from Gordon for submarine-delivered arms shipments was rejected as a "puzzling request," and his recommendation that a carrier task force be dispatched was thought too provocative. The general consensus was that it would be "preferable if we could waffle through to the next election," but Brazil could not be allowed to "dribble down the drain." So, while military options were rejected, oil tankers were prepared in case rebel forces made a move and required fuel, and Gordon was instructed to continue his regular updates. As Rusk explained to him on 30 March, Johnson did not want to appear interventionist, and, if a rebellion was to garner US support, it must have at least a veneer of legitimacy. The president would not be caught out in an "awkward attempt at intervention," the secretary warned, but neither would he "be paralyzed by theoretical niceties if the options are clearly between the genuinely democratic forces of Brazil and a communist dominated dictatorship."[49]

Cognizant of growing opposition to his leadership, and acutely aware of the role of the military in maintaining his position, on 30 March Goulart rescinded the amnesty he had offered to the rebellious sailors. That night he also took to the airwaves to make a heartfelt appeal to the nation to unite, denying that he had any intention of closing Congress, and blaming domestic and foreign business interests for the campaign against him. Unfortunately for Goulart, his appeal came too late; that same day, the CIA reported that a revolution would "definitely get under way this week, probably within the next few days." Mann responded by placing all embassies and consulates on twenty-four-hour alert, and the following day the US outpost in Belo Horizonte reported: "Fourth army has begun move toward Rio with intention deposing Goulart regime." The campaign to oust the president had now begun in earnest.[50]

The initial response in Washington was cautious. As had been the case during the Panama crisis, senior administration officials who usually paid Latin American issues little attention were now following developments closely. The looming presidential election also ensured that any potential domestic impact would be carefully considered. At a hastily convened teleconference, Mann, Dungan, and Undersecretary of State George Ball agreed that, while the opportunity to see the back of "Jango" appeared too good to miss, they were desperate to minimize the risk of getting "out in front on a losing cause" and wanted the rebels to establish "some color of legitimacy" before US aid was forthcoming. Nonetheless, Gordon's request for the dispatch of naval forces was now approved, and the Joint Chiefs of Staff ordered the USS *Forrestal* carrier task group, then stationed in the North Atlantic, to proceed immediately toward Brazil. The journey would take several days, and the group's commander was ordered to "be prepared to carry out tasks as may be assigned" but for the present to "maintain secrecy of destination."[51]

Goulart was most likely unaware of the decisions being made in Washington, but, with numerous state governors declaring for the opposition and little military support, he realized that the writing was on the wall and fled the country the next day. By 1 April, Gordon could report: "We believe it is all over with democratic rebellion already 95 percent successful." The following day Pascoal Ranieri Mazzilli, the speaker of the House, was sworn in as interim president. Mazzilli's appointment allowed Johnson to sidestep the tricky question of recognition as the move possessed enough constitutional legitimacy for him to claim that there had been no break in relations. While Dean Rusk informed the press that the administration had not intervened in Brazil "in any way shape or form," Johnson simply sent Mazzilli a message of congratulations for solving Brazil's difficulties "within a framework of constitutional democracy and without civil strife." With the crisis appearing resolved and civil war averted, the *Forrestal* was ordered to undertake some innocuous maneuvers and return home. From the perspective of Washington, a troublesome leader had been removed without significant bloodshed and with minimal US involvement. In a phone call later that day, Mann expressed his delight at how events had unfolded. "I hope you're as happy about Brazil as I am," he commented. "I am," replied Johnson. "I hope they give us *some* credit, instead of hell."[52]

Initially, it appeared as if Johnson's hopes would be at least partially realized as press coverage of the coup throughout Latin America did not give the US government "hell." Fidel Castro was predictably strident, calling Mann "a known reactionary [and] an archenemy of our revolution," and claiming that the coup was planned "by the Yankee Pentagon and State Department." Some publications in other countries took a similar line, accusing the CIA of planning the moves against Goulart and condemning Johnson's "cynical" support of Mazzilli, but much of the coverage was far less strident, with the American embassy in Montevideo, for example, noting that local "newspapers generally view Goulart's fall with satisfaction or take [the] attitude he fell through his own faults." Had power passed peacefully from Mazzilli to an elected civilian president, such assessments may have become even more prevalent, but, in the days and weeks following the coup, it became increasingly clear that power now rested in the hands of the Brazilian military. Perhaps anticipating such an outcome, George Ball had been cautious regarding communication with Mazzilli, asking Gordon "what level we should play this": "We do not want to tie [the] president on prematurely." Gordon assured him that the military was "wholly free from ambitions" to remain in power, but within days it was clear that he had made a terrible misjudgment.[53]

Mazzilli's presidency would prove short-lived, with the real power in Brazilian politics, the armed forces, rapidly establishing their authority.

Launching a widespread campaign of political reprisals and arrests, the military leaders of the revolt soon installed General Castelo Branco as interim president, in theory until elections could be held the subsequent year. The arrests were committed under the authority of the first Institutional Act, a measure pushed through the legislature by the military that provided for the suspension of political rights and rights of appeal. Gordon viewed events with "considerable dismay," but he was now too committed to the revolt to falter and continued to maintain that the best hope for "avoidance of undemocratic excesses rests in character and convictions of Castelo Branco." By contrast, the *New York Times* was soon reporting that thousands of Brazilians had been arrested in efforts to "root out reds," and the paper also experienced such crackdowns firsthand when its Brasilia offices were occupied by the government and its files searched.[54] After speaking to affected reporters, Mann contacted Gordon asking what could be done to curb such actions as they were "not encouraging for [the] future." Nonetheless, the general feeling in Washington, Mann included, was that these measures were temporary and that normality would soon be restored. Johnson agreed and, despite McGeorge Bundy's warnings that he "ought to be a little careful while this fellow's locking people up," transmitted a warm and public message of congratulations following Castelo Branco's inauguration on 15 April.[55]

A depressing pattern for US-Brazilian relations was now emerging; continued political repression in Brazil would be met with handwringing in Washington, followed by policy makers reassuring each other that these measures were temporary and things would soon improve. By 6 May, almost two hundred people on the Brazilian political scene had their legislative mandates canceled and their political rights suspended, and more than five thousand Brazilians had been arrested. Mann optimistically told Rusk that, while hard-liners were currently in the ascendancy, "the characteristic moderation of the Brazilian is likely to reassert itself increasingly as initial revolutionary enthusiasms wane." That same month, Castelo Branco announced that he was extending his term of office, and, shortly afterward, former president Juscelino Kubitschek joined the ranks of the politically dispossessed. The "pendulum has swung a little bit too far back to the right," Mann admitted, nevertheless still clinging to the hope that Brazil would soon be "back on a moderate road."[56]

Despite the doubts regarding the nature of the new government, US aid was soon flowing into Brazil. As Director of Policy Planning Walt Rostow reminded Mann in late April, the United States now had "an enormous stake" in making the Brazilian government a success. Having supported the coup, the administration was desperate for evidence that Castelo Branco was acting in the best interests of the Brazilian people. Particularly important was for the economic crisis to recede, and Rostow, an expert flatterer, encouraged Mann to get more aid flowing south. "I doubt that [US]AID will move unless it gets a quite unambiguous signal from Tom Mann," he prompted. Mann agreed and in June recommended approval of $60 million from contingency funds to aid with Brazilian debt restructuring, the kind of assistance that had routinely been denied to Goulart. By the year's end, the Brazilian government would receive more than $450 million in Alliance funds, and, by the close of the decade, more aid would be sent to Brazil than to any other Latin American country.[57]

Considering the public criticism that the Johnson administration had received just weeks earlier, with the Mann Doctrine speech interpreted in some quarters as an endorsement of dictatorial regimes, it is perhaps surprising that such clear signals of support were given to a government in Brazil that was growing increasingly repressive. Indeed, the reaction to the events of 31 March gave critics of the administration plenty of ammunition. Reporting from a trip to Italy, Arthur Schlesinger wrote directly to the State Department and explained that he had repeatedly been questioned about Johnson's actions. "I tried to explain why the US government had rushed to embrace the new Brazilian regime instead of following the Kennedy policy of using a suspension of relations," he reported, "and no doubt could have done this better if I understood the reasons for the new policy myself."[58] Schlesinger's sarcasm drew a frosty response from both Bundy and Johnson, but the former aide was not alone in his views.[59] Once Castelo Branco was inaugurated, much of the US press began to take a more critical stance toward both the Brazilian government and Johnson's support for it. The *Washington Post* reported in May that Brazil was now "caught in the grip of an army dictatorship," and a *New York Times* editorial opined that, despite reassurances from the Johnson administration, "there should be no illusions": "Brazil now has an authoritarian military government."[60]

There were several factors behind Johnson's swift support of Castelo Branco's government, none more important that the influence of Ambassador Gordon; his warnings that Goulart was seeking to establish a Perón-type dictatorship and his portrayal of the military as defenders of the democratic process went a long way toward shaping the response in Washington. Castelo Branco was also extremely skilled in maintaining this image, manipulating Gordon's prejudices to his own benefit. Even while implementing the Institutional Act he was assuring Gordon: "The solution to the evils of the left will not be the birth of a reactionary right." In lengthy meetings with the ambassador, the general would regretfully acknowledge that his actions had "distasteful aspects" but assert that they were necessary in order to establish an "honest democratic government" while vehemently denying that he intended to militarize the political process. "My general impression was extremely favorable," Gordon reported after one such meeting. Castelo Branco also knew to stroke Johnson's ego, sending warm messages of congratulations after the Gulf of Tonkin incident in August, and praising LBJ's wider Vietnam policy as keeping the free world safe for democracy.[61]

There was some skepticism in Washington regarding Gordon's reporting and Castelo Branco's fawning. On one telegram, Bundy scrawled a note to Robert Sayre of the NSC staff asking: "Bob: Is Gordon being taken in a bit?" Such doubts were rarely expressed or investigated further, however, as initially Castelo Branco's benefits to the United States far outweighed his costs. As Mann informed USAID director David Bell in June, the new Brazilian government had declared friendship for the United States and support for the Alliance for Progress, loudly opposed communism, and broken relations with Cuba. Following a visit to Brazil in August, Walt Rostow returned full of praise and declaring Branco to be "a remarkable Latin American chief of state." The risk of Brazil becoming the China of the 1960s had disappeared, the new government appearing willing to tackle Brazil's crippling economic problems and welcome US influence. Castelo Branco kept the worst excesses of his government in check long enough to ensure that Johnson's initial support was followed by political and economic cooperation, locking the United States into a close relationship, and ensuring that Washington possessed an "enormous stake" in making the Brazilian government a success.[62]

To the minds of Johnson and many of his advisers, Castelo Branco's government clearly offered a number of benefits, but, in offering support so swiftly in spite of all too obvious political repression, the administration was also appearing to ally itself with antidemocratic forces and strengthening suspicions regarding the US role in Goulart's downfall. While there was little direct US involvement in the events of late March and early April, long-term efforts to destabilize Goulart, such as the islands of administrative sanity program, had been in effect for years, with funding also provided to opposition movements and close links developed with the military. Shortly before the coup, Gordon also informed Washington that the embassy and the CIA were involved in provocations such as "covert support for pro-democracy street rallies," and the dispatch of the USS *Forrestal* suggests that Johnson might have been willing to use force to support the rebellious military if it proved necessary. Certainly, it was clear to the rebels that the United States would not oppose their actions, but one has to be wary of giving too much agency to the "colossus of the North." There was widespread opposition to Goulart, both within Brazil and throughout much of Latin America, and his own political maladroitness and alienation of vital military support fueled that opposition to the point of rebellion. A clear statement of opposition to any attempts to seize power issued by the American embassy may have served to forestall a coup, but, considering US views of Goulart's leadership, it is not surprising that no such statement was forthcoming.[63]

The response to the crisis also demonstrated that, on questions related to potential Communist gains in the hemisphere, there was little difference in viewpoint between the New Dealers and the New Frontiersmen who made up the Johnson administration. Mann, like Gordon, possessed a relatively positive view regarding the character of the Brazilian military, and the removal of a potential Communist dictator without the need for direct US intervention at least partially satisfied both his Good Neighbor and his Cold Warrior instincts. The former Kennedy men who remained in the administration also endorsed Castelo Branco with "complete unanimity," in part reflecting the fact that, since the early days of the Alliance, Latin American militaries had been seen as potential allies in the campaign to modernize the hemisphere.[64]

Indeed, in responding to criticism from Kennedy loyalists now outside government such as Schlesinger and Pierre Salinger, Bundy explained: "[US policy had been] based on the recommendations of Linc Gordon, George Ball, and Dean Rusk—all Kennedy men—and the fact of the matter was that Tom Mann had been in favor of a slightly slower and cooler expression of support." In their eagerness to prevent another loss on the scale of China and shore up the new government of Brazil, the administration became associated with the military leadership and tied itself to the actions that followed. Although Mann and others were troubled by the Institutional Act and associated abuses of freedom, the security and relative economic stability provided by Castelo Branco meant that US support never seriously wavered. While Gordon and the rest of Johnson's advisers may have truly believed that Goulart intended to establish himself in a dictatorship—and indeed he may have—this theoretical possibility pales next to the reality of the decades of brutal military rule that followed the coup of 1964.[65]

On one count at least the Johnson administration's assessment of the situation proved accurate; Castelo Branco's government did improve Brazil's economic performance. Inflation fell, GDP rose, and an October 1965 State Department memo ranked Brazil's economic self-help efforts as "outstanding." However, a similar report assessing the progress of Latin American nations toward good democratic government compiled a month later ranked the region's largest country as "poor," the same rating received by Cuba. Any lingering hope that the Brazilian military intended to return its nation to civilian rule disappeared in 1966 when Castelo Branco's minister of war, General Artur da Costa e Silva, took the presidency, "elected" by the Congress. Described by Johnson's agriculture secretary Orville Freeman as "short tempered, sensitive, power conscious, and prone to alcohol," Costa e Silva ushered in a period of repression and violence that eclipsed that of his predecessor.[66]

Considering the long-term consequences for the Brazilian people, Johnson's handling of the coup was far from his most admirable moment. The speed with which he expressed public support for the new government severely limited any future ability to restrain the behavior of a repressive military that would soon set about entrenching itself in power. This response also meant that those looking for evidence that US support for democracy in the hemisphere was dead and buried were provided with a perfect example. Yet it is difficult to argue that US actions represented a significant break with previous policy. A focus on the Mann Doctrine in the case of Brazil implies either that Mann had introduced new policies toward Goulart in the precoup period or that his doctrine guided the response to the military seizure of power. Instead, the Brazilian case demonstrated that, when it came to issues of hemispheric security, both Johnson and Mann were happy to follow long-established patterns. The Good Neighbor policy had tacitly endorsed relations with right-wing authoritarian leaders, and both Eisenhower and Kennedy had demonstrated that they preferred a military government with a chance, however slim, of a return to civilian control over the possibility of a Communist-influenced dictatorship. Even more appealing in this case was that Goulart's downfall did not require substantial US intervention. Inso-much as the Alliance for Progress had any influence over decision making, Castelo Branco was actually more open to US aid programs than Goulart had been, but Alliance-related idealism played little part in the events of March and April 1964.[67]

Establishing a Johnson Policy for Latin America

The first months of Mann's and Johnson's stewardship of Latin American pol-icy had been challenging to say the least. A major administrative reorganiza-tion, internal opposition, and press criticism inflamed by the Mann Doctrine incident had made for an uncomfortable domestic scene. Concurrently, two significant and overlapping crises had tested the fledgling administration's ability to respond diplomatically to hemispheric events. With the Brazilian and Panamanian issues negotiated to a relatively satisfactory outcome, at least from the administration's point of view, and Mann's bureaucratic reorganiza-tion in place, the remainder of 1964 gave an administration with one eye firmly fixed on the November presidential election the chance to establish a clear direction in its Latin American policy. The president wanted his Mr. Latin America to continue constructing a more sustainable framework for development than the modernization-theory-driven rhetoric of the early days of the Alliance. Utilizing the breathing space afforded by the ensuing period of relative calm, Mann and Johnson seized the opportunity to implement their vision of a hemispheric policy that incorporated the best aspects of both the Good Neighbor policy and the Alliance for Progress.

Considering its turbulent beginning, 1964 ultimately provided some evi-dence for cautious optimism regarding hemispheric affairs. Both Johnson and Mann had entered office determined to cut the red tape surrounding aid authorizations and to increase the efficiency of the Alliance for Progress. Mann's back-to-back reorganization of State and USAID soon appeared to be fulfilling those goals and paying dividends, despite the negative coverage it had received. In May, USAID reported that the Alliance expected to dis-tribute 97 percent of its funds that fiscal year, a vast improvement over the performance of the Kennedy administration. "Your prodding is beginning to show results," Bundy congratulated the president. The following month, Mann reported that USAID and State were demonstrating a satisfying level of cooperation and proudly boasted: "We have processed more loans [in the past six months] than the World Bank does in a year for the entire world." In addition, Mann informed Johnson, increased cooperation with private industry had resulted in direct investment in Latin America rising by $26 million in three months, compared to a decline of $8 million in 1963 and $37 million in 1962.[68]

Alliance for Progress statistics are notoriously unreliable, but, nonetheless, Johnson's staff were soon able to report some impressive-sounding numbers to him as a result of increases in financing.[69] By the end of 1964, Gordon Chase noted, Alliance funds had built 20,000 classrooms, trained 80,000 teachers, and published 10 million textbooks. In the field of health care, 850 hospitals, medical centers, or mobile health units had been produced, reaching 11 million people throughout the hemisphere. More than 1,200 water and sewer systems affecting 27 million people had been either built or improved, 330,000 homes had been constructed, 8,000 miles of roads laid, and 250,000 agricultural loans dispersed, and the number of credit unions and rural cooperatives had tripled. Other Alliance goals also had some limited success, with tax collections improving, basic land reform programs passed by around a dozen nations, and ten finally submitting national development plans. Most significantly, the per capita GDP growth rate for 1964 was around 2 percent, still short of the targets established at Punta del Este but an improvement compared to a decline of around 1 percent in 1963.[70]

The launch of CIAP also suggested at least a limited commitment to multilateralism. Although CIAP would not have direct control over assistance funds, all US embassies were instructed to do everything in their power to help the body acquire "sufficient prestige" as "without such a collective instrument . . . we doubt that [an] adequate political base for [the Alliance] can be built and sustained." The new US CIAP representative, Walt Rostow, reported after his first meeting with his counterparts in Mexico in July that Latin Americans were keen to take on greater leadership roles, to provide the Alliance with better coordination, and to develop a code of conduct to guide transactions between national governments and private investors. CIAP could be a "vital multilateral instrument," he told Johnson. "I am more of an optimist about the Alliance for Progress than I was when you appointed me a few months ago."[71]

The positive developments regarding the Alliance for Progress meant a slight easing in the barrage of press criticism that Mann had received for the first months of his tenure. In May, *Newsweek* ran a special report, written by the former Eisenhower aide and speechwriter Emmett John Hughes, focusing on Mann's return to Washington. The piece attempted to explain why Mann had received such a rough welcome and concluded that, as "a strong principled, literal-minded Texas Puritan," the new assistant secretary had come to personify "all the subtle differences, in both substance and style, between the old New Frontiersmen of the Kennedy administration and the new Old Frontiersmen of the Johnson Administration." Goodwin and Schlesinger had dismissed Mann as a "visionless reactionary," Hughes noted, but only because Mann's views served to "challenge the premises of his liberal critics, to contend that their seeming altruism only assures diplomatic futility, and to warn that the idealistic jargon of an Anglo-Saxon political vocabulary cannot sensibly be applied to the raw realities of Latin politics." "And in all this," he concluded, "[Mann] has a lot of modern history on his side." The *Newsweek* story was a welcome fillip for Mann, but he and Johnson were well aware that much still had to be done to redress the damage inflicted by the Mann Doctrine episode and events in Brazil. "Schlesinger's going all over telling people that we've changed our Latin American policy and lost interest in the Alliance," Johnson reminded Mann in May. "We should answer him."[72]

Mann intended to answer his critics in a lengthy speech to be delivered at American University in May. He envisaged it as a "nuts and bolts" definition of the direction needed in inter-American policy, balancing hope for what might be achieved in the long term with the reality of limited American power and influence. His drafts particularly emphasized the need for nations to help themselves, the importance of commodity agreements and technical assistance, and the vital role of both North and South American private investors. Despite adding more lyrical touches than he was accustomed to, Mann found that his drafts met with disapproval from Bundy. Informing him that, while the content was sound, he had "serious reservations about its tone and balance," Bundy warned against the danger of appearing as if he was delivering "a moral lecture from on high." "I think Tom has to be particularly careful about tone," Bundy reminded Johnson, "because there are many people who are all too willing to unjustifiably paint him as a reactionary, and who will seize every opportunity or phrase to do so." Still smarting from the backlash to his speech in March, Mann reconsidered, eventually deciding to state his case at a commencement address to be read at Notre Dame University in June.[73]

The speech that Mann delivered on 7 June was a reworked version of one he had read at Baylor University four years previously, "The Democratic Ideal in the Latin American Policy of the United States." The address was essentially a statement of policy regarding political developments in the hemisphere and an attempt to refute the most damaging accusations that had accompanied the Mann Doctrine controversy and the administration's handling of the Brazilian coup. Just as he had in 1960, Mann argued in favor of Good Neighbor–style nonintervention wherever possible, citing the unforeseen consequences of Theodore Roosevelt–era meddling in other nation's political affairs. This did not mean, he clarified, that the United States would "abandon its firm policy to discourage any who conspire to overthrow constitutionally elected governments" or would ever stop encouraging nations to hold "free and fair elections." The United States would, he pledged, continue "quiet, unpublicized efforts" to foster democracy throughout the hemisphere and would consider multilateral action against repressive regimes that "outrage the conscience of mankind." Without making specific reference to Brazil, he also announced that the response to coups would be a "careful, dispassionate assessment of each situation," that there would be no doctrinaire straightjackets, but that refusal of recognition would still be an option. "Finally," he concluded, "let there be no mistake about our consistent and complete devotion to the principles of human dignity and freedom."[74]

Copies of Mann's speech were distributed to all ARA embassies as a "policy information statement," but attempts to publicize the clarification of Mann's views in the United States were not particularly successful. The only mention of the speech in the *New York Times* was buried on page 22, whereas the Mann Doctrine had been front-page news. The *Washington Post* gave the story a little more coverage, reporting Mann's comments on page 10 but providing no analysis or explanation of their significance. Bill Moyers worried that, while Mann had made an admirable attempt to "introduce *reason* into the debate," he might have come across as attempting to justify a "hard line" policy. Fortunately for Mann, some responses in Latin America were more positive, with his talk of nonintervention and multilateral solutions garnering more favorable coverage. *La Republica* of Costa Rica commented that his words had "categorically given the lie to those who charge there has been a return to the past," reports in Peru praised his "plan against dictatorships," and *El Diaro* of Bolivia described the case-by-case approach to coups as "a valid and realistic doctrine." Although there were of course publications that condemned Mann's words as the lies of "an expert in overthrowing popular governments," the more favorable reactions suggested both that Good Neighbor–era terminology had a lingering appeal and that the damage done to his reputation by the Mann Doctrine episode was not irreparable.[75]

Lyndon Johnson was also making efforts to dispel claims that he cared little about foreign policy and less about the Alliance for Progress.[76] In May, he called a meeting of Latin American ambassadors and CIAP members to the White House to announce Rostow's appointment as US representative to the Alliance's multilateral committee. He swore to those gathered that "not for a single moment or by a single act have our purpose or our principles shifted since the signing of the Charter of Punta del Este" and promised to fight Congress with "every resource of [the] government" to obtain the maximum funding for Alliance programs. Tying the Alliance into FDR's legacy as well as his own Great Society and civil rights programs, he painted a picture of a hemisphere united for change "because morality commands it, justice requires it, and our own dignity as men depends on it." Speech delivered, Johnson invited Carlos Sanz de Santamaría, the CIAP chairman, and all the ambassadors for a meeting with himself and Mann. The gathered Latin American representatives were treated to a classic Johnson performance, one encompassing deepest sincerity, bawdy humor, and sympathetic understanding. Latin America would always be a priority, he promised; there was "not a man living who cared more than he did, and no one more competent to work for the Alliance than Tom Mann." In response to queries about specific loans or legislation, he would pick up the phone to call the officials responsible, making a show of hurrying them along, and pausing to make jokes to the gathered ambassadors. The meeting ended with a reminder from Johnson to keep the faith—"a sure way to lose an election is to predict you'll lose it"—and to come to Mann with any concerns as he was now the "jefe" for inter-American affairs in Washington.[77]

The gathering was largely successful, with Chase reporting to Bundy that the ambassadors were impressed with both Rostow's appointment and Johnson's obvious concern for the Alliance. The *New York Times* quoted one ambassador as remarking: "These were the words we were waiting to hear. . . . [T]he United States has returned to the political leadership of the Alliance." For a president notoriously reluctant to meet with foreign representatives, Johnson also kept up in the following months an impressive degree of contact with the Latin American ambassadors. Hoping to maintain the good feeling generated at the May discussions, he hosted similar meetings in July and

Johnson and Mexican president Adolfo López Mateos unveil the new boundary marker following the resolution of the Chamizal dispute, 25 September 1964. (National Park Service, US Department of the Interior.)

September, interspersed with occasional visits from heads of state, and followed by a gathering of CIAP representatives in October. He would also travel to Texas to unveil a new boundary marker as part of the successful resolution of the Chamizal dispute the previous year. Between them, Johnson and Mann were working hard to prove that the administration was not failing in its commitment to hemispheric affairs.[78]

The administration received a major fillip on 26 July when a long-running OAS action brought by Venezuela against Cuba resulted in multilateral sanctions against Castro's government.[79] The sanctions called for the mandatory severing of relations with Havana and further reduced the scope for Latin American trade with Cuba. Commenting on the "perversion" of Castro's 26 July movement, Congressman Armistead Selden (D-AL) rejoiced that, because of the OAS vote, the "date has again been elevated to an honorable place in the Western Hemisphere." Selden's hyperbole aside, the

OAS vote appeared to endorse the administration's Cuban policy, which had sought to isolate Castro without provoking direct confrontation. As Mann explained to Averell Harriman in April, "the ultimate US objective is the replacement of the present government in Cuba by one fully compatible with the goals of the United States," but, unwilling to use force, Johnson would seek the "economic, political and psychological isolation of Cuba from the free world." Mann's memo to Harriman had been marked "top secret," yet the public statements of US policy differed very little from the private, with the continued use of intelligence-gathering overflights the major excision from documents designed for public consumption.[80]

As with security policy in general, there was a large degree of continuity with the Cuban policy of the Kennedy administration. The one notable exception was that Johnson and Mann scaled back many of the programs of subversion and covert action that had developed under their predecessors. In meetings with CIA director John McCone early in his presidency, Johnson had agreed to continue intelligence gathering, distribution of propaganda, and economic sanctions but ruled out any further CIA attempts to kill or otherwise remove Castro from power. Under the previous administration, Operation Mongoose had been something of an obsession with Robert Kennedy, and perhaps this had some bearing on Johnson's decision.[81] More important, however, was the president's temperamental distaste for the intelligence community, or as he put it: "That's what these intelligence guys do. . . . [Y]ou work hard to get a good program or policy going, and they swing a shit-smeared tail through it." Mann also had little interest in covert action, telling McCone that, even if the CIA were given free rein to implement all its schemes, he doubted that it would result in Castro's downfall. He believed that nothing short of a full-scale invasion—which he opposed—would oust Castro, at least for the foreseeable future, and that the best policy was to attempt to quarantine his influence.[82]

Aside from a brief rise in tensions early in his presidency over the seizure of Cuban fishing boats in American waters and Castro's subsequent cutting of the water supply to the US military base at Guantanamo Bay, US-Cuban relations under LBJ were relatively calm, particularly considering the drama of the preceding years. Although the threat of Castro's brand of communism spreading throughout the hemisphere would be a constant worry, direct antagonism was rare. Indeed, Mann and Johnson seemed to treat Castro as they did other leaders whom they felt were too extreme for any form of US cooperation, such as "Papa Doc" Duvalier, the brutal dictator of Haiti. Duvalier was, according to Mann, "at the Trujillo stage," having "gone so far now he has lost all sense of balance"; consequently, no aid would be forthcoming "unless we can figure out something that would help the people without putting a nickel in his pocket." Political isolation and economic pressure, rather than direct overt or covert intervention, was the favored position to be taken toward truly unpalatable regimes, and the July OAS vote appeared to give multilateral weight to the approach.[83]

If the OAS decision indicated success in restricting the spread of Castro's influence, events in Chile in September suggested that the other major aspect of the Alliance's political goals—the spread of stable democratic regimes—might also be gaining traction. National elections on 4 September saw the defeat of the Socialist candidate, Salvador Allende, and brought the leader of the Chilean Christian Democrat Party, Eduardo Frei Montalva, to the presidency. Frei having run a campaign based on moderate reforms to tackle poverty and social inequality, his presidency was described by Pat Holt of the Senate Foreign Relations Committee as "the epitome of liberal democratic non-military civilian government." In short, he was exactly the kind of leader the Alliance for Progress called for, and in defeating Allende, seemed to represent the victory of the center-left over more radical opposition. According to Johnson, Frei's victory was "a good omen for the success of the Alliance for Progress," and the majority of the media concurred, with the *Washington Post,* for example, declaring: "Chile landslide is boost for democracy."[84]

While it was true that Frei was a moderate reformer who would do much to tackle Chilean poverty, his victory over Allende was not so clear-cut as Johnson suggested. Although the election itself was conducted fairly, the Christian Democrats had been secretly receiving funds from Washington since mid-1962, when Richard Goodwin had begun championing their cause. Throughout 1963 and 1964, a number of covert campaign contributions were made to Frei's party with the stated intention being to "deprive the Chilean Communist Party of votes" and to "achieve a measure of influence over Christian Democratic Party policy." Although Johnson would announce that the election "was an internal matter in which the people of Chile were the only judges of the issues," intelligence reports contradict that viewpoint entirely. CIA memos listed attempts to keep a third party in the race, financial and organizational assistance to the Christian Democrats, and propaganda campaigns against Allende as "indispensable ingredients of Frei's success."[85]

Mann supported the efforts to ensure Frei's electoral victory, believing that Allende was not a Communist but that, had he won, he would have been a "prisoner" of the extremists. However, he would be uncomfortable with continued covert funding on a larger scale, disagreed with CIA suggestions that Frei's party was the "only effective force fighting Communists," and worried that US financing would be used to suppress "other non-Marxist parties." "Tell them not to expect any help to beat other non-Commie groups. Tell them we helped them fight Marxists. This is different. This would be intervention," he would later declare when asked about possible funding for congressional elections in 1965.[86]

The Chilean election was nonetheless a victory for Johnson's and Mann's Latin American policy. A campaign that began in 1962 bore fruit in September 1964 with the election of a responsible, left-of-center democratic government in one of the hemisphere's most strategically important nations. That campaign, however, raised worrying questions about the administration's attitude toward intervention. Mann again demonstrated his conviction that combating Communist influence neither constituted intervention nor contradicted his often-repeated commitment to avoiding such entanglements. Although in this case the short-term results were relatively benign, that might not have been the case had there been no viable democratic alternative to Allende. The campaign also firmly established Allende in the minds of US policy makers as a political opponent and potential Communist, something that was not lost on their Chilean allies. Allende would win the presidency six years later, but the pattern of US opposition to his rule was already established and would contribute to the military coup that prematurely ended his government and his life in September 1973.[87]

Despite a difficult beginning, 1964 had offered some signs of encouragement for Mann and Johnson. The goal of a more efficient Alliance seemed attainable, and efforts to restrict the spread of communism while allowing democracy to flourish appeared to be showing signs of success. As early as May, Mann felt able to reassure his president that they were "making good progress—better than anyone could have hoped." His satisfaction was not entirely misplaced, but there were also other developments that could discourage even the most ardent optimist. In particular, two major disputes threatened to derail the administration's hopes of fostering sustainable economic growth in the hemisphere.[88]

On 15 November 1963, Argentine president Arturo Illia declared void his nation's contracts with foreign, mostly US-based oil companies, offering $70 million compensation and the possibility of negotiating new contracts on terms more favorable to his nation, an offer that had still not been accepted well into 1964. Illia remained open to negotiation, and, as Mann observed, "everything [was] open and above board as far as we know," but the process was complicated by the need to coordinate fourteen separate oil companies, some of whom appeared unwilling to listen to any form of compromise deal.[89] A concurrent dispute was taking in place in Peru, where the government accused the US-based International Petroleum Company (IPC) of owing more than $70 million in taxes and obtaining its drilling sites illegally. Although President Fernando Belaúnde Terry had promised in July 1963 that the issue would be settled "within 90 days," the threat of expropriation by the Peruvian government hung over proceedings throughout 1964, prompting Johnson to continue Kennedy's policy of reducing aid appropriations to Belaúnde's government.[90]

Mann's major concern regarding both disputes was the damaging effect that the expropriation of US property could have on the future of private investment in Latin America. On handing over the reins of ARA, Ed Martin had warned that to allow Argentina to break its oil contracts without sufficient compensation would encourage other nationalists hostile to outside investment, "particularly that of the Yankee variety," to do the same, provoking a fierce backlash in the United States. Indeed, the Kennedy administration's failure to take a strong initial stand on the issue of expropriation had sparked a damaging domestic reaction, with the *Wall Street Journal* blustering that it appeared "stealing is alright, provided the government is the thief," and Congress passing the restrictive Hickenlooper Amendment. Mann was just as concerned about an economic domino effect as Martin had been, and he also feared fiscal conservatives in Congress invoking the Hickenlooper Amendment and cutting off all financial assistance to both Argentina and Peru. He believed that, if the disputes ended in nationalization, the result could be a spate of similar actions throughout the region and a congressionally mandated reduction in Latin American aid programs, either of which would be a disaster.[91]

In Mann's attitude toward both disputes, the importance of his experiences during the Good Neighbor era once again came to the fore. Mann was not inherently opposed to state involvement in industry, supporting the idea of joint public-private ventures in Mexico while ambassador, and telling a meeting of the Inter-American Economic and Social Council in December 1964: "I do not wish even for a minute to minimize the great importance of the public sector in the process of progress. It is not only important, it is indispensable." However, he also shared with his president the New Dealer's faith in the role of private industry to boost economic growth, provided it was regulated and overseen by a government willing to curb excesses and mediate disputes. The Johnson administration was therefore just as committed as any of its predecessors to encouraging US investment in the hemisphere. "Capital brings in not only just the capital itself," Mann noted, "but it invests that capital in productive enterprise, it creates jobs, it increases exports, earnings, it pays taxes, and, therefore, does a pretty good job of promoting delivery." In Latin America, Mann believed, many of the state-run enterprises were inefficient as governments were scared to raise prices, and hence private investment was discouraged and "chronic, galloping inflation" ensued.[92]

Both oil disputes illuminated a problem that the Kennedy and Johnson administrations failed to deal with effectively—the growing strength of economic nationalism and the resultant resentment of perceived US economic imperialism. The irony was that Mann felt that private investment would provide economic growth without the need to dictate how Latin American nations should distribute their budgets or spend the aid money received through the Alliance for Progress. "Either they're sovereign states and capable of managing their own affairs or they're not," he would later reflect. "I think the Latin Americans know better how to manage their affairs than we do. I'm sure they do." This attitude did not extend, however, to the breaking of contracts or the expropriation of property. Whereas nationalists in Peru and Argentina saw themselves righting historic wrongs and reducing Yankee influence, Mann, along with the majority of North Americans, saw only illegal seizures and breaking of contracts. Such fundamental differences would prove difficult to resolve, and neither issue would be decided that year. Similar economic disputes would continue to plague the Alliance for years to come.[93]

Mann's worries regarding potential congressional interference with the oil negotiations reflected another issue that continued to trouble the administration. While the actual implementation of Alliance programs had little to do with Congress, their funding was entirely reliant on approval from the legislature, something made abundantly clear by the cuts to Kennedy's final foreign aid budget. Frustrated at the influence of House conservatives on his ability to fund his policies properly, Johnson was raging at his congressional allies just weeks into his presidency. "I'm really humiliated that I'm president and I've got a friendly speaker, and I've got a friendly majority leader . . . and [Louisiana congressman] Otto Passman is king," he complained bitterly in December 1963. "I think it's awful that a goddamn Cajun from the hills of Louisiana has got more power than all of us." Johnson was exaggerating, of course, but disputes with Congress did provide some minor setbacks for the administration. A notable example was Mann's failure to obtain approval for a coffee agreement that would have stabilized global prices for a fixed term, a project that was still close to his heart. Despite his best efforts to convince the House leadership, Mann had to apologize to Latin American colleagues in December for the lack of a result and promised that the president would resubmit legislation the following year.[94]

Mann believed that pressure from Congress limited his freedom of action and endangered the Alliance's economic program—and not just via the threat of the Hickenlooper Amendment. In a telegram to Lincoln Gordon, he outlined how in the early days of the Alliance much of the aid to Latin America had been in the form of grants but pressure from Congress had resulted in an increase in soft loans with low interest rates and flexible repayment options. Even soft loans were now being assailed by conservatives as grants by another name, and Mann feared congressional efforts to remove USAID's ability to authorize loans of any kind. Indeed, such a measure had only recently been defeated in the Senate by a vote of 42–41. Mann was now faced with striking a balance between creating a record that was "defensible and justifiable" to aid skeptics and pushing too hard for Latin American aid recipients to make unrealistic commitments that would alienate those nations as well as liberals in Congress. As a result, during meetings with congressional representatives, he would strongly urge continued support for the Alliance, arguing that there was "no time for disillusionment," that "we must live in the world as it exists and try to make it better," and stressing the need for "strong, consistent US leadership."[95]

Despite Johnson's tantrums and Mann's worries, relations with Congress throughout 1964 were actually relatively good, and, the coffee agreement aside, conflicts were mostly minor. Nonetheless, tensions that were brewing throughout 1964 would greatly increase the following year, eventually crippling Johnson's ability to manage foreign affairs, and contributing to the dramatic end to his presidency.[96]

Seemingly insurmountable problems also continued to undermine some of the efforts of the Alliance, none more so than the rate of population growth in Latin America. Speaking at the Planned Parenthood annual banquet in November, Mann pointed out that a population growth rate of almost 3 percent meant that economic output had to grow at 5.5 percent a year to hit Alliance targets, a daunting figure. Of more immediate concern, he suggested, was the strain placed on water and food supplies and on a housing deficit that was already at 40 million units when some cities were growing at 14 percent a year. He admitted that little had been done to address the problem but noted how easy it would be to "offend others by statements which might be misinterpreted as contrary to their ethical, moral, or religious convictions." Although the Foreign Assistance Act had recently been amended to allow for research into population growth, Johnson would not allocate any funds toward education in family planning until 1966, and the Latin American birthrate would continually be a challenge to all the efforts of the Alliance for Progress.[97]

The year 1964 still had one more minor crisis in store as an unexpected coup in Bolivia served as a reminder of the political instability of much of Latin America. Since 1952, Bolivia had been governed by the MNR, the party that had overthrown a conservative oligarchy in a popular revolution. The MNR had been receiving significant amounts of aid from the United States ever since, with economic leverage used to isolate the party's radical wing and allow limited US investment.[98] After President Víctor Paz Estenssoro amended the Bolivian constitution to allow himself to remain in office for consecutive terms following an election in May 1964, he was overthrown by a military junta headed by General René Barrientos in November, a series of events that seemed to take Washington largely by surprise. The administration considered ways of assisting Paz, but, with the military against him, he stood little chance. A circular telegram to all ARA posts reported: "Paz Estenssoro has fled the country and arrived in Lima with his family afternoon November 4." It also noted: "Our overriding objectives in the present situation, therefore, are to prevent the collapse of authority, civil war and a Communist takeover, and to protect U.S. lives and property."[99]

The United States had little direct influence over the events in Bolivia, although pressures exerted through years of economic meddling had helped fragment the MNR leadership, opening the door for just such a military takeover. On 7 December, relations were reestablished after Barrientos restored political rights and promised to hold elections. Denying diplomatic relations served little purpose, Mann argued, and the United States might as well follow the lead of Argentina and Brazil, as well as most European nations, in recognizing the new government. Still, Paz's downfall was not a welcome development and served as a reminder of the limits of American power; a decade of close US assistance had led only to another Latin American coup and continued political instability.[100]

Events in Panama, Brazil, and Bolivia had made for an eventful first year in inter-American relations for the Johnson administration, but they should also be considered within the context of preceding years. There was no Bay of Pigs–style embarrassment and no global drama such as the Cuban Missile Crisis. Lyndon Johnson won a landslide victory over the Republican candidate, Barry Goldwater, in November, and, unlike in 1960, Latin American issues were barely mentioned during the campaign. Still, the record of the Johnson administration was definitely mixed, with optimism often tempered by anxiety and frustration. In May, Mann was confident enough to remark that the administration was "making good progress," but the following month he lamented to LBJ in a moment of particular frustration: "You wonder if some of these countries are capable of governing themselves."[101]

Such ambivalence was not wholly surprising. The success of Mann's bureaucratic reorganization, the launching of CIAP, and gradually improving statistics all suggested that the Alliance for Progress was finally approaching a reasonable level of success. Negotiations were under way with Panama to settle disputes over the functioning of the Canal Zone, a potential left-wing dictatorship had been avoided in Brazil, and the favored candidate of the United States had won a significant electoral victory in Chile. Johnson could be forgiven for looking toward 1965 with cautious optimism, particularly as inter-American affairs were being overseen by an assistant secretary whose opinion he had quickly learned to respect and trust. Unfortunately, the Alliance was also still beset by many of the problems that had plagued the program under Kennedy. The sheer scale of the challenges in Latin America that the program aimed to address made any successes limited at best, and the rapid rate of population growth suggested that achieving the goals announced at Punta del Este would prove to be a Sisyphean task. Disputes over economic investment demonstrated the failure of Washington to align its goals with Latin American nationalism, and every setback brought increased scrutiny from Congress. In addition, Brazil's slide into the grip of a military dictatorship and the overthrow of a long-term ally in Bolivia demonstrated that a stable, democratic hemisphere was still well out of reach. All these problems would combine with the tendency, still prevalent in Washington, to seek military solutions to potential Communist threats, as well as with the continued suspicions provoked by the Mann Doctrine, to make Latin American policy a source of controversy and conflict in 1965. The administration's efforts in the hemisphere and relationships with Congress and the press, as well as Mann's career and reputation, would never fully recover.

4

No More Cubas

The Dominican Republic Intervention

"LBJ for the USA" was the slogan, and, on 3 November 1964, the country went to the ballot box and elected Lyndon Baines Johnson president of the United States of America in his own right. Dedicating himself to solving America's social ills through his Great Society programs while portraying himself as a foreign policy moderate who would keep America safe without risking nuclear confrontation, LBJ trounced his Republican opponent, Barry Goldwater, carrying forty-four states, and receiving over 60 percent of the popular vote. Mandate in hand, Johnson would set about expanding his already ambitious legislative agenda, creating a record unrivaled since the days of his political hero, Franklin Roosevelt. His domestic successes in 1965 and 1966 came at a cost, however; as the Great Society demanded much of his attention, other responsibilities would inevitably take something of a backseat. The year 1965 was also one of major escalation in the Vietnam conflict. In March, the "Rolling Thunder" bombing campaign against North Vietnam began, and the first US combat units landed soon after. For the next four years, "that bitch of a war" would be Johnson's preeminent foreign policy concern, eventually enveloping and devouring his presidency and leaving the former master of the Senate a broken man.

Focused on domestic issues, and distracted by an increasingly troublesome foreign conflict, Johnson did not place Latin America at the top of his agenda. Having brought Mann back from Mexico to oversee the Alliance for Progress, he hoped his fellow Texan would do most of the heavy lifting, requiring only the broad direction of policy to be set from the Oval Office, with occasional speeches and meetings with heads of state his most onerous responsibilities. Instead, a crisis in the Dominican Republic would place

Johnson's Latin America policy under more scrutiny than ever, hindering other efforts in the region for the remainder of his presidency. The decision to dispatch troops to the Caribbean would expose long-standing hypocrisies and contradictions of US policy, cripple Johnson's relations with Congress, and undermine his credibility as a leader. Mann's involvement would deliver more ammunition for his critics and provide a controversial epitaph to a long and varied career.[1]

Promotions

The pinnacle of Lyndon Johnson's political life arrived on an overcast and chilly January day in Washington, DC. Johnson had first taken the oath of office in a hurriedly arranged ceremony on board Air Force One in the aftermath of his predecessor's murder. This time, on 20 January 1965, he could enjoy the moment. He adopted a modest tone in his inaugural address, promising: "I will do the best I can." The Great Society that he sought to build was based on a few simple beliefs, he noted: "In a land of great wealth, families must not live in hopeless poverty. In a land rich in harvest, children just must not go hungry. In a land of healing miracles, neighbors must not suffer and die unattended. In a great land of learning and scholars, young people must be taught to read and write." He largely avoided foreign affairs but did pause to acknowledge the extent of US global commitments, warning: "If American lives must end, and American treasure be spilled, in countries we barely know, that is the price that change has demanded of conviction and of our enduring covenant." The speech made clear that solving America's domestic problems would be LBJ's primary focus and that his concern over "countries we barely know" was oriented toward Southeast Asia rather than conflicts within his own hemisphere. Johnson did have at least one substantial change in mind for inter-American policy, however, and, within days of his inauguration, he would reveal it.[2]

The year 1964 had been an eventful one in Latin American relations and one that had provoked criticism from the press and former Kennedy aides aimed at both Johnson and his new assistant secretary of state for inter-American affairs, Thomas Mann. Nonetheless, Mann had negotiated hemispheric crises, reduced bureaucratic infighting, and even begun to coax some encouraging statistics from the Alliance for Progress. Crucially, he and Johnson had also developed a healthy rapport and a level of trust that the president, never the easiest man to work for, did not share with many of his other advisers. As early as February 1964, Johnson had been teasing his stoic, bespectacled, and bow-tied aide: "You'll have to help me dance with the ladies [at official functions]." It was not long before other State Department employees were complaining that "only [Secretary of State Dean] Rusk, [Undersecretary of State George] Ball and Mann have personal meetings with the President." Mann was not immune from the less pleasant sides of Johnson's personality and would receive his share of criticism, but he was never subjected to the kind of verbal assaults to which longtime Johnson aides were forced to grow accustomed. Indeed, National Security Adviser McGeorge Bundy was surprised by how close Mann and Johnson became, confiding to Ball in April 1964 that he had thought Johnson's "activist" nature would not mesh well with Mann's natural caution. Yet, in an administration where so many possessed close ties to the Kennedys, Mann offered no hint of divided loyalties. He was not a Harvard like Bundy or Defense Secretary Robert McNamara but a fellow Texan who had quickly demonstrated his willingness to make decisions that would be unpopular with the Kennedy loyalists. In part because of his Texas background, in part because he had been Johnson's first major appointee, but largely because the president respected his style and abilities, Mann had a level of access to the Oval Office that few individuals shared.[3]

Demonstrating the value that he placed on their relationship and the job that Mann had performed the previous year as well as the confidence in his own position that came with a landslide electoral victory, five days after the inauguration Johnson telephoned Mann to discuss a promotion. With much of his time to be focused on the Great Society, but keen to see improvements in the Alliance, he wanted Mann to have more freedom of action than ever in shaping hemispheric policy. He initially considered Mann trading roles with Bundy but, having been advised by Mann that this would not go down well with the national security adviser, revised the offer to instead replace the Democratic Party stalwart Averell Harriman as undersecretary of state for political affairs. The offer was accepted, but only on the condition that Rusk and Ball approved. Mann also ended the conversation with a warning to find Harriman an alternative position as despite being "garrulous and vain . . . he understands the Commies and he understands power . . . [and] could cause a lot of trouble on the outside." Johnson took Mann's advice; Harriman would be appointed ambassador-at-large, later serving as Johnson's chief negotiator during the Vietnam peace talks.[4]

Mann called the following day to inform Johnson that both Rusk and Ball had given their blessing and that he would accept the position, under the alternative title of undersecretary of state for economic affairs, if the president still approved.[5] Johnson did and made it clear that, as far as he was concerned, economic affairs "was a title"; what he wanted was somebody "who can help . . . with the assistant secretaries and get his ideas across and get the policy planning group working." In short, Mann would be number three in the State Department, and his title was irrelevant. Agreeing, Mann suggested Ambassador to Panama Jack Vaughn as his successor in ARA as he had "good political instincts . . . a liberal image and . . . might even be able to convert Schlesinger." Left unsaid was that Vaughn had more experience with the Peace Corps than with the State Department and would be happy to defer to Mann on most policy matters. A tougher and more experienced candidate, the former Kennedy assistant secretary Ed Martin, did not appeal to Mann as he would not represent a "Johnson approach" to hemispheric affairs.[6]

Mann's new role would be announced in mid-February, but not before Johnson laid some groundwork with the media. On 3 February, the president invited members of the press to observe a meeting with himself and Mann in which they would discuss "general economic matters in the world," and he made sure to remind the gathered reporters of Mann's previous experience in the Economic Bureau of the State Department. If he was attempting to forestall criticism similar to that which had followed Mann's previous promotion, he need not have worried; the press was far more interested in Harriman's reassignment and rumors of a dispute between the president and Dean Rusk. The *New York Times,* so often critical of Mann, simply noted that he "would continue to devote a great deal of attention to Latin America" and that Vaughn was "not expected to bring to the Latin American post views significantly different from those of Mr Mann." Indeed, Vaughn would continually struggle to convince anyone that it was he, and not Mann, who exercised the greatest influence over hemispheric policy.[7]

No doubt contributing to the lack of interest in Mann's promotion was the relative stability of inter-American affairs in early 1965. Economic disputes with Argentina and Peru were an irritation but well short of crisis level, and negotiations with Panama regarding a new canal treaty were progressing slowly and not widely followed by the press now that the crisis had subsided. Economic growth in the hemisphere was still short of Alliance targets but appeared to be improving, helped enormously by the stabilization measures implemented by the Castelo Branco government in Brazil. Other encouraging signs came from Mexico, with Mann able to comment in early February that, thanks to the Chamizal and salinity agreements, relations had "never been better," while Argentina, Chile, Venezuela, and Ecuador provided examples of moderate governments implementing much-needed reforms.[8]

Undersecretary of state for economic affairs was the highest position that Mann would attain during his lengthy government career. In theory, he now had wide-ranging geographic authority, but at heart he was still a Foreign Service officer specializing in Latin American politics and economics. Although he would exercise some influence on global economic policy, he continued to focus the majority of his time and attention on Latin America. Persisting in his attempts to implement a more sustainable approach to development than that pursued by the early Alliance for Progress, he remained the administration's most influential voice on Latin American issues. In effect, he would fulfill the powerful role that Kennedy had envisaged in 1963, undersecretary of state for Latin America.[9]

Mann's priority in his new role was to build on recent improvements in the economic performance of the hemisphere, which still remained short of Alliance targets. The best example of how to do so, he believed, was provided by the success of the Central American Common Market (CACM). Established in 1960, and incorporating Guatemala, Costa Rica, Honduras, El Salvador, and Nicaragua, the CACM was described by USAID officials as "a pioneer venture in economic integration among the underdeveloped countries of the free world." By encouraging economic cooperation and close trading links, the CACM would, it was hoped, help nations pool investment capital and reduce overreliance on certain exports while encouraging the development of vital infrastructure such as improved transport links. Although he remained skeptical regarding the viability a hemisphere-wide common market, Mann hoped that a broad network of trade agreements and multinational endeavors would maximize the effectiveness of the funds provided through the Alliance. A reduction of tariffs and the subsequent increase in trade could only be of benefit to the entire hemisphere, he believed, and, in February, he encouraged Dean Rusk to "not let our traditional trade policy stance bar the road to a major political advantage." The secretary agreed to refer the ideas to an interagency working group but initially showed little enthusiasm for pursuing Mann's initiatives.[10]

While it would take several months for hemispheric integration to be publicly endorsed by the president, Mann's first notable success in the path toward his goal of greater economic cooperation was the passage of the fixed-term coffee commodity agreement that he had pursued for so long. In a statement before the House Ways and Means Committee in April, Mann reassured congressmen that recent international efforts at stabilization had actually resulted in lower prices for the American consumer. The free market was nice in theory, he continued, but was simply not feasible at the moment, and, if the legislation resulted in an "unwarranted increase" in prices, then Congress had a right to terminate it. Since he had already gained approval from the Senate, the House's decision to pass the legislation marked the culmination of his efforts dating back to 1957 and was a significant step toward the cooperative economic approach that he hoped would benefit the hemisphere. "More than 20 million persons depend directly on coffee for their livelihood," Johnson noted on signing the bill into effect. "The United States is now in a position to do its full part."[11]

In addition to seeking new methods of boosting hemispheric productivity, Mann and Johnson both began 1965 keen to build on the gradually improving reputation of the administration in Latin America and to pacify some of their domestic opponents. Criticism of Johnson's policies still grated, and he continually encouraged his staff to produce evidence of his commitment to the Alliance for Progress. In early March, for example, when the administration was ready to announce an increase in funding for the IADB, the close Johnson aide Jack Valenti identified "an excellent opportunity for the right kind of statement which would show [former Alliance coordinator Teodoro] Moscoso how wrong he is."[12]

Efforts to improve the administration's reputation included organizing seminars for leading academics to meet with government officials and sending representatives of the State Department along with members of the business community to Latin America for informal economic discussions. Serious consideration was also given to Johnson making a substantial visit to Latin America, a notion prompted in part by calls from Castelo Branco for a presidential meeting in Brazil to demonstrate the warm relationship between the two. Mann believed that some kind of trip could be beneficial but was wary of a grand tour for both security reasons and the potential offense caused if the president had to leave any countries out. Besides, he told Bundy in February, FDR and Kennedy were popular in the Americas not because of "barn-

,storming trips" but because of their identification with the Good Neighbor policy and the Alliance for Progress. His preference would be for a gathering of hemispheric leaders in Brazil in an "informal atmosphere" that would encourage discussion of substantive issues. At the same time, he was also aware of the criticism that would follow a state visit to a government widely viewed as "dictatorial in character," even if he shared the view common within the administration that Castelo Branco was largely doing a good job and would soon return Brazil to "democratic procedures."[13]

In spite of such mixed feelings, it was decided that the potential benefits of backing Brazil while also meeting with democratic leaders outweighed the likely criticisms, and planning for the trip reached a relatively advanced stage before events elsewhere prompted its cancellation. Increases to the US commitment in Vietnam in February and March meant that Mann was forced to cable relevant embassies and order them to halt consultations with their host governments on a potential meeting in Rio owing to "new developments in the international situation, particularly in Asia." He made a similar point in person to the Brazilian ambassador, Juracy Magalhães, assuring him that the trip's postponement did not reflect any change in the president's "full support" for Castelo Branco's government.[14]

Despite the public and private support offered to Castelo Branco's military regime in Brazil, broader efforts were also made to downplay US links with foreign armed forces. "There is no misunderstanding or disagreement in Washington," Mann wrote in a telegram to all ARA embassies, "that a basic objective of the United States' policy in Latin America . . . is democratic governments. . . . [T]he actions and words of every American official should be consistent with that goal." Political intervention by the military could occasionally preserve these goals, as would, it was hoped, turn out to be the case in Brazil, but it could also be carried out "capriciously and irresponsibly," he warned. It was therefore the duty of the US embassy to maintain good relations with Latin American armed forces, using their influence "wisely and discreetly" to discourage "political adventures."[15]

The administration's charm offensive continued in April via two productive, albeit quite different, conferences. The first was a week-long gathering of US officials involved with the Alliance held in Washington and chaired by William Rogers, the program's deputy coordinator. The reports that emerged were almost uniformly positive, predicting that 1965 would be "the year of noticeable advances" as the hard work of the recent past began to bear fruit.

Downplaying the importance of US aid, and talking up the efforts of Latin American self-help programs, Rogers pointed to promising economic developments in Brazil, Chile, and Peru while also praising the efforts of the CACM as "a dramatic example of self-help under the Alliance." His comments were supported by CIAP chairman Carlos Sanz de Santamaría, a Colombian diplomat and civil engineer, who promised the continued expansion of self-help efforts by the countries of Latin America and suggested that their contributions would reach the level of $12 billion by the end of 1965.[16]

Running concurrently with the meeting in Washington was a Ford Foundation–sponsored conference in Cuernavaca, Mexico, featuring economists, diplomats, politicians, and academics from fourteen nations, including Germany and the United Kingdom. The conclusions of this meeting were unsurprisingly more mixed than were those of its Washington counterpart, with a number of Latin American participants expressing frustration at poor communication between the United States and its neighbors and reporting widespread suspicion at the motives behind the Alliance. Despite these and other criticisms, there were points of general agreement. Almost all delegates concurred that more attention must be given to the issues of population growth and military interference in political processes, and proposals to see a wider variety of nations taking on roles of hemispheric leadership were met with unanimous approval.[17]

None of the issues raised in Cuernavaca would have come as a surprise to Mann, given his recent attempts to address relations with the hemisphere's militaries and improve inter-American communication. He had also long been concerned that unchecked population growth could destroy efforts at Latin American development. The conference signified the Johnson administration's willingness at least to listen to Latin American complaints, and the points of agreement that emerged suggested that, while much work remained to be done, inter-American communication was gradually improving and US policy might be headed in a direction that was more genuinely cooperative. At the same time, however, the discussions regarding a potential presidential trip to Brazil had demonstrated that, while the administration would work to improve relations "between the northern and southern halves of the globe," the conflict "between the East and the West, between freedom and communism," remained the priority. Events would soon see Cold War security concerns push all other considerations aside, dashing any hope that 1965 could in fact be "the year of noticeable advances."[18]

The Dominican Republic Intervention

A January 1964 CIA report described the Dominican Republic as "one of the Latin American countries least prepared for representative government": "Its past has been characterized by a succession of foreign occupations, coups, and despotic administrations. . . . [T]hirty years of Trujillo's dictatorship . . . [have] warped the political and economic framework of the country." The report failed to note, however, that a degree of responsibility for much recent Dominican history lay with the United States. For the majority of his brutal reign, Rafael Trujillo had enjoyed the backing of powerful allies in Washington, and the United States had also assisted in his downfall when the Eisenhower administration's decision to distance itself from the hemisphere's worst dictatorships led to OAS sanctions and the breaking of relations in 1960. The Dominican dictator had by that time become a dangerous embarrassment, attempting to assassinate his political nemesis, Venezuelan President Rómulo Betancourt, and raging against what he viewed as betrayal by the United States. When he was assassinated in May 1961, possibly with weapons supplied by the CIA, few tears were shed in Washington. Instead, attention turned to ensuring political stability. As a small Caribbean country with an economy almost entirely reliant on sugar exports and subject to a lengthy and repressive dictatorship, the Dominican Republic bore inescapable similarities to Cuba. Partly owing to fears of a "second Cuba," it soon became a major recipient of Alliance assistance. When the interim president, Joaquín Balaguer, announced that the nation's first democratic elections would be held in December 1962, it was hoped that the small nation might become a model of how to rebuild a society after a long dictatorship.[19]

The election of 1962 saw the Partido Revolucionario Dominicano (PRD; the Dominican Revolutionary Party) win a resounding success, with its leader, Juan Bosch, elected the nation's first truly democratic president. A talented historian and writer, Bosch had been exiled under Trujillo but had returned to his homeland promising a new constitution and dramatic changes to the system of land ownership. The Kennedy administration viewed Bosch uneasily. While supporting him publicly and providing his government with substantial aid, Ambassador John Bartlow Martin was soon cabling the State Department regarding Bosch's tolerant attitude toward Communists. "Unrealistic, arrogant, and erratic," began George Ball's scathing assessment of the Dominican president, "a muddle-headed, anti-American pedant committed

President Kennedy meets the president-elect of the Dominican Republic, Dr. Juan E. Bosch, in the Oval Office, and neither appear overly happy about it, 10 January 1963. Assistant Secretary of State Edwin Martin stands in the background. (Abbie Rowe, White House Photographs, John F. Kennedy Presidential Library and Museum, Boston.)

to unattainable social reforms." Bosch's mistrust of the military and his attempts to reform Dominican society created powerful enemies, and he was overthrown in a coup in September 1963. "This is a sick destroyed nation," commented Martin.[20]

Bosch was replaced by a military-backed triumvirate led by Donald Reid Cabral, a member of the Dominican social and political elite. Although disappointed that another coup had occurred in the hemisphere and ended a constitutional government, the Kennedy administration was not entirely displeased to see the erratic Bosch depart. The coup provoked a break in diplomatic relations, but State Department discussions made it clear that they would be restored once the triumvirate had been "given time to sit and worry," the idea being that the new government would be prompted to schedule elections. Following Kennedy's death, one of Lyndon Johnson's first tasks as president was to dispatch Ambassador Martin back to Santo Domingo.[21]

Despite the resumption of diplomatic relations, political unrest in the Dominican Republic remained a concern during the first months of Johnson's administration. The CIA reported that small groups of organized Communists, including the Moscow-oriented Dominican Popular Socialist Party and the Castro-influenced Fourteenth of June Political Group, were growing in popularity, a development that Mann blamed on the ruling triumvirate. Corruption and police brutality were rife, he told Rusk, and, despite substantial Alliance aid, the new government's economic policies had led to unemployment as high as 30 percent while pressing needs in education, health, and other services were ignored. When widespread strikes and an explosion at a government arsenal resulted in crackdowns by the police and military in June 1964, Mann cabled the embassy in Santo Domingo to inform the new ambassador, William Tapley Bennett, that events were "all too reminiscent of Trujillo days" and that he should impress the need for restraint on Reid Cabral. Despite his misgivings, Mann also worried that the only alternative to the triumvirate, which at least included civilians, would be an even more repressive military junta. While the Communist groups were a concern, they did not seem to present any immediate threat, with CIA reports predicting that government security forces could put down any potential insurgency. The only realistic option, Mann informed Rusk, was to "urge moderation on all who will listen" and "pressure . . . the triumvirate to be flexible and patient in dealing with the country's grave problems."[22]

Subsequent months witnessed little change in the attitudes of the Dominican leaders, however, and, on 24 April, while Ambassador Bennett was in Washington to brief his superiors, reports emerged that forces loyal to Bosch had launched a revolt against the triumvirate. The Johnson administration's response would destroy most of the goodwill it had painstakingly sought to recover after the Mann Doctrine incident, proving beyond a doubt that Cold War fears still outweighed all other priorities in Latin American policy. The Dominican Republic crisis had begun.

On the afternoon of 24 April 1965, Deputy Chief of Mission in the Dominican Republic William Connett cabled Washington to inform the State Department that Santo Domingo was "rife with rumors of a coup." Radio Santo Domingo had briefly been seized by a group claiming to be "young and honest military officers" who had broadcast a call for all "constitutional" citizens to unite and overthrow the regime in favor of former president Bosch. The incident marked the beginning of a conflict between the forces opposed to Bosch's return known as "Loyalists," made up largely of members of the military and the upper classes of Dominican society, and the "Constitutionalists" (the rebel forces), consisting of many younger elements of the military, students, workers, and members of Bosch's party, the PRD. Over the next two days, violence escalated, with reports of Loyalist planes bombing civilian targets and strafing the Constitutionalists occupying the presidential palace in downtown Santo Domingo. Revolt had rapidly become civil war. Connett did not, however, recommend intervention by US forces to restore order, noting instead that the dispatch of troops would have "serious repercussions in Latin America." He did have one worrying warning for his superiors, however: "We all know that communists are deeply involved in [the] rebel movement."[23]

Mann agreed with Connett's warnings regarding the use of armed forces to intervene in a Caribbean civil war. Despite tentative enquiries from the Loyalists regarding the possibility of military assistance, he informed Connett that his priorities were to encourage a return to constitutional government without "bloodshed and political risk" and to secure a cease-fire that included a guarantee of no reprisals by either side. Calls for a truce grew increasingly urgent the following day when foreign nationals were evacuated to American warships anchored not far from the Dominican coast. A large group of mostly US citizens had gathered at the Hotel El Ambajador and were badly shaken when a group of armed men entered the building and, according to Connett, "shot up the place." Although no one was hurt in the incident, it sparked increasing concern regarding the safety of US citizens and the ability of the Dominican authorities to protect them. Nonetheless, there still seemed little chance of US intervention in the conflict. That would soon change, however; Ambassador Bennett was on his way back to Santo Domingo.[24]

William Tapley Bennett was appointed ambassador to the Dominican Republic in March 1964, replacing the thoroughly disillusioned John Martin. Bennett was raised in Georgia and had served in the army during World War II. A State Department biography from 1964 described him as "experienced, versatile and able . . . at age 47, one of our youngest Ambassadors." Bennett had known Mann since the Truman days; both specialized in Latin American affairs, and they had worked on State Department projects together as early as 1950. They developed a friendly relationship, spending time together with their families, and, following his return to Washington in 1963, Mann had received a request from Bennett asking: "Isn't it about time I had an autographed picture of the Coordinator of the Alliance for Progress to add prestige to my piano?" Mann replied that he thought a picture of himself would add very little "prestige" but complied with his friend's request nonetheless.[25]

The historian Alan McPherson has described Bennett as a "gentleman-diplomat from Georgia with a reputation for mixing only with the crème of Dominican society." Certainly, Bennett relied far too heavily on the triumvirate and the military for his information, a shortcoming that would have serious consequences during the US intervention, but he was not entirely oblivious to the problems of the nation to which he was posted. Writing to Mann in May 1964, he condemned the Dominican military as "venal and corrupt" and expressed concern about Reid Cabral, whom he believed to have a "gnawing" ambition to ensconce himself in a dictatorship. Like Mann, however, he saw few viable alternatives. He lamented the lack of a "Dominican Betancourt," dismissed Bosch as an "émigré" out of touch with his own nation, and warned that a change in government would only hasten the return of "Trujillo elements" to positions of power. He firmly believed that the Loyalists offered the only feasible leadership, and his attempts to preserve their position would see US involvement in the Dominican crisis rapidly escalate.[26]

The ambassador's return to Santo Domingo on 27 April resulted in a marked change in the tenor of the reports sent back to Washington. Arriving at the embassy around midday, Bennett was soon convinced that Loyalist forces under General Elías Wessin y Wessin (air force) and General Antonio Imbert Barrera (army) were on the brink of victory. He was also certain that he understood the nature of the Constitutionalist movement, informing Mann that the "role being played by the commies was very evident and getting clearer all the time," despite a lack of evidence to support his assertions. Overconfident of a Loyalist victory, and convinced of the radical nature of the opposing faction, Bennett made a serious misjudgment on the afternoon of his return when several key Constitutionalist leaders visited the US embassy in Santo Domingo. Sharing the ambassador's assessment of their prospects of victory, they hoped that the United States would be willing to act as intermediary in discussions of a cease-fire and potential provisional government. Ignoring the orders Mann had given Connett to seek a cease-fire, Bennett instead informed the Constitutionalists that they had "initiated this fratricide," accused them of giving "Communists free rein" by distributing arms, and refused to mediate with the Loyalist junta. Offered no hope by the US ambassador, a number of the most senior figures fled to other embassies, seeking escape from the retribution likely to be dished out by the Loyalist military, while others returned to the conflict. Bennett had not only passed up a potential opportunity for bringing the fighting to an early end; he had also driven away the Constitutionalist leaders most willing to negotiate the cease-fire that Mann and Johnson desired.[27]

Bennett's rash misjudgment was exposed when the tide of the conflict shifted away from the Loyalist military. Shortly after the meeting at the embassy, an assault on downtown Santo Domingo was repelled by the Constitutionalists, and the Loyalists were forced to retreat to the military barracks of San Isidro. Despite the crushing defeat, General Wessin issued an immediate call for an unconditional surrender from the "rebels" and formed a new junta to rule the Dominican Republic. His announcement impressed Bennett, who assured Mann that Wessin's forces would launch a fresh assault on the twenty-eighth and that "it would all be over within five hours."[28]

Lyndon Johnson had been paying close attention to developments in the Dominican Republic. On the twenty-sixth, concerned at press stories claiming that his administration was backing the Loyalists, he asked Mann to emphasize US neutrality publicly and begin considering means of reestablishing a government once the fighting was over. Both Johnson and Mann were clear that they did not want Bosch to return, agreeing that the former president was "no good at all" and overly influenced by Communists in his political circle. As Bennett began to report greater Communist involvement in the conflict, Johnson's worries increasingly focused on the possible embarrassment of another Cuban-style revolution. He made his concerns clear to Mann on the twenty-eighth, stating that he did not want the potentially Communist-led "rebels" to win but was wary of intervention: "[I have] just about lived down the Bay of Pigs and I don't want you to get me involved in another spot like that." Mann agreed, rejecting a request to distribute walkie-talkies to the Loyalist forces, and reminding Jack Vaughn: "We should honor our treaties on non-intervention." He did, however, offer the caveat that, if a Communist takeover of the Dominican Republic looked likely, that position might have to be reconsidered.[29]

Despite Bennett's increasingly shrill warnings regarding the radical nature of the Constitutionalists, as late as 5:00 P.M. on 28 April, Mann, Johnson, and the majority of the administration were still opposed to the use of force in the Dominican Republic. That resolve would soon be tested, however, as that same day the broken and dispirited Loyalist military began to call for US intervention. Aware that "the first thing the president will ask is 'what does Mr. Mann think?'" McGeorge Bundy immediately telephoned his colleague to consult on how best to advise Johnson. Bundy believed that while the balance of the conflict was "still on the side of the angels"—probably the only time the Dominican military was described as heavenly beings—calls for assistance were growing more insistent. "I'm against it," Mann replied simply. Shortly after that exchange, however, the State Department received the text of an official request from the Loyalists, carefully worded to provoke the worst fears of every US policy maker. Claiming that they represented "democratic institutions," the Loyalists warned that the Constitutionalists were "directed by communists" and that the result of a rebel victory would be to "convert this country into another Cuba." The only way to prevent this, the junta claimed, was by "unlimited and immediate military assistance" from the United States.[30]

A request from an embattled and desperate military junta might not, by itself, have been enough to force Johnson's hand, but a few minutes later a crucial telegram from Ambassador Bennett arrived. Bennett reported that the situation on the ground was "deteriorating rapidly," with most of the Loyalist military "dejected and emotional." The Dominican authorities could no longer protect evacuees; therefore: "Country team [is] unanimously of [the] opinion that, now that we have request from military junta for assistance, time has come to land the marines. American lives are in danger. . . . I recommend immediate landing." Bennett's previous concerns about the growing influence of Communists within the Constitutionalist ranks had now crystallized into a stark warning that what had begun as a civil war was fast becoming a Communist revolution and one in which the lives of American citizens could be at risk. Serious consideration would now be given to landing US forces.[31]

Bennett's request transformed the tone of discussions among Johnson's key advisers from wary watchfulness to crisis management, with Mann and Bundy speaking immediately to consider the ambassador's recommendations. Mann admitted that his old friend was probably "excited" but that they had to "go on what the boys on the ground said." Bundy recalled

Winston Churchill's warning to "never take the advice of the man on the spot" but did not challenge Mann's judgment. Mann then spoke to Deputy Secretary of Defense Cyrus Vance about the practicalities of a potential landing, noting that, with more than two thousand foreign nationals still left to evacuate, to "do nothing" would be unthinkable. The two former lawyers were also aware that their other option was to "re-establish order in the most illegal way possible—there is no precedent." Unsure as to what, if any, legal justification the United States would have for landing troops, Mann told Vance that he had to call the president back.[32]

The speed with which the administration's position had evolved was remarkable. At 5:45 P.M., in a conference call with Mann, Bundy, and Rusk, Lyndon Johnson made the decision, with unanimous support, to endorse his ambassador's request and send US Marines into the Dominican Republic. Initially focusing on the threat to American citizens, the plan was to secure an evacuation route from the Ambajador while calling on Loyalists and Constitutionalists to "negotiate terms of a ceasefire and agree on the way we restore law and order and a democratic government." Mann agreed that a landing was now necessary but advised against mentioning "the Communist angle," instead suggesting that a simple statement be obtained from either Bennett or the junta announcing that American lives were in danger and that an evacuation was therefore needed. Johnson agreed, and ten minutes later Mann was on the phone to Bennett, securing the statement from the junta later that evening.[33]

Decision made, Johnson turned to his next task: informing Congress. While he did not need legislative authorization to send troops on such a mission, he was, as ever, desperate for consensus. At 7:30 p.m., fifteen influential congressmen, including the majority and minority leaders of the Senate, were given a persuasive presentation that incorporated testimonials from Defense Secretary Robert McNamara, Dean Rusk, the recently appointed CIA chief, William Raborn, and the president himself. While extremist influence was mentioned, greater emphasis was placed on the breakdown of order and the immediate danger to American citizens. The pitch had the intended effect, with even J. William Fulbright, later a vehement critic of the intervention, offering support for Johnson's decision. The only note of caution came from Senate majority leader Mike Mansfield, who recommended greater OAS involvement in operations. Following the congressional briefing, Johnson telephoned Mann to say that "the Goodwins, Adlai Stevensons, and Fulbrights" had echoed Mansfield's concerns regarding OAS involvement. He ordered Mann to make sure that the hemispheric council was fully informed, to send a circular to all ARA embassies, and to brief the press. At around the same time, 8:30 P.M., the first US Marines landed on a polo field close to the Ambajador. It would be the first time US armed forces had openly intervened in the hemisphere since Johnson's idol, Franklin Roosevelt, had declared in the 1930s that his nation would from now on be a "good neighbor."[34]

At 11:45 P.M., Johnson called Mann for the final time that day. The president was agitated, having heard rumors that Bosch had seventeen thousand troops loyal to him in the army, and was worried that the intervention could escalate into full-scale warfare. Ten thousand at most, Mann reassured him, "and this was composed of all the rag-tags, scum, riff-raff and commies, everybody they could fool"; he would not be surprised if the figure was closer to two thousand. The press briefing had gone well, Mann offered as further comfort, and explained how he had focused on the need for immediate evacuations and presented the Ambajador incident as evidence. "There were no hard questions," he concluded. Despite his attempts to reassure the president, Mann also had to deliver some prescient words of warning. "The real trouble will come when we are finished with the evacuation," he cautioned. "Tomorrow will be the day."[35]

In assessing Johnson's decision to intervene in the Dominican Republic, it is clear that, as was publicly claimed, his thinking was at least partly shaped by the need to evacuate American citizens. The incident at the Ambajador has at times been subject to exaggeration and distortion, but it is almost certain that some kind of confrontation between evacuees and Constitutionalist forces took place. Bennett's frantic telegrams regarding the safety of evacuees and reports of sporadic sniper fire on the US embassy further fueled these fears. Despite this, the threat to American citizens alone was not enough for Johnson to send in the marines. As the commander of the US forces was informed by the chairman of the Joint Chiefs of Staff, Earle Wheeler: "Your announced mission is to save US lives. Your unannounced mission is to prevent the Dominican Republic from going Communist."[36]

Perhaps unsurprisingly, then, several analyses of Johnson's decision making have drawn parallels with his agonizing escalation of US involvement in Southeast Asia. His fear of appearing weaker than his predecessor, his desire to placate domestic conservatives who might threaten his Great Society legislation, and his dedication to preserving American global credibility have all

An emergency meeting in the White House Cabinet Room during the first hours of the US intervention, April 28 1965. *Left to right:* George Ball, Secretary of State Dean Rusk, President Lyndon B. Johnson, Jack Valenti, Richard Goodwin, unidentified, George Reedy, McGeorge Bundy, unidentified. (LBJ Library photo by Yoichi Okamoto.)

been identified as factors in his handling of both the Dominican Republic and the Vietnam conflicts.[37] Certainly, Johnson perceived the Dominican crisis to have wide-reaching political implications, complaining: "If I send in the marines, I can't live in the hemisphere. If I don't, I can't live at home." Nor was he alone in his fears. Special Assistant Jack Valenti warned him: "If the Castro-types take over the Dominican Republic, it will be the worst domestic political disaster any Administration could suffer." Johnson was aware of the damage to his hemispheric reputation that an intervention could cause, but, as had been the case during the Brazilian coup, he was far more concerned about facing domestic charges that he had lost another nation to the enemy. Worries about the global reputation and credibility of the United States also played on his mind. As he later exclaimed: "What can we do in Vietnam if we can't clean up the Dominican Republic?" In his judgment, domestic pressures and global credibility outweighed the importance of continuing to rebuild his administration's reputation in Latin America.[38]

Johnson's fears of a Communist revolution were not entirely without foundation. There were small groups of Communists among the rebels, but their influence was grossly exaggerated in the reports the president was receiving. It was not only Bennett, overly reliant on his Loyalist contacts, warning of the likelihood of another Cuba, but the intelligence services as well. "The CIA were ahead of us on this all the way," Mann reminded the president on the evening of the twenty-eighth. "They were sending in memos predicting doom if we did not send in the marines."[39] In addition, having apparently decided that events in the Dominican Republic were within his purview, FBI chief J. Edgar Hoover began inundating the White House with intelligence reports. According to Hoover, not only was there "extensive active participation on the part of Communists and pro-Castro groups during this Dominican revolution," but Juan Bosch, whom the Constitutionalists wished to reinstate as president, was considered a "communist leader" by Soviet intelligence.[40]

Given his lack of faith in the intelligence services in general, Johnson should have viewed these warning with more skepticism, but it appears that any risk of another Cuba was considered unacceptable. Johnson also understood that the Good Neighbor policy of nonintervention had, in the context of the Cold War, largely ceased to be applicable. The Eisenhower administration had privately reserved the right to intervene unilaterally in Latin America if US interests were threatened, and Johnson had been fully briefed on the deliberations of the Kennedy Doctrine group that had produced the no more Cubas maxim. Indeed, both those administrations had supported covert interventions designed to remove governments believed to be Communist or Communist dominated in Guatemala and Cuba. It is understandable, then, that Johnson believed a tough, uncompromising line on communism, either indigenous or Soviet, to be fully in line with the policies of his predecessors. Once Bennett supported the junta's assertion that the Dominican Republic was on the verge of becoming another Cuba, Johnson's fears allied with recent precedent, and the backing of his senior advisers was more than enough to see US forces mobilized.[41]

If Lyndon Johnson felt that the pressures of global and domestic politics, combined with the weight of policy precedent, left him little option but to intervene, Mann's abrupt volte-face on the afternoon of 28 April can be explained by his views on how the Good Neighbor policy should be interpreted within the context of the Cold War. As committed as Mann was to nonintervention in the political affairs of Latin American nations, he would later justify his change of attitude in the following terms: "Once I became convinced, and it didn't take me very long, (in fact, everybody was convinced) that if the rebels won, the Communist military component in the rebel movement . . . would take over—that you would have another Cuba—then all my problems disappeared, because I didn't think we were dealing with the problem of intervention; we were dealing with a problem of self-defense."[42]

This position reflected Mann's long-standing concern with the language of international law and inter-American treaties regarding the definitions of *intervention* and *aggression*. In a top-secret memo from July 1964, Mann had criticized the "outdated" definition of *aggression* that referred only to armed attack by another nation, such as existed in the Rio Treaty signed in the wake of World War II. In the new reality of subversion, guerrilla warfare, and ideological conflict, he believed that *aggression* should now encompass subversion sponsored by an outside power, such as Cuban-trained revolutionaries attempting to overthrow their own governments. If this issue was not addressed, he warned in the memo, "we shall find ourselves as frustrated and divided as we were at the Bay of Pigs when another crisis arises," recommending a full review of "our individual right of self-defense as it relates to communist subversion in the Western Hemisphere." While it does not appear that such a review took place, the memo does help explain Mann's thinking, however convoluted, regarding the necessity of sending troops into the Dominican Republic. In his view, a Communist revolution in the Western Hemisphere equated to an outside attack on the nation in question; the principle of collective self-defense therefore justified US intervention to prevent a victory for the forces of global communism and trumped the Good Neighbor commitment to noninterference.[43]

Mann's willingness to believe that the Constitutionalist forces had been subverted from within by Communist revolutionaries also reflected his background as a Foreign Service officer and his experiences in the field. As he had with Lincoln Gordon during the Brazil crisis a year before, Mann gave great weight to his ambassador's judgment and recommendations. In addition, his history with his friend "Tap" Bennett increased the likelihood that he would take much of the ambassador's reporting at face value. When Johnson enquired as to Bennett's character, Mann replied that he was "a Georgia boy, in the service twenty years, fine record, solid, level-headed, believes as you believe." In reality, Bennett was exaggerating evidence as he had seen the

Johnson and Mann listen to updates during the Dominican Republic crisis, 29 April 1965. (LBJ Library photo by Yoichi Okamoto)

damage that failure to predict previous Communist takeovers had done to the careers of other Foreign Service officers, effectively adopting a better-safe-than-sorry attitude. There is no reason to think that, on receiving this already-inflated risk assessment, Mann, a Foreign Service officer himself, would not be afflicted with the same worries as Bennett. Indeed, Mann had worked closely with Roy Richard Rubottom, whose apparent failure to fully appreciate the threat of Fidel Castro in 1959 had effectively ended his career.[44]

Considering the information available to them and their belief that a Bosch return would lead to a Communist victory, Johnson's and Mann's decision to dispatch troops to the Dominican Republic is not altogether surprising. Contingency plans for intervention had been established during both the Panamanian and the Brazilian crises but had proved unnecessary. The apparent urgency of the situation in the Dominican Republic meant that this time those plans were implemented. Recent policy doctrine, domestic pressures, and personal convictions all combined to make intervention seem the only viable option. Understandable it may have been, but the intervention was still a mistake. Obvious weaknesses and flaws in the intelligence were overlooked, and a failure to consider domestic radicals as anything other than outside agitators meant that a Dominican civil war was quickly subsumed into dominant Cold War paradigms. The shaky foundations on which the decision to intervene was built would soon be revealed as Johnson and Mann set about extending and justifying an intervention that would rapidly become an occupation.

Occupation and Justification

Once the decision to intervene in the Dominican Republic was taken, the Johnson administration faced two major challenges. First was the matter of what US troops would actually do once they had landed. The second, and eventually more problematic, was how to justify the intervention and best deflect the inevitable criticism it would provoke. From an operational point of view, the landing of marines was a success. From the few hundred soldiers who landed on the evening of 28 April and efficiently carried out the remaining evacuations, numbers increased to more than six thousand by 1 May. The additional forces allowed for the implementation of a plan devised by Admiral Kleber Masterson that expanded the evacuation operation to create a "line of communication," placing US forces between the opposing factions. The Loyalists, led by Wessin and Imbert, were still based out of the San Isidro barracks, while the Constitutionalists, now coalescing around Colonel Francisco Alberto Caamaño Deñó, were effectively hemmed into downtown Santo Domingo.[45]

The initial priority in Washington was to appear neutral; peacekeeping and preventing bloodshed would be easier to justify than intervening to save a corrupt military from an indigenous rebellion suspected of harboring Communists. Wessin and Imbert did not make that an easy task, however. On 2 May, Mann ordered Bennett to remind Wessin that US forces were not there to prop him up. "FYI," he added, "it would be particularly helpful if he could be persuaded to stop playing the Star Spangled Banner over San Isidro Radio Station." With the two factions seemingly entrenched, the first major diplomatic effort was to send John Bartlow Martin, the former ambassador, back to Santo Domingo. Martin, accompanied by the papal nuncio, was able to visit both the Constitutionalist and the Loyalist leadership and negotiate an uneasy cease-fire. At the same time, the initial security zone established by US forces steadily grew, creating a troubled and sporadically violated peace.[46]

Attempting to downplay the unilateral nature of the intervention, Johnson promptly sought assistance from the OAS. A full briefing was given to the OAS Council the day after US troops first landed, resulting in retroactive OAS approval of Johnson's decision. Under pressure from the White House, a meeting of foreign ministers on 6 May also approved the creation of the Inter-American Peace Force (IAPF), which was to be sent to the Caribbean, but there was no escaping the fact that US forces had landed without multilateral approval. Former Venezuelan president Rómulo Betancourt reminded Mann and Vaughn of this in a meeting on 1 May. While accepting that the OAS Council would have been unable to approve action swiftly enough, Betancourt nonetheless believed that it had been a "political blunder" not to call an immediate meeting, even if it had been at "2 am." He also worried about the political future of the Dominican Republic, warning against any association with the "ineffective" Wessin, and dismissing Bosch as a "good personal friend" but "completely unqualified to govern a country." He was not optimistic about the prospects for a positive outcome for the Dominican people or the United States, disdaining the OAS commission that was about to be dispatched to the Dominican Republic as lacking any "real force."[47]

Johnson and Mann shared many of Betancourt's worries, particularly regarding the establishment of an effective Dominican government. With a provisional cease-fire agreed to and OAS involvement assured, Johnson was soon demanding that Mann devise a workable political solution to a situation in which there seemed to be few acceptable candidates for leadership. On 2 May, the president ruled out the possibility of Constitutionalist forces leading a provisional government, as some aides had suggested, owing to the risk of "a Castro take-over," and warned Mann to think of something quickly before they were stuck with "a Schlesinger or Goodwin plan."[48] Nor were there appealing candidates among the Loyalists. John Martin had proposed Imbert as a figure to build a provisional government around, but Mann believed the general to be a "thug," not suitable for leadership, and the president agreed, ordering Mann to find a solution that did not involve "communists or fascists."[49]

Johnson was clearly willing to manage the formation of a provisional government closely, but he was also desperate to avoid the presence of those he considered extremists from either side. What he failed to grasp was how difficult a task this would be. When McGeorge Bundy and Jack Valenti telephoned Mann in quick succession to press him for the names of some "good Dominicans" or "non-rebel liberals," Mann vented his frustration. Most Dominicans were "so damn partisan and bitter for so long it is hard to think of someone who wouldn't cut across all kinds of lines," he complained. The best candidate, he told Valenti, was former president Joaquín Balaguer, whom he believed to have overseen the immediate post-Trujillo period with a "certain dignity and integrity." Mann was aware that Balaguer would "arouse [both] support and opposition" owing to his Trujillo associations, but he was struggling to find alternatives. His only other suggestion was to water down the junta through the addition of neutral civilians, a suggestion that was, he noted, "frankly . . . the best I have been able to come up with" and one put forward only because "Martin says reconciliation between these two groups is absolutely impossible." Keenly aware that, the longer the United States acted unilaterally in trying to establish a provisional government, the greater the risk of getting "deeper and deeper in trouble on the intervention side," Mann soon cast his net wider in search of a workable solution. On 5 May, he proposed establishing a committee of respected Central American political leaders who could oversee the formation of a viable provisional government. Men such as Betancourt, Alberto Lleras Camargo, and José Figueres were all moderate, anti-Communist, and respected within the inter-American system. He hoped that their involvement would help take the sting out of accusations of US imperialism.[50]

Mann's growing desperation to maintain at least an appearance of neutrality was not aided by the actions of Tap Bennett, with whom he was becoming increasingly frustrated. Bennett refused to look further than the Loyalist junta for a political solution, repeatedly recommending that it be recognized as the legitimate government of the Dominican Republic. Both Mann and Bundy were entirely against this course of action, with Mann informing US representative to the OAS Ellsworth Bunker that such recognition would be "disastrous." Open support for the Loyalists would "take all the fig leaves off" regarding US suspicion of the Constitutionalists, and, when it became clear that Imbert would be a central figure in any Loyalist government, Mann dismissed recognition out of hand. Indeed, by 11 May, Johnson and Mann were discussing the possibility of building a provisional government around the Constitutionalist leader Francisco Caamaño. Mann believed Caamaño to be independent of Bosch and, unlike others in his movement, free from Communist influence. Bennett had made "an error of judgement," Mann concluded, in refusing to talk to Caamaño and the other Constitutionalist leaders on the twenty-seventh, but, perhaps by courting

The senior foreign policy team receives an update on the Dominican intervention, 29 April 1965. *Left to right:* Admiral William F. Raborn (partly obscured), Thomas Mann, Dean Rusk, President Johnson, Robert McNamara. (Lyndon Baines Johnson Library photo by Yoichi Okamoto.)

Caamaño, the administration could split the genuine PRD supporters away from the extremists.[51]

By mid-May, none of the US initiatives had advanced the situation beyond the cease-fire stage. Mann had given up on the idea of a commission of respected political figures as the OAS was not prepared to grant them sufficient powers to be effective and both factions appeared more entrenched than ever. Both Imbert and Caamaño were proclaimed the legitimate leader of the nation by their respective sides, and the United States was supplying food and medical supplies to all parties, even paying the wages of many Dominicans in an attempt to keep basic public services running. It was also becoming increasingly difficult to appear fully neutral when the Constitutionalists were hemmed in downtown and subject to sporadic attacks from the Loyalist military. Mann was frustrated; he had been unable to prevent the United States getting drawn in "deeper and deeper" to the occupation, and there appeared little sign of a solution on the horizon. The pressure to find a workable compromise would be intensified further by growing public criticism and his president's clumsy attempts to deflect it.[52]

A report produced by the think tank the Center for Strategic Studies in July 1966 described the Dominican Republic intervention in the following terms: "The actions of the U.S. government in the Dominican Republic were more successful than its public explanation of these actions. Our government's failure to communicate effectively the rationale for its actions had damaging effects in the U.S. and throughout Latin America." Lyndon Johnson was primarily to blame for the damaging miscommunication that the report correctly identified. Desperate for blanket domestic approval for what was always likely to be a divisive operation, the president would make pronouncements that contradicted all available evidence, seriously damaging both his personal credibility and that of his administration.[53]

During his first public address on the Dominican crisis on the night of 28 April, the president set the terms of US involvement as an operation to evacuate American citizens and other foreign nationals. He also emphasized that his administration had "appealed repeatedly in recent days for a cease-fire between the contending forces of the Dominican Republic in the interests of all Dominicans and foreigners alike." Two days later, however, he would ominously announce: "There are signs that people trained outside the Dominican Republic are seeking to gain control." These "people" were not identified explicitly, but soon Johnson would dispense with any ambiguity. "What began as a popular democratic revolution, committed to democracy and social justice," he informed the nation during a televised address on 2 May, "was taken over and really seized and placed into the hands of a band of Communist conspirators." He explicitly linked his actions to the policies of his predecessor, invoking Kennedy's promise: "We in this hemisphere' must also use every resource at our command to prevent the establishment of another Cuba." As evidence of the Communist usurpation of the Constitutionalist movement, Johnson noted: "The original leaders of the rebellion . . . took refuge in foreign embassies because they had been superseded by other evil forces." But he failed to mention that they had been turned away from the US embassy by Bennett. Most dramatically, he also claimed to have a list of fifty-eight Communist agitators involved in the uprising that he subsequently provided to the press.[54]

Mann observed the president's speeches with growing unease. He had personally approved Johnson's first address, recommending a bold statement that avoided any mention of potential Communist involvement, but had gradually lost control of the messages being delivered to the public and the intelligence on which the president was basing his claims. He, along with other senior advisers, was aware of how little proof the administration possessed regarding Communist subversion, with Robert McNamara, for instance, warning Johnson: "[The intelligence services] haven't shown any evidence that I've seen that Castro has been directing this." Jack Valenti also cautioned against unverifiable statements, reminding the president that there must be "NO DOUBT as to our evidence."[55]

Unfortunately, Admiral William Raborn, who had been appointed CIA chief barely a week before the crisis erupted, lacked a firm grasp of the nature of the intelligence emerging from contacts within the Dominican Republic.[56] He was soon informing the president: "In my opinion this is a real struggle mounted by Mr. Castro." Yet he offered little evidence to support his claims. J. Edgar Hoover also continued to inundate the White House with reports, many of which were increasingly bizarre. One account ostensibly dealing with the Dominican situation provided a detailed description of a small protest at the Federal Building in Los Angeles that was opposed by "three fully uniformed members of the American Nazi Party" carrying placards that read "Death to Communist Traitors . . . and one picket [that] picketed all demonstrators with a placard reading 'Joe McCarthy Society.'" It is difficult to believe, therefore, that Johnson fully trusted Hoover's or Raborn's judgment, yet the list of names that was brandished before the press appears to have been cobbled together from information provided by them both. That Johnson could have felt certain the list was entirely genuine is unlikely, particularly given his general suspicion of the intelligence services, but, in his desperate desire for approval, it appears that he felt that some kind of evidence, no matter how unreliable, was necessary to secure it.[57]

Johnson's claims regarding the subversion of the Constitutionalists were not approved by Mann, who was convinced that the intelligence services were "sending figures but no caution to go with them." "[The list was] phony . . . everyone knew that all along," he remarked to Valenti after the president's speech, but now they would have to go "all out" to find evidence that supported Johnson's assertions. That would prove difficult, with even attempts to obtain photographs of "rebels wearing Fidel Castro caps" unsuccessful. Mann was forced to inform Johnson that the task might prove impossible, reminding him that underground Communist organizations were, by their nature, secretive and that any reliable information could take months to verify. The list that Johnson provided the press did, of course, prove to be as phony as Mann had feared, with certain names repeated twice and some of the supposed agitators either dead or imprisoned. Raborn had failed to grasp "the difference between raw information and evaluated information," Mann would later reflect, noting also that Johnson's claims "were not supportable by the evidence." The embarrassment would only add fuel to the fire of what was already a suspicious and increasingly hostile press reaction.[58]

Johnson's Joe McCarthy–like brandishing of the list of agitators gave elements of the press already critical of much of his Latin American policy plenty of ammunition for renewed attacks. Early support for the evacuation operation in both the media and public opinion polls soon turned to skepticism and outright suspicion once the president began painting the civil war as a Communist revolution. As the majority of the press coverage shifted from ambivalent to hostile, Johnson's invocation of Kennedy's promise to prevent more Cubas ironically became known as the "Johnson Doctrine" and was roundly criticized for overcommitting the United States to military action.[59] In response, Mann was dispatched to appear on the *Today Show,* denying that there was any change in policy, and arguing that in preventing outside interests from hijacking the Dominican political process the administration was in line with decades of policy. When Cyrus Vance appeared on ABC's *Issues and Answers* a few days later, however, he dismissed the idea of a Johnson Doctrine by focusing on the evacuation of American citizens. The failure of two of the administration's senior figures to maintain a consistent position in rebutting the Johnson Doctrine demonstrated just how clumsily justifications for the intervention were being articulated. The *New York Times* was particularly critical, but soon even publications that had previously displayed little in the way of an agenda regarding the administration's Latin American policy, such as *The Economist,* were accusing Johnson of "hitting first and seeing afterwards who precisely got hit."[60]

The situation was exacerbated by the volume of US reporters flooding into Santo Domingo—more than 150 by 7 May, according to embassy figures. Most of the correspondents were soon commenting on signs of cooperation between the US forces and the Loyalist military and questioning the degree of Communist influence in the Constitutionalist camp. One embassy report described the atmosphere at press briefings as "full blown and ugly," with reporters demanding "incontrovertible proof" of the administration's claims that the Constitutionalist cause had been subverted. Critical press reports also piqued the interest of members of Congress, with Wayne Morse, Joe Clark, and Robert Kennedy, now a member of the Senate, prominent among those requesting regular updates and openly questioning Johnson's decision making.[61]

In addition to domestic criticism, the administration was facing growing outrage from elsewhere in the hemisphere. Within the Dominican Republic itself, attitudes were often ambivalent, even among the Constitutionalists. As the historian Alan McPherson has observed, for the Dominicans encircled downtown, the US cordon was protecting them from the tanks of the Loyalist military. "As a man who selfishly wants to live, I am glad the American troops are here," one young Dominican told a reporter, "but as a nationalist, I deplore their presence." For the majority of other Latin American media, removed from the immediacy of the conflict, the issue was less complex. Most outlets took the view that, regardless of potential Communist threats, there had been a "deplorable" disregard for OAS charter provisions. *La Prensa* of Mexico was typical in describing the intervention as a "Yankee incursion" and running a cartoon that depicted a boulder marked "militarism" crushing the forces of democracy. Outrage was stoked further by Juan Bosch, who, from his temporary home in Puerto Rico, made his views clear in columns and interviews. Bosch repeatedly denied any Communist affiliation, supported Caamaño's leadership claim, and attacked the intervention as "a violation of the sacred right that each nation has to forge its own future." "I have no doubt that they have killed Dominican democracy," he told one Uruguayan newspaper, "at the very time when the people were creating it with their blood in an epic achievement."[62]

The combination of attacks from the domestic press, the legislature, and elsewhere in the hemisphere began to take its toll on Johnson, a man who never dealt well with criticism. "We are just mean sons o'bitches and outlaws and they are nice, virtuous maidens," he complained sarcastically to Bundy at a point of particular frustration. With domestic pressure building and the situation on the ground seemingly at a stalemate, he began to press harder for a solution that would enable US forces to withdraw.[63]

The Path to "Democratic Purity"

By 15 May, the president was thoroughly dispirited with all the efforts made to resolve the deadlock in the Dominican Republic. Mann had failed to identify an acceptable provisional government, and a five-man commission the OAS had dispatched appeared to making little headway. Discussions with Juan Bosch through Abe Fortas, Johnson's longtime legal counsel and close confidant, had also been unproductive, while communication with the Loyalist military had been conducted largely through Bennett, whose opinions Mann and Johnson were learning to treat with caution. Johnson's solution was to launch a diplomatic offensive headed by some of his most senior advisers. McGeorge Bundy, accompanied by Cyrus Vance, would visit Bosch in Puerto Rico before traveling to Santo Domingo to meet with the Constitutionalist leadership. Meanwhile, Mann, along with Jack Vaughn, would head to San Isidro to consult with the Loyalists as well as serving as liaison with the OAS commission. It was hoped that, through consultation with all parties, an acceptable provisional government could be formed and US forces, now numbering almost twenty-four thousand, could begin to withdraw.[64]

Bundy was not initially optimistic about his allotted task. He shared the widely held view that Bosch was overly idealistic and ineffective and thought the Constitutionalist demands for reform of the Dominican government were totally unrealistic and entirely unpalatable to the Loyalist forces. Nonetheless, Bundy "gave it a good college try," as one of his colleagues observed, and spent several days in Santo Domingo negotiating with the Constitutionalist forces. Eventually, he thought he had found an acceptable solution—a provisional government led by the moderate Constitutionalist Antonio Guzmán that incorporated elements of both factions. The only potential sticking point, from Bundy's perspective, was that Guzmán refused to exclude more radical members of his side, such as Héctor Aristy, from the process.[65]

Despite feeling the pressure of the continued occupation, on 22 May, the president vetoed the compromise deal. Observers, both at the time and since, have suggested that Mann, committed to the return of Balaguer and overly sympathetic to the Loyalist forces, "torpedoed" Bundy's agreement.[66] Abe Fortas, for instance, believed that Mann's favored solution was simply "to turn Imbert loose completely" on downtown Santo Domingo and eradicate the Constitutionalist forces. It is undeniable that Mann's views were influential, with Johnson confiding to Fortas: "I have more confidence in Mann's judgement than I do in Bundy's." However, Mann was just as keen as Bundy to find a prompt political solution, and his skepticism regarding the compromise deal appears to have stemmed not from Loyalist sympathies but from his own experiences in Santo Domingo.[67]

Mann arrived in the Dominican Republic on 15 May and immediately met with the Loyalist leadership at the San Isidro barracks. The exchange that followed demonstrated the difficulties that any compromise plan would face. Mann opened by informing the assembled generals—to much protest—that there would be no operation to clear out downtown by force. The Constitutionalists included many "well intentioned youngsters who had been tricked by the extremists," he said. "[The] shedding of their blood would be a tragedy." Next, he announced that every measure would be taken to keep Communists out of power. However: "The Dominican people were tired of government by oligarchy, unjustified privileges for the few and general corruption. They wanted equality, reforms and constitutionality." In this, he promised, the American government would support them, and the first step in this process would be the formation of a provisional government under Guzmán. Rebel military units should be reincorporated with "no reprisals or vengeance," and the armed forces had to clean up their corrupt image and give their full support to a provisional government, or else "all might end in chaos and hatred." Mann's presentation was direct and unsympathetic, with one aide noting that the generals suffered the experience "with some pain." Nonetheless, the Loyalist leadership remained stubbornly hostile to any form of compromise deal. Their protestations ranged from the selection of an armed forces representative in the government, potential persecution of Catholics if the 1963 constitution were reinstated, and one general's conviction that Caamaño had personally burgled his home. Their entrenched attitudes were summarized by General Martinez Arana, who concluded that he had nothing against Bosch personally, apart from the fact that he was "sick and crazy."[68]

Frustrated, Mann called a number of the more senior figures aside into a private meeting. If they hoped that Johnson's envoy wished to deliver a secret message of support, they were to be disappointed. Emilio De Los Santos and Francisco Rivera Caminero, the respective heads of the navy and the air force, were instead informed that, for the provisional government to succeed, they would have to leave the country entirely. They eventually gave their reluctant agreement—if it proved to be "absolutely essential"—but not even that degree of cooperation would be forthcoming from Imbert. During a private meeting later that evening, the "shocked and angry" Loyalist leader rejected the idea of a Guzmán government outright and accused Mann and Johnson of carrying out a treacherous "double-cross."[69]

Mann's experience with the Loyalist military suggests an alternative explanation for his reluctance to endorse Bundy's compromise deal. Bundy had spoken only to Bosch and some elements of the Constitutionalist leadership, not to the generals at San Isidro. As Mann would explain to a Senate hearing in July, he believed that if a provisional government was formed that did not have some degree of acceptance from the Loyalist military, that military would simply overthrow it—unless, that is, the United States was prepared to remain in the Dominican Republic indefinitely, propping up a government through force. As a consequence of the line of communication that the US forces had established, the position of the Constitutionalist forces hemmed into downtown Santo Domingo had grown increasingly weak, while the Loyalists, with their relative freedom of movement, had been able to regroup and reorganize. That the Loyalists were allowed such freedom of movement undermines claims that US forces were ever fully neutral, but, as the transcript of his meetings with their leadership demonstrates, Mann was not in favor of unleashing Wessin's and Imbert's forces on the increasingly bedraggled Constitutionalists. Indeed, as restraining the generals at San Isidro became ever more challenging, it appears that Mann believed Bundy's proposals would be more likely to provoke further conflict than lay out a road map to peace.[70]

Ultimately, even Bundy had doubts regarding the viability of a Guzmán-led provisional government, and suggestions of a power struggle between two of Johnson's most influential advisers are somewhat exaggerated. Bundy may have been frustrated that days of complex negotiations had come to nothing, and there is no way of knowing whether Mann was correct in his belief that the compromise would fail, but, having been sent to gauge the attitude of the Loyalists, that was what he did. Uneasy about the continuing presence of what he viewed as the most radical elements of the Constitutionalists, Johnson accepted Mann's judgment and began to hunt for an alternative plan.[71]

The collapse of Bundy's negotiating efforts meant a new round of searching for potential solutions, with the president increasingly desperate for signs of progress. The situation on the ground was not promising, however. The Constitutionalists remained entrenched in downtown Santo Domingo, Johnson's advisers being unable to devise any practical means of either

Mann delivers an update in the Cabinet Room following his trip to Santo Domingo, 19 May 1965. (Lyndon Baines Johnson Library photo by Yoichi Okamoto.)

encouraging or pressuring them to disperse. Equally frustrating was the stubbornness of the Loyalists, with Mann willing to threaten Imbert with everything short of military force to get him to agree to a compromise deal. Johnson was by now convinced that "every hour the Marines stay there, it takes something off me," and confided to Mann in late May that he feared the press would soon be looking for "scapegoats." One of the few encouraging developments was the increasingly prominent role played by other Latin American nations in the IAPF, and both Johnson and Mann were desperate to reduce the specter of a unilateral United States by promoting the role of the OAS.[72]

The diplomatic effort that would finally result in the formation of a provisional government was indeed an OAS initiative, albeit one with a strong US influence. In early June, a new three-man OAS commission—including both Brazilian and Salvadoran representatives and spearheaded by the vastly experienced US ambassador Ellsworth Bunker—was dispatched to the Caribbean. "They worked together beautifully," one colleague observed. "They were the ones who carried through the negotiations with both sides, setting up a provisional government, the elections, and finally the withdrawal of the troops." The recommendation of the committee was to work toward closely supervised elections but with the "formation in the meantime of a provisional government of technicians who, governing under an institutional act with strong OAS support, could take [the] country to elections." Bunker believed that this would almost certainly be opposed by both Caamaño and Imbert and probably Bosch, but he advised Washington that it would be possible to forge ahead without their consent. After all, the Constitutionalists remained trapped in the city with no chance of winning a military victory, while the Loyalists owed their position of relative superiority to ongoing US support. Both were susceptible to pressure from negotiators.[73]

While it would take almost three months of discussions to conclude, on 31 August, the Act of Dominican Reconciliation was signed, with even Caamaño and Imbert adding their signatures. The agreement dispersed controversial figures on both sides overseas and established a provisional government under Bosch's former minister of foreign affairs, Héctor García-Godoy. In contrast to his earlier micromanagement, Johnson had afforded Bunker a great degree of freedom during the negotiations. In part this was due to his desire to see the OAS take on a more prominent role, but it also reflected that he had a more pressing problem to deal with—attacks from his own party in Congress.[74]

Congressional dissent over the Dominican intervention had been a concern for the administration since the troops first landed but had truly emerged onto the national stage a week later via familiar sources. On 6 May, in a speech penned by Arthur Schlesinger, Senator Robert Kennedy attacked Johnson for acting unilaterally and delaying consultation with the OAS. Kennedy's actions were termed "absolutely outrageous" by Averell Harriman, but for the first weeks of the intervention Kennedy was an exception, and Johnson largely had the backing of the legislature. As press scrutiny increased, however, so did congressional interest in the administration's actions, eventually peaking in mid-July with a series of hearings that called Johnson's senior advisers before the Senate Foreign Relations Committee. The president was wary, particularly of the attitude of his old Senate ally J. William Fulbright, but nonetheless instructed Mann not to be "apologetic about anything."[75]

Mann appeared before the committee on 14 July, on 15 July, and again on 29 July. The hearings were cagey affairs, marked by some sharp exchanges with Fulbright, who was openly skeptical regarding the administration's justifications for both the intervention and the delays in withdrawing. "Maybe the Communists are the only solution," he suggested provocatively during one particularly spiky session. "We don't want another missile base," Mann answered bluntly. The most controversial line of questioning dealt with the issue of neutrality, and on this neither Mann nor Vance, who appeared alongside him, were particularly convincing. Vance claimed that there was some initial cooperation with the junta as it was the "only government available" but that, once a cease-fire was established, any violations of neutrality were "isolated cases." Mann declared that there was cooperation with all parties, except for known Communists, and dismissed questions about "switching sides" as a matter of "semantics." Unable to disguise that the priority of the intervention had been to prevent an outright Constitutionalist victory, Mann and Vance unsurprisingly failed to persuade the more hostile members of the committee to support the administration's actions.[76]

The role of Tap Bennett was also scrutinized during the hearings, and, although he did not appear in person, the ambassador submitted a statement that further provoked those senators who believed the administration's reporting to be exaggerated. During the crisis itself, Bennett had demonstrated a gift for hyperbole, informing Johnson at one stage: "We have reports of churches being attacked. . . . [I]t's a real holocaust." In his written statement to the committee, this talent was once again on show. He claimed that "countless lives had been saved through this action and that an extremist take-over, directly or indirectly, had been averted." While he may have had a point about preventing further loss of life, language such as "there was a blood fever in the streets" and an exaggerated description of the Ambajador incident served only to further undermine his and the administration's credibility.[77]

Bennett was not the only administration representative guilty of hyperbole. The day after the ambassador's statement was submitted, the president held a disastrous but luckily for him untelevised news conference in which he put Bennett to shame. Clearly feeling the pressure of the Senate hearings and the media scrutiny, Johnson turned, as he often did, to exaggeration as a means of emphasizing a point. Attempting to evoke the chaos of Santo Domingo in the buildup to the US intervention, he described headless bodies lying in the streets, fifteen hundred civilians murdered, and Bennett cowering under a desk as insurgents strafed the embassy. Quizzed about Johnson's remarks during the hearings, a plainly uncomfortable Mann weakly pointed out that he could comment only on official White House statements, not off-the-record opinions. "Johnson was a man given to exaggeration and hyperbole anyway," the committee's chief of staff Pat Holt later commented. "I don't think Mann ever really believed this business about fifteen hundred people having their heads cut off, . . . but one of Mann's characteristics is absolute loyalty to whoever was president."[78]

Following the Senate hearings, the committee was divided, unable even to issue a report. Fulbright had drawn his own conclusions, however, deciding that Bennett had overreacted and that the administration had subsequently lied regarding its level of neutrality. Aware of Fulbright's hostility during the hearings, Johnson attempted to court his erstwhile ally by sending him on a diplomatic mission to Brazil with Mann for company. He hoped that, during the flight, Mann could convince Fulbright to soften his stance, but instead the senator locked himself in a cabin and refused to come out. The president also tried to apply pressure through his contacts in Congress, but all to no avail. On 15 September, the chairman of the Foreign Relations Committee delivered an incendiary speech on the Senate floor. Administration policy, Fulbright declared, had been characterized "initially by over-timidity and subsequently by overreaction . . . [and] throughout the whole affair . . . by a lack of candor." The degree of Communist involvement, he concluded, was not proved "at the time and has not been established since."[79]

Fulbright's speech destroyed his relationship with the president beyond repair. A furious Johnson had Bundy draft a letter that "hit him with everything but the kitchen stove," banned his old friend from the White House, and encouraged other senators to denounce him. For Johnson, Fulbright was now part of the Schlesinger group of intellectuals who opposed him unswervingly and was therefore not worth his time to try and court. Of even greater consequence was the damage done to the reputation and credibility of both Johnson and his administration, effectively called reactionaries and liars by the Senate's most senior foreign policy spokesman. Battles with Fulbright and accusations of dishonesty would plague Johnson for the remainder of his presidency.[80]

Congressional activity on the Dominican Republic had one last headache in store for the Johnson administration, although it was intended, ironically, as a statement of support. In September, Congressman Armistead Selden (D-AL) successfully introduced a resolution to the House that fervently supported the right of the United States to intervene in the hemisphere, without OAS consultation, to combat Communist subversion. For an administration that had been attempting to deflect charges of unilateralism and gunboat diplomacy, the resolution was a disaster. William Bowdler of the State Department unsuccessfully begged Selden to withdraw it, and Mann hurriedly drafted policy statements announcing that the congressman spoke for neither the White House nor the State Department. Their worries were well founded. A State Department research memo from 30 September noted: "[The resolution has] aroused fears [in Latin America] that the U.S. may be returning to a 'big stick' policy. . . . [N]o favorable reactions have been received." Bundy warned the president: "We are likely to feel the shock-waves for some time to come." If Fulbright was tarnishing Johnson's reputation at home, Selden was unintentionally doing likewise in Latin America.[81]

The concluding act of the Dominican Republic crisis was, for Johnson at least, the election of June 1966, in which Joaquín Balaguer defeated Juan Bosch in the contest for the presidency. The García-Godoy government had managed to limp along from September 1965, largely propped up by the United States. Johnson had initially been wary of García-Godoy, wondering whether he was a "stooge of Bosch" and whether a military government might be better equipped to see the nation through to the elections. "That's no solution," Mann warned. García-Godoy needed support while the provisional government "clean out the top on both sides." Mann's fears about the danger posed by the Loyalist leadership had also been confirmed by an attempted military uprising led by Wessin, averted only when the general received a US marine escort to the nearest airport and was forced into exile. Wessin's ignoble departure helped with Mann's "clean out," as did the announcement in March 1966 that Bennett was to be reassigned to Portugal. Press guidance for administration representatives stated that his relocation in no way reflected dissatisfaction with his performance and that the president had full confidence in his abilities. In reality, Bennett was too closely associated with the Loyalists and despised by Bosch. While Johnson and Mann steadfastly refused to throw him to the wolves, his departure reflected the need to get him out of Santo Domingo before the elections began in earnest while not openly admitting that he remained part of the problem.[82]

In his memoirs, Lyndon Johnson wrote that the elections of June 1966 were "an outstanding act of democratic purity," reflecting the will of the Dominican people. Some historians have, broadly speaking, agreed with him, while others have argued that the elections were marred by violence, intimidation, and widespread fraud.[83] Available documentation appears to suggest that, while the voting process itself was relatively fair, particularly by the standards of past elections, the campaigning most certainly was not. Johnson's claims were based largely on the presence of OAS observers during the electoral process. In addition to the OAS teams, international press coverage was intense, further reducing the likelihood of widespread fraud. Analysis of the process throughout the hemisphere was also generally positive, with one State Department report noting that there "was a widespread feeling of relief that the elections had taken place" and an acceptance that Balaguer was "the free and democratic choice of the Dominican people." Even the more radical media outlets were relatively free of accusations of fraud. Finally, the Johnson administration was also drawing up contingency plans for a Bosch victory suggesting that the United States would "be forthcoming in attitude and deed in support of him." As the Johnson aide Bill Moyers explained to Bowdler, this was largely because "if a rightist coup should overthrow him after he is the victor in free elections . . . the criticism of LBJ by the liberal community of this hemisphere will be scathing" but nonetheless reflected a belief within the administration that a Bosch victory was at least a possibility.[84]

Unfortunately, any claims of "democratic purity" are undermined somewhat by the preferential treatment shown to Johnson's and Mann's preferred candidate, Joaquín Balaguer. CIA memos are clear that the president had indicated whom he wanted to win and that he expected "the Agency to arrange for this to happen." Throughout the first months of 1966, "the Agency" carried out extensive polling, the results of which were used to formulate campaign strategy for Balaguer's camp. Consequently, successful aspects of Balaguer's campaign, such as a major voter registration drive in rural areas where he enjoyed widespread popularity, were a direct result of planning by the US intelligence agencies. Bosch, by contrast, was offered no support, barely leaving his house during the campaign owing to justified fears for his safety. Complaining to reporters that he was running only out of a sense of obligation to his party, he would bitterly inform Ellsworth Bunker: "The elections offered a way out for the U.S., but not for the Dominican people."[85]

Balaguer took around 56 percent of the vote to Bosch's 39 percent, winning, as the CIA had predicted, almost the entire rural vote. The presence of OAS observers guaranteed a veneer of American impartiality, but there was no doubting that Johnson's favored candidate had won and owed much to his

Left to right: Thomas Mann, the papal nuncio, Monsignor Emanuele Clarizio, the apostolic delegate, Egidio Vagnozzi, and President Johnson, the Oval Office, 6 October 1965. The papal nuncio had recently been attempting to broker a cease-fire in the Dominican Republic. (Lyndon Baines Johnson Library photo by Yoichi Okamoto.)

Langley-trained campaign team and the widespread awareness that he enjoyed the backing of Washington. Although he would thankfully fall short of Trujillo's level of brutality and notoriety, Balaguer would nonetheless establish an authoritarian rule that saw him go on to dominate Dominican politics for three decades. As Bosch had predicted, the outcome was far from ideal for the people of the Dominican Republic, but it was more than good enough for the Johnson administration.[86]

Ultimately, the decision to intervene in the Dominican Republic in April 1965 had deeply unpleasant consequences for both the Dominican people and Lyndon Johnson's presidency. The intervention opened fissures in the delicate congressional coalition that Johnson had built in order to pass his Great Society legislation, and he would never again have consistently good relations with the legislature as the cracks were widened by escalating commitments in Vietnam. Relations with the press mirrored this decline, with Johnson increasingly embattled and unable to dispel the idea of a credibility gap between his words and his actions. The intervention also severely damaged the administration's reputation in the hemisphere, an outcome that both Johnson and Mann had resigned themselves to at an early stage of the crisis. Regardless of justification, the United States dispatched thousands of troops, without OAS approval, to intercede in what many observers were convinced was a Dominican civil war, not a Communist uprising. Any goodwill and respect that Johnson and Mann had managed to establish in Latin America was dealt a far greater blow by this than by either the Mann Doctrine or the response to the Brazilian coup of 1964. Johnson once remarked that the OAS "couldn't pour piss out of a boot if the instructions were written on the heel," and his obvious disdain for the hemispheric council and apparent lack of respect for inter-American treaties crippled hemispheric cooperation and undermined what little authority the OAS possessed.[87]

The harshest critics of the Dominican Republic intervention have tended to condemn Johnson's actions in symbolic terms. Walter LaFeber has argued that it represented a return to traditional US policies of "overt military power, open economic pressure, and the unilateralism of the Monroe Doctrine." Others have also positioned the intervention within the context of more immediate policy precedent, such as William Walker III, who has portrayed it as "the apotheosis of the U.S. obsession since January 1961 with subversion" and the "logical culmination" of Washington's commitment to hemispheric security. Johnson certainly appears to have believed that his actions were guided by a long-established commitment to opposing Communist influence in the hemisphere, a commitment that predated his presidency. Yet, even as he followed through on that commitment, he was aware of the damaging nature of the historically loaded image of US marines landing in the Caribbean and the resulting accusations of a return to a gunboat policy. As domestic and international criticism of his actions increased, Johnson bemoaned to aides that he would now be seen as an "intervenor" or, in his more melodramatic moments, a "Führer" stamping his "brand on this satellite state."[88]

Some of Johnson's frustration may have stemmed from the fact that, unlike Eisenhower with Guatemala or Kennedy with the Bay of Pigs, the Dominican intervention was not a planned covert operation but a crisis situation requiring an immediate decision and resulting in the open use of the US military. Subsequent analysis has suggested that there was little chance of the Dominican civil war evolving into a Cuban-style revolution, but that was a risk, however small, that neither Johnson nor his advisers were willing to entertain. As Bundy reassured his president the day after the first troops landed: "We'll never be sure they wouldn't have won without us. We only know that we couldn't take that chance." Mann, Bundy, McNamara, Rusk, and all the most influential voices in the administration endorsed the intervention, but ultimately the decision rested with the president. Presented with evidence, however flawed, that a Communist revolution might be in the offing, Johnson delivered on his predecessors' guarantees and then dealt with the consequences as best he could.[89]

Johnson's clumsy handling of media and public opinion, fueled by his hypersensitivity to criticism, was disastrous, but this has, to some extent, masked the complexity of the postintervention challenges facing his administration. Unwilling to cede full control of the situation to Dominicans or the OAS, but desperate to avoid further accusations of imperialism, Johnson tried to walk a policy fine line that he hoped would result in a provisional and then permanent government that was, as he put it to Abe Fortas, "anti-communist and pro-liberal." No one understood this better than Mann, ordered by Johnson to find a solution that excluded both "communists" and "fascists." A second Cuba was unthinkable, but, after intervening and enforcing a cease-fire, so was a military coup or a resumption of fighting once US forces departed. Mann was not, as some critics have painted him, simply the figure who sabotaged Bundy's compromise deal and consistently favored the Loyalist military but a beleaguered diplomat struggling to find the elusive and possibly nonexistent "third force" that his president demanded.[90]

The intervention laid bare the simple truth that, no matter how much policy makers in Washington favored hemispheric cooperation and development, the security concerns of the United States would always lie at the heart of the nation's inter-American policy. Priorities that dated back to the Monroe Doctrine were augmented by Cold War fears of Communist subversion and national humiliation to fuel a situation in which Johnson was convinced that he had little choice but to send in the marines. Considering the policies of his predecessors both recent and in the more distant past, it is not difficult to understand why. Nonetheless, the intervention would have dire consequences for the administration's reputation, its relationships with the other nations of the Americas, and Thomas Mann's career. Struggling for foreign aid funding as he waded deeper into Vietnam, and soon shorn of his chief adviser, Johnson would continue to find inter-American relations a frustrating challenge.

5

New Alliances

The Post-Mann Era

Lyndon Johnson's decision to send US Marines to the Dominican Republic has often been treated as the concluding act of his administration's Latin American policy, final evidence of the dominance of the Mann Doctrine and confirmation that any hope for the Alliance for Progress was lost. In part, this reflects the fact that the intervention was the last major hemispheric crisis of the Johnson years, but other factors have been of greater relevance in shaping such a narrative. Most pertinently, by the end of 1965, there were more than 200,000 American military personnel in Vietnam, accompanied by the first stirrings of the domestic protest movement that would soon divide the nation. Furthermore, international crises in the Middle East, the Indian Subcontinent, and Indonesia that followed the Dominican intervention would provide compelling diversions for both the policy makers and the historians concerned with foreign relations during the remainder of Johnson's presidency.[1]

For Thomas Mann too, the drama of April and May 1965 has often been taken to be the last significant event of his career, prompting a steady decline in his influence until he departed government service in the spring of 1966. Contributing to this impression was the fact that, despite his position as number three in the State Department, he steadfastly and, in hindsight, sensibly refused to wade too deeply into the quagmire of Vietnam policy. "Any ideas on Vietnam?" Johnson would occasionally ask hopefully. "[I've been] too far removed from that," Mann would typically reply. "I don't have any ideas." Consequently, as administration, public, and media attention swung inexorably toward Southeast Asia, his profile and influence commensurably declined. Nonetheless, despite his distance from the defining foreign policy issue of Johnson's presidency, he remained in office for almost a year after the Dominican crisis; he would grow ever closer to the president, ending his career as a confidant to and comrade of an increasingly embattled leader before leaving government in early 1966.[2]

Similarly, the decline in prominence of hemispheric issues after the Dominican intervention does not mean that relations with Latin America ceased to concern the administration. The remaining years of Johnson's presidency would in fact see him spearhead one final attempt to revitalize the Alliance for Progress even as a series of military coups served to underline the great challenges faced by the hemisphere as whole and the costs and limitations of American development efforts. While LBJ's attempts to encourage greater economic and physical integration via an inter-American summit in 1967 were not entirely successful, they demonstrate a leader who remained far more engaged with the hemisphere than is commonly acknowledged. They also reflected the blend of New Deal and New Frontier thinking—the continued commitment to development marked by a degree of caution and pragmatism—that was present in Johnson's administration. As British ambassador to the United States Patrick Dean observed in 1967, this period saw the Johnson administration realize that its "best interest lies in encouraging, but not being too closely enmeshed in, the development of collective regional endeavors in all areas of the non-Communist world." While the implementation of this realization would have its limits, the efforts made to shape a new vision for inter-American affairs deserve more recognition than simply to be forgotten among the aftermath of the Dominican Republic crisis and the trauma and tragedy of the Vietnam War.[3]

Picking up the Pieces

For several months following the Dominican intervention, the Johnson administration's priority in Latin America was to attempt to repair the damage done by the unilateral show of force in the Caribbean. As part of these efforts, Mann's public profile steadily declined, a process accelerated by the adverse reactions to an address in October 1965 that further confirmed that public relations were not his forte. The speech was effectively a rebuttal to Senator William Fulbright's criticisms of the administration's conduct in the Dominican Republic, and, although Mann's defense of the intervention and claims that the United States sought to follow a path that bisected "reaction and leftist extremism" met with a mixed reaction in Latin America, it was widely condemned at home. The *New York Times* in particular dismissed the speech as "the most emphatic statement to date of the so-called 'Hard-line' policy . . . of which he is widely regarded as the architect." The response convinced Mann that he could best serve his president by maintaining a low profile, and it would consequently be the last major public address of his government career.[4]

The president's attempts to gain ground on his critics would, in some instances at least, be marginally more successful than those of his Latin American chief. On the fourth anniversary of the Alliance for Progress, 17 August 1965, Johnson delivered a speech that was designed, according to Assistant Secretary of State Jack Vaughn, to counter charges that "the Alliance died with Kennedy . . . [or that] our Dominican policy overshadows it." In an ambitious address, the president guaranteed continued commitment to the Alliance and promised improvements, particularly in trade agreements and multinational projects designed to further regional integration. He also promised that more attention would be given to "efforts toward those things which directly touch the lives of individual human beings—housing, education, health, and food." These things were "the common thread which runs through the Great Society in [this] country and the Alliance for Progress in all countries."[5]

Unlike Mann's efforts, the speech was met with considered praise both in the domestic media and throughout the hemisphere. One State Department report noted that foreign press coverage was generally positive and that "the presidents of Venezuela, Colombia and Peru made very favorable comments." Even the *New York Times* supported Johnson's endorsement of expanded regional markets as "a constructive effort to improve hemispheric relations" and recognized the "many solid achievements" of the Alliance. Glad of a distraction from the continuing negotiations in the Dominican Republic, and keen to build on the goodwill generated by his speech, Johnson dispatched Vaughn on a two-week tour of the hemisphere. The trip was designed to meet citizens, not governments, and to witness Alliance projects in action. "We are not bringing our tuxedoes this time," quipped one member of the party.[6]

The administration's efforts to mitigate the damage done by the Dominican intervention culminated in November 1965 at an inter-American conference in Rio de Janeiro. Dean Rusk represented the United States, and his rare foray into the world of hemispheric relations reflected the degree of importance Johnson accorded the meeting. Throughout the conference, Rusk supported the establishment of new cooperative mechanisms to safeguard democracy "from the extreme right or the extreme left," emphasized the need for all nations to support each other financially and militarily, and, most significantly, extended the life of the Alliance by announcing that President Johnson wanted "no calendar end to the program." As a result, the conference produced the Act of Rio de Janeiro, which made some adjustments to the charter of the OAS but also declared that the Alliance would exist "as long as it is needed." Reporting on the meeting, the State Department official and CIAP representative Walt Rostow observed that, while the extension of the Alliance had been well received, the most welcome development had been the widespread acknowledgment that the hemisphere consisted not of a rich United States and a poor Latin America but of a variety of nations with differing economic statuses. According to Rostow, that acceptance "immediately affected the vocabulary used in the committee meetings," with "mutual aid" a recurring theme, and an increase in technical assistance and short-term loans between Latin American nations was now a "realistic expectation."[7]

The removal of the ten-year limit on Alliance programs and the emphasis on Latin American mutual assistance reflected not only the desire of the administration to heal the wounds of the spring but also the fact that wider-ranging developments were in store for the management of inter-American policy. One significant change came in the form of personnel, with Lincoln Gordon replacing Vaughn as assistant secretary of state for inter-American affairs and Alliance coordinator in early 1966. Mann had found Vaughn to be "not a very good administrator or a very profound thinker," but he also feared that Robert Kennedy, now an influential senator, had his "knife sharpened" for the assistant secretary and thought that he would benefit from a return to the Peace Corps. Despite his prominent role during the Brazilian coup, Gordon still had "some lines out to the left," and Mann argued that he represented Johnson's best option. Gordon's return to Washington was widely taken to mark the end of Mann's control of Latin American policy, but in truth his influence had begun to wane even before the personnel change. Mann's less prominent role in the administration following the Dominican intervention reflected a desire to avoid any further media attacks but also preparation for his long-delayed retirement. Gordon had been a prominent ambassador, had helped plan the Alliance, and was generally a far more forceful and opinionated character than Vaughn, who had deferred to Mann on most matters of policy. Gordon's return marked the beginning of Johnson's preparations for a Mann-less administration.[8]

Mann's departure would deprive the president of more than just his Latin American expertise; in the months following the Dominican intervention, the two men had grown increasingly close. Mann was a regular guest at the White House and the Johnson Ranch in Texas, where he made a particularly good impression on the First Lady. Writing in her journal, Lady Bird Johnson commented that Mann seemed to have "had a strange life about which he is quite silent" and possessed a deep love of Mexico that had not been affected by the loss of one of his children to "an amoebic disease contracted on one of the South American tours of duty." To her, he seemed "made of tough fiber, but a loveable man," and she noted that his presence helped "make our Administration feel more closely knit."[9]

Beyond the dinners, the president also developed the habit of engaging Mann in wide-ranging telephone conversations that would often begin by focusing on specific hemispheric issues before wandering into lengthy analyses of Washington politics and candid discussion of members of the administration and troublesome congressmen. He particularly valued Mann's input on appointments and promotions. When considering George Ball for UN representative, for example, he was dissuaded by Mann, who argued that the undersecretary needed to remain where he was as he "made ninety percent of the decisions that have to be made" in the State Department. The two would also vent their long-standing frustrations with their liberal critics, "Schlesinger and Goodwin and that crowd," with Mann indulging Johnson to the point of describing himself as "the most anti-Kennedy man in the USA." Fulbright also received particularly harsh treatment, now belonging, in the president's opinion, "intellectually and emotionally" to the Robert Kennedy camp. Ignore him, Mann advised Johnson during one particularly therapeutic conversation; Fulbright was "emotional and vain," lazy and overly influenced by his aides Holt and Marcy, "who are no friends of the president or Mr. Mann." "He does not work, he loafs," Mann concluded acidly.[10]

These conversations involved more than just indulging in cheap shots at critics. Mann's opinions mattered to Johnson; retaining Ball, recalling Gordon from Brazil, and appointing John Crimmins to succeed Tap Bennett as ambassador to the Dominican Republic were all actions suggested by Mann and implemented by the president. On one important decision, however,

Johnson chose not to take Mann's advice. In late 1965, the president was considering potential replacements for McGeorge Bundy, who would depart his role as national security adviser in February 1966. Keen to have Mann stay in the administration, Johnson once again offered him the position. When Mann refused, ostensibly on health grounds, Johnson changed the subject, eventually asking for an assessment of Walt Rostow.[11]

Rostow's influence and range of responsibilities had been growing steadily throughout Johnson's presidency, and his position on CIAP meant that he and Mann had crossed paths fairly regularly. The two had worked particularly closely on an effort to resolve the ongoing petroleum dispute in Peru, with Rostow dispatched by his "Latino pals," as he referred to Mann, Jack Vaughn, and Lincoln Gordon, to negotiate directly with President Belaúnde Terry. "Useful" was Mann's initial take on the erstwhile modernization theorist: "[He] has a liberal image, big heart, the Latins love him." Johnson edged closer to his point, asking Mann whether Rostow was loyal to him. Mann responded that he had never heard rumors of disloyalty but that Rostow's only real allegiance was "to Walt himself." Well, what about Rostow for national security adviser? Johnson finally asked. Perhaps reflecting his long-standing distrust of those he considered overreliant on theory to guide their policy decisions, Mann responded with one word: "No."[12]

On this point Johnson failed to heed Mann's advice, selecting Rostow as his replacement for the influential Bundy. With Mann leaving government shortly afterward, "America's Rasputin," as Rostow was memorably christened by Averell Harriman, with his hawkish views on Vietnam soon replaced Mr. Latin America in the president's confidence. Furthermore, despite his personal endorsement of Cyrus Vance for the role, there would be no direct replacement for Mann, and the nearest equivalent role, undersecretary of state for political affairs, would be taken in October by Rostow's brother, Eugene. Walt Rostow would, in effect, replace both Thomas Mann and McGeorge Bundy, two of Johnson's most powerful advisers. Unsurprisingly, then, his influence over administration policy, inter-American affairs included, would be considerable.[13]

In April 1966, Thomas Mann finally secured his retirement from government service, effective from June. "I don't know of another public servant who has been more valiant in defending the national cause of freedom and integrity of purpose," Johnson wrote on accepting his resignation. "You . . . leave with the deep regret of your president." In one of their final conversations, the

"Mr. Latin America" and "America's Rasputin," Walt Rostow, enjoy each other's company at Mann's leaving party, 25 May 1966. Mann's departure greatly increased Rostow's influence within the administration. (Lyndon Baines Johnson Library photo by Yoichi Okamoto.)

two men reflected on their record in Latin America, lingering over events in the Dominican Republic. "If we had it to do over," Johnson asked, "would we do it the same way?" "Yes," Mann replied bullishly. "I never had any doubts we were right. . . . [S]ome people don't understand because they don't want to."[14]

Many of those people whom Mann had in mind would have been representatives of the fourth estate, yet his departure went relatively unnoticed by a press more concerned with events in Southeast Asia. In a piece of, presumably, accidental symbolism, the most in-depth consideration of his retirement in the *New York Times,* so long his bête noire, was buried within a longer piece on the growing US commitment in Vietnam. Mann's exit, it was noted, occurred almost simultaneously with the resignation of one of the Alliance for Progress's advisory bodies, the Council of Nine, formed during the "euphoria" of the early days of Kennedy's presidency. For the *Times,* Mann was "the man who instinctively deplored that euphoria, and did a great deal to dispel it," although it was acknowledged that he was "a complicated man of private charm and public abrasiveness." Another brief *Times* article simply

Thomas and Nancy Mann and Lady Bird and Lyndon Johnson at Thomas Mann's leaving party, 25 May 1966. Congressman Henry B. Gonzalez stands to the right. (Lyndon Baines Johnson Library photo by Yoichi Okamoto.)

noted that Mann had been a controversial and divisive appointment but "withdrew perceptibly from hemispheric matters" in recent months.[15]

A contrasting view was provided by William S. White, a Texan and long-time associate of Lyndon Johnson's, in his *Washington Post* column. "No official has more ably served the legitimate hemisphere interests and needs of this nation," White enthused, before turning on the critics who had reduced Mann to a "cardboard caricature of the bad old Yankee type, forever hostile to democratic reforms, . . . a grossly erroneous picture." There were of course elements of truth to both perspectives, but confirmation of the esteem in which Mann was still held within government was demonstrated at his leaving party on 25 May, attended by the president and the first lady as well as the vice president and the majority of Johnson's senior foreign policy team. His departure from the administration was far less dramatic than his entrance.[16]

The following month, Johnson telephoned Mann to solicit his opinion on the upcoming elections in the Dominican Republic, but they were soon discussing retirement plans. Mann informed the president that he hoped to write two books, one about the Dominican crisis and another on "economic and social development" policy, and planned on traveling to Latin America for research. He was soon ensconced in an office at Johns Hopkins University, but the proposed books would never be published as he soon abandoned the academic life to accept a job, after seeking Johnson's approval, as president of the Automobile Manufacturers Association. The role would not entirely preclude Mann from returning to certain forms of government service, and he remained alternate US governor of both the International Monetary Fund and the International Bank for Reconstruction and Development until 1967 and was a regular witness before congressional committees. In July 1967, for instance, he appeared before the Senate Subcommittee on Foreign Economic Policy to emphasize that, while primary responsibility for development lay with the Latin American nations themselves, the United States could not abandon the Alliance, an aid program that was needed to lay the foundations for sustained progress. Speaking to the House Foreign Affairs Committee a week later, he also made the case for approving a new Panama Canal treaty. "I see . . . no reason for maintaining exclusive unilateral United States control over affairs within the Zone just for the sake of maintaining the status quo," he noted, before explaining that the United States never exercised true sovereignty in the zone and that therefore "we cannot relinquish that which we never had." In both cases, he was advocating Johnson's policies and attempting to deflect criticism from congressmen who had grown impatient with seemingly ineffective aid programs and were hostile to any potential concessions made in a new canal treaty. Such difficulties were indicative of the problems that post-Mann inter-American affairs would continue to face.[17]

The "Johnsonian Dimension"

The first major challenge the administration faced in Latin America following Thomas Mann and McGeorge Bundy's departures took a familiar form when the government of Arturo Illia in Argentina was overthrown in June. In responding to yet another military takeover, the administration would maintain its case-by-case recognition policy while also demonstrating the new Rostow-dominated structure of decision making that would characterize US foreign policy, with its continuing challenges and contradictions, for the remainder of Johnson's presidency.

The relationship between the United States and Argentina had often proved a difficult one, most notably during the height of Juan Perón's anti-Americantinged populism in the 1940s, and it remained so in the 1960s. Tensions between the supporters of the now-exiled Perón and the military had already resulted in one coup during the Alliance era when Arturo Frondizi was ousted in 1962, and similar problems had threatened to undermine the government of Arturo Illia ever since his election the following year. Illia's decision to declare all oil contracts with foreign corporations void and negotiate new ones had challenged Washington's regional economic policy but also prompted worries that the resulting instability could lead to political turmoil, with Mann commenting as early as mid-1964: "The oil controversy may be the straw that brings on a coup." The basic stance of Johnson's administration had therefore been to pressure Illia toward resolving the contract dispute through the slowdown of aid disbursements but without undermining his government to the extent that it prompted a military coup d'état. The problem with attempting such a middle-ground approach was that it provoked the ire of those on both sides of the equation, with many in Argentina resenting American interference and conservatives in the United States critical of the perceived softness of Johnson's response. For instance, a February 1965 speech by Rostow at a Buenos Aires university was disrupted by "Yankee go home type shouts and chants together with coin throwing" from a large group of students, yet the following month Senator Bourke Hickenlooper was badgering the State Department demanding to know why his amendment requiring the suspension of all direct aid in response to seizures of private property had not been enforced in the case of Argentina.[18]

While the oil dispute dragged on, senior members of the Argentine military became increasingly frustrated with Illia's economic policies and concerned about the growing influence and electoral prospects of the Peronistas. As early as May 1965, the CIA was reporting that a group of both active and retired military officers considering action "along the lines of the Brazilian coup which unseated the Goulart regime," was being restrained only by the powerful figure of General Juan Carlos Onganía, whose patience was "wearing thin." The US intelligence services were kept well informed by the plotters throughout the following year until early June 1966, when General Julio Alsogaray, a key figure among the disgruntled officers, provided a detailed outline of the proposed action, stated that Illia would be gone by the end of July, and justified the proposed coup on the grounds of "the government's complete failure to solve the economic problems facing the country, its failure to combat increased Communist subversion and infiltration," and the likelihood of a Peronist victory in the 1967 elections.[19]

Despite claims by the Argentine military that, like its Brazilian counterpart in 1964, it was acting in the best interests of the people, the response from Washington was not supportive. In the Brazilian case, Ambassador Lincoln Gordon had been convinced that President João Goulart was plotting to install himself in a dictatorship and viewed the military, however mistakenly, as the best option for preserving some form of democracy. Now assistant secretary of state for inter-American affairs and under orders from his president to try and "keep the Argentine military in line," Gordon now explicitly opposed any attempt to remove Illia, making this clear in his communications with Ambassador to Argentina Edwin Martin. Following the CIA's June report, he informed Martin that, while he appreciated the "strenuous efforts to make known both generally and to key Argentine figures our position of strong opposition to [a] coup against [the] Illia government," he worried that leading figures like Onganía thought that the United States was "making QUOTE the expected noises UNQUOTE and that, after a brief hiatus we would continue business as usual." Pressing the ambassador to make clear that "our opposition to a coup is not merely philosophical . . . but also strongly based on [the] belief that [a] military coup would be [a] serious setback to Argentina's economic and political development," he authorized Martin to threaten the withdrawal of military-assistance programs. While the armed forces might actually offer an effective alternative to Illia, he concluded, "stability is perhaps more important in this regard than efficiency."[20]

Such efforts ultimately proved ineffectual, and, on 28 June, the commanders in chief of the army, navy, and air force removed Illia from power, soon installing Onganía as the new president of Argentina. Unlike the Brazilian coup, the Argentine coup met barely any opposition or protest from either military or civilian sources, and very little violence ensued in establishing Onganía and his hastily appointed cabinet in power while dismantling the majority of democratic institutions.[21] The takeover was nonetheless widely condemned throughout the Americas, and, despite accusations from Cuba that the new regime was "a creature of the Pentagon," it was not welcomed in Washington either. Shortly after Onganía installed himself in power, Walt Rostow informed Johnson that the "unjustified military coup is a serious setback to our efforts to promote constitutional government and representative democracy in the hemisphere" and suggested that it would be "necessary to re-examine our whole policy towards Argentina."[22]

Despite such concerns, recognition was extended to Onganía's regime on 15 July, although by that stage all the NATO countries, eight OAS members, and the Soviet Union had already done likewise. In part, this was because, aside from the notable exception of violent crackdowns on universities, christened "the night of the long batons," the removal of a president lacking in popular support was efficient and relatively bloodless. Onganía's swift establishment of a "bureaucratic-authoritarian state" in Argentina would have damaging longer-term consequences, however, furthering a cycle of coups and military juntas that would become increasingly brutal and repressive in subsequent years.[23]

Unlike in Guatemala in 1954, the US government had not been actively plotting the removal of an elected leader in Argentina or even, as the case had been in Brazil, offering tacit approval to the forces coalescing in opposition. US policy nonetheless affected and was in turn affected by the Argentine coup of 1966. First, it was clear that the ongoing oil dispute played a role in the military's opposition to Illia, with one general informing the American embassy that the president had caused his own downfall through a series of mistakes and that "the first was the cancellation of the oil contracts." Despite efforts by the Johnson administration to moderate its impact, the oil dispute had angered various factions in both countries, ultimately contributing to the Argentine military's frustration with Illia's economic policies.[24]

The regular and accurate information that State Department and CIA officials were being provided by the Argentine military also reflects a second strand by which US policy was entwined in the coup. A crucial element of the Alliance for Progress had been to reorient Latin American militaries to be less concerned with external defense and more focused on both internal subversion and their own role in helping modernize their nations. In some cases, such as in Bolivia in 1964, this had resulted in a more efficiently trained and equipped military deciding that it was in fact the best-placed force to implement the modernization ideals that the Alliance for Progress called for.[25] One embassy assessment of the Argentine military from April 1966 told a similar story, noting that, while the armed forces had focused on "modernization and professionalization under U.S. guidance," this did not rule out the chance that they "might seek to usurp civilian powers under a given set of circumstances." Indeed, as the historian William Michael Schmidli has observed, in "redefining the military's mission to encompass virtually all aspects of Argentine life, and elevating anticommunism to the center of his administration's agenda," Onganía was effectively putting into practice the lessons learned via inter-American military cooperation as part of the Alliance.[26]

The administration's swift recognition of the Brazilian military government in 1964 may also have served to encourage the plotters, with one aide to Onganía expressing confusion at the lack of a warm reception from Johnson as it was "thought the Pentagon favored a grand anti-Communist alliance between the military governments of Brazil and Argentina." Still, there had been military coups in Argentina before 1964 that had received recognition from Washington, and it is unlikely that administration policy in Brazil played a decisive role. Ultimately, events in 1966 reflected the lack of US influence on Argentine internal politics as pleas to the military to abandon its plans fell on deaf ears. As one embassy report observed, US influence was minimal, and it was "Argentine political forces, Argentine economic pressures, and local attitudes which determine Argentine policies." In delaying recognition of the Onganía regime, the administration demonstrated that some lessons had been learned from Brazil but also that it felt that its only real option was eventually to reestablish relations once a coup had taken place. Onganía's seizure of power demonstrated the limited nature of US influence in the Americas while further undermining any sense of progress in establishing a more democratic hemisphere.[27]

The Argentine coup was also the first major hemispheric event requiring high-level attention following Mann and Bundy's departures, and a clear pattern of internal communication was established during the administration response. In previous years, Bundy had been highly influential in controlling what information crossed the president's desk, but regarding Latin American issues Johnson would speak directly with Mann. During the Argentine coup, however, Gordon tended to report to Rostow, who would then keep the president updated, with instructions also often flowing along the same route in reverse. Gordon and his eventual successor, Covey Oliver, would continue to operate on a similar basis for the remainder of Johnson's presidency, with Rostow firmly in charge of the information that reached the president. Ultimately able to exercise little influence over events in Argentina, this new organizational hierarchy would enjoy greater success with an aspect of inter-American policy over which more direct control was possessed—the Alliance for Progress.

The first years of the Alliance under Johnson and Mann had been turbulent and not without controversy, but there had also been positive indications that the program was becoming more effective. The annual per capita GDP growth rate for Latin America, widely acknowledged as the barometer of the Alliance's economic success, had averaged less than 1 percent under Kennedy, but the figure was 2.2 percent between 1964 and 1967. State Department figures for the same period also suggested that tax collections in the region increased by nearly $3 billion, and total exports rose by almost $2 billion. US private investment—admittedly a double-edged sword—rose from $242 million to $457 million, while levels of private charitable aid, mostly from the Rockefeller, Ford, and Kellogg Foundations, rose from a total of $81.1 million between 1961 and 1963 to $125.3 million in the subsequent three years. More tangible accomplishments—notably the construction of houses, schools, hospitals, and roads—also significantly increased during the same period. Finally, although aid in the form of soft loans had begun to replace grants, more Alliance money was disbursed at a faster rate than it had been before, with an increase in overall aid of around 30 percent on the Kennedy years. Although still a long way from reaching most Alliance targets, the program was showing some encouraging signs of improvement.[28]

Walt Rostow was consistently upbeat regarding the performance of the Alliance, informing Johnson in November that, "except for the Argentine setback, representative democracy has been considerably strengthened" and that "the hemisphere is moving out of the economic crisis stage and can now increasingly devote its attention to and energies to development." Nonetheless, he argued, the Alliance was at a "crossroads": "Economic and social progress must be accelerated if the present gains are to be consolidated." However, in the aftermath of the Dominican intervention, and with commitments in Vietnam growing, the administration—particularly the new coordinator of the Alliance, Lincoln Gordon—would face a challenge in building on the modest gains of recent years. By October 1966, Gordon would be complaining to the president that Bureau of the Budget proposals would result in US aid contributions the following year falling short of the commitments made at the Alliance's founding, and subsequent years would see even greater cuts imposed by Congress.[29]

Without the continued availability of loans and grants on a large scale, the model established during the first few years of the Alliance would no longer be viable. In part driven by these budgetary concerns, the administration would progress farther down a path set by Mann and Johnson the previous year to reorient the focus of the Alliance by concentrating on inter-American physical and economic integration. The shift would, for some observers, be further evidence of failure to promote the political and social elements of the program, with Johnson's talk of integration dismissed as a cheap alternative to direct aid, a means of furthering the interests of US investors, or simply lacking in genuine commitment.[30] While such criticisms are not entirely without foundation, the 1967 Summit of the Presidents of the Americas at Punta del Este—the same Uruguayan coastal resort where the Alliance was first agreed on—would see the administration submit a set of proposals that indicated a readjusted approach to hemispheric development. At the very least, Johnson's emphasis on integration would demonstrate a relatively coherent vision, a potentially more sustainable framework for economic growth than the initial direct-aid-centered efforts of Kennedy's early Alliance, and a president who retained a genuine interest in the program's success.

In an August 1966 speech to mark the five-year anniversary of the Alliance for Progress, President Johnson announced that hemispheric development required a new approach that placed advances in economic integration at the very top of the political agenda, promising his fellow American presidents that, if they chose to "move boldly along this path," then "the United States will be by [their] side." While Johnson's speech reflected his continuing campaign to repair his critically damaged reputation with neighbors to the south, it also demonstrated the ongoing development of the administration's approach to the Alliance that incorporated a greater focus on economic and physical integration as well as agricultural and educational programs. The administration's initial interest in increased hemispheric integration owed much to Thomas Mann. Throughout 1964 and 1965, Mann had been impressed by the achievements of the fledgling CACM and, while unconvinced that a hemisphere-wide equivalent could be achieved, envisaged the development of a broad network of trade agreements and multinational endeavors supported by funds provided through Alliance machinery.[31]

There was growing statistical evidence to support Mann's views, with annual trade among the Central American nations steadily rising from $32 million in 1960 to $260 million in 1969. The CACM reflected widespread interest in economic integration among technical planners in several nations of the hemisphere who sought to revive earlier examples of inter-American cooperation and was soon followed by the Latin American Free Trade Association (LAFTA), which incorporated Argentina, Chile, Mexico, Paraguay,

Peru, and Uruguay. Launched in January 1962, LAFTA also enjoyed early success, with trade among its member nations rising by around 40 percent between 1961 and 1963. Hence, Mann's interest was largely a pragmatic acknowledgment that initiatives driven by other nations of the hemisphere were achieving results and that traditional US opposition to regional trading agreements was counterproductive. Increased integration, Mann believed, could potentially provide a sustainable engine for economic growth that was not reliant on the mood of the US Congress, as aid appropriations were.[32]

Once Mann had departed Washington, both Gordon and Rostow would continue to support the focus on integration and trade agreements despite their association, as part of Kennedy's Alliance task force, with the more idealistic rhetoric and emphasis on economic, social, and political change in the growing urban areas of the hemisphere that had been envisaged during the Alliance's conception. By the mid-1960s, Rostow in particular—a prominent modernization theorist in his own right—had begun to embrace "the national market concept" that considered it just as important to harness agricultural and rural resources as urban and industrial. Similarly, he was fully in agreement that public funds and technical assistance alone could not provide the impetus much of the hemisphere needed for sustained growth and was increasingly in favor of expanded private investment and self-help initiatives. Hence, the positions that Mann had been advocating, along with a greater emphasis on agriculture and taking advantage of the "internal frontiers" of Latin America, were fully in line with Rostow's modified vision for the Alliance for Progress, and support for integration soon rose to the top of Washington's development agenda for the hemisphere.[33]

The mixing of New Dealers and New Frontiersmen that had been so problematic in the early months of Johnson's administration would now result in a new approach to the Alliance that had initially been suggested by Mann before being embraced and furthered by Rostow. The focus on cooperation and integration seemed a neat fit with the Alliance's ethos, yet it emphasized economic improvements while remaining vague on social and political change, which had proved much more problematic to instigate and support. In theory, the approach promised economic improvements that, while requiring substantial investment from the United States in the short term, suggested independent sustainability in the long run. The emphasis on internal frontiers also appealed to the New Dealer in Johnson, given its promise of improving the lot of some of the hemisphere's most impoverished rural populations through programs of electrification, road building, and agricultural improvements, and, as part of a wider review of foreign aid programs in January 1966, the president tasked Rostow with producing a "preliminary assessment of the potentialities of developing the frontiers of South America." The following May, Rostow could report: "South America is at a stage of historical evolution where the further development of its frontiers can contribute to food production, a widening of markets, regional integration, and the settlement of various bilateral disputes." He enthusiastically advised that, after further investigation, it would be wise to "establish Alliance for Progress policies based on this review." In response, Johnson issued National Security Action Memorandum no. 349, which authorized Gordon and the inter-American desk of the State Department to develop the report into concrete proposals to form part of the "overall program of assistance" for Latin America.[34]

These changes did not, however, represent a dramatic or sudden shift in aid policy or conceptions of the envisaged path to modernization. Indeed, they reflected the fact that the approach to development in the Kennedy-Johnson era was rarely fixed or carefully defined but was instead being continually refined and adjusted, subject to changes in personnel, global priorities, and theoretical reconfigurations. This is a process that had occurred during Kennedy's administration and would continue under Johnson. The basic idea that had driven the launch of the Alliance—that trying to modernize the economies and societies of the hemisphere would ultimately be of benefit to the United States as well as to the recipients of its aid and expertise—remained intact. Thus, it is possible to identify an approach emerging in this period that, while bearing the marks of Mann's and Johnson's influence, was still largely in line with recent policy. This moderately reconfigured view of international development would be encapsulated in the program drafted for the 1967 Summit of the Presidents of the Americas.

The 1967 presidential summit has received little sustained scrutiny from historians, often being dismissed as simply an attempt on Johnson's part to generate positive publicity that produced few tangible results.[35] Initially proposed by Argentine President Arturo Illia, it was not welcomed at first by Gordon, who observed scathingly: "This strange and totally unwarranted initiative stems from Argentine domestic politics." Despite Gordon's reticence and Illia's precarious position, which would soon see him deposed, a hemisphere-wide summit appealed to Johnson, who publicly endorsed the idea during a visit to Mexico in April 1966 and instructed his staff and a panel of experts that included Mann and Milton Eisenhower to begin drafting a program. Part of the appeal certainly lay in the potential boost to Johnson's image, with internal communications often reflecting frustration at the president's lack of popularity in the hemisphere, mostly blamed on his failure to "project the sparkling intellectual image of Kennedy" and "the distasteful—but necessary—job of sending troops into the DR." Along with a goodwill tour by one of his daughters, the summit meeting was viewed as the best possible counter to this. It was also hoped that such an event could garner positive domestic coverage and spark renewed enthusiasm for the Alliance. As Dean Rusk put it to the president: "Our own people have been hearing almost nothing else but Viet-Nam, President de Gaulle and China, and hemispheric affairs have dropped somewhat into the background."[36]

Even if image-related concerns were paramount, substantial effort also went into drafting a relatively coherent set of proposals intended to revitalize a flagging Alliance and reflect recent administration thinking regarding development. Rostow made this point clear to Johnson during the planning stage, arguing; "[The] summit theme should be built around this concept: charting the historic transition of Latin America from a decade of national planning and development (the 1960s) to a decade of regional integration and accelerated progress." Similarly, Milton Eisenhower, as familiar with the recent history of inter-American relations as anyone, suggested that Johnson make clear his enthusiasm for integration and the "dramatic shift in policy which this represents for us." "Historically, we have discouraged it," he observed. "You would be the first President to give it a major thrust forward." Unsurprisingly, then, the central plank of the program was to secure a commitment to increased Latin American integration through a variety of channels, including reductions in tariffs, an increase in multinational development projects, and, ultimately, a regional common market formed through a merger of the CACM and the LAFTA. In addition, the proposals included higher Alliance targets and increased funding for agriculture and education, a reduction in military spending, and a continued commitment to private investment. In order to help finance this rejuvenated Alliance and support physical integration projects, Johnson optimistically envisaged that additional funding totaling $1.5 billion could be procured from Congress.[37]

While Rostow remained the dominant voice in the planning for the summit, Johnson also sought the views of an old friend. Thomas Mann's input would be less exuberant and more cautious than Rostow's, neatly encapsulating the contrast in style and temperament between the two advisers. Mann worried that little of substance would be agreed on at the conference, an outcome that would be embarrassing for the president given his efforts in bringing it about, and advised Johnson to be wary of other leaders "ganging up" to press for maximum economic concessions from the United States. He was more positive regarding a potential commitment to regional integration, "probably the most significant thing that could come out of this meeting," and believed that, in terms of increases in aid levels, "we certainly ought to do what we can." The greatest challenge he envisaged, however, was the "growing reluctance on the part of Congress to appropriate large additional sums in view of the other demands on our resources," particularly the "military burden" of Vietnam.[38]

Heeding Mann's warning, Johnson drew on his experience as Senate majority leader steering through the Senate Eisenhower's request for Congress to approve $500 million for the Social Progress Trust Fund in advance of the Bogota Conference. Aware that any promises of increased funds he made at Punta del Este would be reliant on his securing appropriations on his return and thus potentially viewed as meaningless by other leaders, Johnson sought to secure a similar preemptive financial commitment from the legislature. In a special message to Congress delivered on 13 March 1967, he eloquently outlined the great achievements of the Alliance, the challenges that still remained, and his vision of a cooperative, integrated hemisphere that was "within reach" with just a little more financial assistance. Noting that he was "going to you in the Congress not after a commitment has been made, but before making any commitment," he called on the legislature to endorse not only his vision but his request for $1.5 billion.[39]

The response in the House was swift and positive—the proposal was approved 210–147—but progress was not so smooth in the Senate. Condemning the request as another Gulf of Tonkin–style "blank check," the chair of the Senate Foreign Relations Committee, J. William Fulbright, led the opposition, redrafting the resolution to remove references to the common market, stress congressional control of foreign aid appropriations, and promise only to "consider" increases in funds. "Worse than useless" was the administration's public judgment of the revised resolution, and the president would head to the summit lacking the financial backing of the legislative branch.[40]

Johnson's struggles with the Foreign Relations Committee reveal less about the wisdom of his proposals than they do about the fractious nature of his congressional relations by early 1967. The administration had already clashed with Fulbright over Vietnam policy and the Dominican intervention, and the latest request, viewed by some as encroaching on congressional prerogatives, prompted other senators to exercise long-held grudges. The *New York Times* observed that, in many cases, Republican senators appeared the most supportive of the resolution, quoting one senior Democrat as complaining about the president's "bullying" tactics, which may have worked when Johnson was majority leader but would no longer be tolerated. While Johnson may have misjudged the degree of antipathy in the Senate, his very public efforts to secure the necessary increases in funding nonetheless suggest an administration committed to making the summit a success. The combination of these factors made for mixed press coverage in the days preceding Johnson's departure. Criticism of the administration's handling of Congress and the lack of a prominent social plank in the conference program was counterbalanced by occasional votes of confidence, such as Walter Lippmann's belief that the president's commitment to economic and physical integration provided "the true alternative, probably the only alternative, to stagnation and revolution."[41]

Despite Johnson's inability to commit to specific financial contributions, the summit, held in Punta del Este between 11 and 14 April, was as successful as the administration had dared hope. Before departing for Uruguay, Johnson hosted a large group of Latin American ambassadors at his ranch to discuss the conference program, an event that Rostow assured him would be given "maximum play" in the media through the production of "special TV clips and a color film." On his arrival in Punta del Este, a series of bilateral meetings were followed by larger-scale consultations and a round of rousing public addresses. The bilateral meetings addressed specific national problems, and the private group consultations allowed Johnson to raise the increasingly thorny issue of balance-of-payments problems before a major public address that sought to generate widespread enthusiasm for a readjusted Alliance. In a speech sprinkled with references to Simón Bolívar and Franklin Roosevelt, the president highlighted Alliance achievements and pointed out that he had consistently increased the program's funding, before going on to outline his vision for the future and urging the nations present to "join your energies, your skills and commitments in a mighty effort that extends into the farthest reaches of this hemisphere."[42]

Most importantly, the final day of the conference saw all but one of the leaders present sign the Declaration of the Presidents of America, which

The conference in session during the Meeting of American Chiefs of State, Punta del Este, Uruguay, 13 April 1967. (Lyndon Baines Johnson Library photo by Frank Wolfe.)

President Johnson and Secretary of State Dean Rusk at the Meeting of American Chiefs of State, Punta del Este, Uruguay, 13 April 1967. (Lyndon Baines Johnson Library photo by Frank Wolfe.)

endorsed a common market, multinational projects to facilitate integration, increased emphasis on agriculture and education, a promise to limit military expenditures, and a commitment from the United States to increase assistance and explore the establishment of generalized trade preferences. In short, the declaration included all the Johnson administration's proposals, along with additional initiatives such as an inter-American science program. Although a number of the other participants departed somewhat disappointed at the lack of progress made toward securing preferential access to North American markets, most assessments of the summit fell somewhere between the El Salvador delegation's measured view of it as "sound and productive rather than spectacular" and President Frei of Chile's belief that it was an "unqualified success."[43]

While Johnson's public addresses at the summit were moderately well received, it was his quieter diplomacy that was the most effective. Even before the summit began, for example, he had secured the attendance of Peruvian president Belaúnde Terry, who was concerned at proposed reductions in military expenditure, by arranging to fly his recently deceased uncle's body from

New York City to Lima on Air Force One. Both Rostow and Mann had emphasized the potential impact of Johnson's personal diplomacy at the summit, with Mann recommending the president "set aside a day or two . . . for you and the other presidents to visit informally." Keen to dispel his image as the trigger-happy bully who had crushed a popular uprising in the Dominican Republic, Johnson was more than happy to follow this advice, and, once in Punta del Este, he welcomed other presidents for lengthy and informal chats by the pool of his rented villa. Listening more than he spoke, and responding to complaints with promises to seek constructive solutions, he made, according to James Reston in the *New York Times*, "an impression on the other presidents with his patience and sympathetic understanding."[44]

When his formidable political attributes were utilized in the manner that suited him best—in small and informal meetings—Johnson could be a skilled and subtle statesman, and this was clearly in evidence at Punta del Este. Even the President of Ecuador, Otto Arosemena, who refused to sign the declaration, returned home claiming that the two had established a warm personal rapport. Ralph Dungan, the US ambassador to Chile and later a regular critic of Johnson's, observed: "I thought the President was masterful [at Punta del Este], myself, I really thought he did a hell of a job, considering the lost ground that he had as [a] result of the Dominican Republic and so forth."[45]

Desperate to exploit the increasingly rare commodity of positive press coverage, Johnson made sure to maximize the good publicity that accompanied his performance at Punta del Este. Within days of his return to Washington, members of the administration appeared on *Meet the Press* and the *Today Show* to talk up the achievements of the summit, while USIA began producing pamphlets and a television documentary to do the same. In his own public pronouncements, Johnson emphasized the transformative nature of the conference, announcing that the "first phase of the Alliance" was over and "the second phase is now underway." He also could not resist a jab at his critics, commenting that "we have long since abandoned the view that rhetoric could alter a social system" and that "we know now that transforming the lives of over two hundred and fifty million people requires a commitment to specifics." Seeking to strike while the iron was hot, he also turned his attention back to Congress, with Rostow preparing a detailed list of factors that might convince legislators to approve the increases in funding. Having previously failed to obtain the money with inspirational rhetoric, Rostow now recommended a more pragmatic approach, one emphasizing that a relatively

President Johnson meets with President Gustavo Díaz Ordaz of Mexico and an interpreter during the Punta del Este conference, 11 April 1967. This was one of many informal meetings that Johnson arranged while in Uruguay. (Lyndon Baines Johnson Library photo by Yoichi Okamoto.)

small amount—in this case increasing IADB funding by $900 million over three years—would serve as "cheap insurance" against the political, economic, and military disaster of another Cuban-style revolution. Given the unwillingness of the Senate to endorse such increases before the summit, a great deal of effort was put into lobbying, with support sought from a variety of businessmen, academics, union leaders, and prominent Republicans. The outlook was not promising, however, with one aide's report noting that, in addition to those Democratic senators who were becoming increasingly antagonistic to the administration, others worried about "the looming deficit and the cutback in domestic social programs." A difficult and potentially unsuccessful floor fight was predicted. Unfortunately for the president, the warnings proved accurate, and, in a clear indication of the struggles the Alliance would continue to face, the legislature slashed his requests in half.[46]

Despite the struggle for funding, there were signs in the months following the summit that pledges made there were being fulfilled and that the readjusted vision of development assistance was being implemented. In June, the United States lent the Central American Bank for Economic Integration $20 million, and, in October, Johnson approved the offer of another loan to assist with the establishment of the Caribbean Development Bank, which would fund regional programs. The following month, the head of the IADB was announcing that he had overseen $174 million in loans and technical assistance toward the integration process, including road building, hydroelectric projects, and funding for feasibility studies of several multinational ventures. Further signs of cooperation included the creation of an inter-American panel on scientific development, a regional energy plan devised by the Atomic Energy Commission, new task forces within the administration charged with developing physical integration plans, and the Inter-American Cultural Conference, which was to approve programs to carry out summit directives on education, science, and technology, all with funds eventually totaling $25 million pledged for the first year.[47]

Reflecting the renewed dedication to education and agriculture promised by the declaration as well as his hope that the summit could spark fresh optimism about the Alliance, Johnson appointed Covey Oliver to succeed Lincoln Gordon, who took up a position at Johns Hopkins University in June 1967, as his chief Latin American adviser. A legal scholar and former ambassador to Colombia, Oliver was a Texan who had known the president since the days of FDR, had lived in Brazil as a Fulbright-Hayes professor, and was known to favor the social as much as the economic facets of the Alliance. While Johnson remained keen to emphasize "the soundness of the policy-making and administrative arrangements worked out in 1964" by Mann, his instructions to the new assistant secretary were to "broaden and deepen the scope of the Alliance" using the integration blueprint established at Punta del Este and to "maintain a stance of idealism; stay out in front on social as well as economic development; and [not] be outflanked from the left rhetorically." Hence, Oliver would make a series of well-publicized speeches that echoed his president's positioning of the summit as a crucial turning point that signified a new era of the Alliance, a "second phase" wherein "the emphasis will be on human needs and hopes, on institution building and modernization."[48]

In January 1968 Johnson entered the final year of his current term of office, and hemispheric affairs were considered an area in which a positive narrative could be stressed ahead of the November election, providing a contrast to the increasingly dire situation in Vietnam. Keen to maintain the momentum of Punta del Este, the president regularly pressed Rostow for ways to "dramatize" US efforts and approved suggestions for regular tours of the hemisphere by senior administration officials, an increase in visits to the White House by Latin American politicians and journalists, and a reorganization of both CIAP and the IADB to increase their prominence. As part of these efforts, Covey Oliver would tour Latin America with Milton Eisenhower in February 1968, attending the Inter-American Cultural Conference, and emphasizing the administration's continued interest in the region. The president too made efforts to highlight Alliance developments, agreeing with Rostow that a meeting with several hemispheric dignitaries would be an ideal opportunity to celebrate the new Inter-American Task Force on Physical Integration. The task force would emphasize Johnson's contributions to Latin American relations. Rostow enthused: "The Johnsonian dimension to the Alliance for Progress is integration."[49]

As promising as such developments were, the progress report Johnson received in April 1968, the first anniversary of the Punta del Este summit, painted an ambiguous picture. While temporary "sub-regional" groups were implementing trade agreements and a plan was slowly coalescing for a merger of LAFTA and the CACM, progress toward a common market remained slower than anticipated. In terms of funding, while Congress had not provided the full amount requested, US contributions to the IADB special operations fund had still increased by $50 million a year. The report noted that even this limited increase meant that $70 million had been assigned to programs like highway building and electrical systems, with a further $2 million in loans and grants for feasibility studies that included telecommunications networks, air cargo links, River Plate basin development, and various transport projects. Positive signs could also be found in a new coffee-price-stabilization agreement and the fact that technical assistance and loans focused on agriculture, health, and education now made up 62 percent of total US assistance, up from 42 percent in 1967. The key to greater achievement, the report concluded, was to "dispel growing Latin doubts about the firmness of the U.S. commitment to the Alliance, and galvanize the Latin American governments to move forward more rapidly on bold economic and social reforms and on integration."[50]

A major effort on the president's part to dispel those doubts was soon to follow in the form of a visit to El Salvador to meet with the presidents of Central America at the headquarters of the Organization of Central American States (ODECA). The small summit reflected a combination of Johnson's desire for some form of Latin American tour, possibly including Brazil and Colombia, and several invitations from Central American nations to attend events in the region. As the president's domestic situation grew increasingly fraught throughout 1968 with widespread protests and riots and the tragic assassinations of both Martin Luther King Jr. and Robert Kennedy, a lengthy absence from Washington appeared unwise, but a brief escape looked ever more appealing. Consulted once again in an unofficial capacity, Thomas Mann encouraged Johnson to visit Central America, arguing that it was the region of the hemisphere "traditionally . . . most sympathetic to us," and suggesting that Mexican president Gustavo Díaz Ordaz be invited as well. In this, he was overruled by Rostow, who dismissed the retired undersecretary "as out of touch with public reactions in Latin America to recent events in the United States." Rostow argued that Mexico's presence would overshadow the discussions with other countries and also advocated holding a mass at San Salvador's cathedral in memory of the recently assassinated Robert Kennedy to set the tone for the visit. Johnson agreed, telling Rostow to "get this thing rolling," and the summit would be limited to just the ODECA members, El Salvador, Honduras, Guatemala, Costa Rica, and Nicaragua.[51]

Despite the restricted guest list, the messages delivered at the event were intended to reach a much wider audience. Johnson would use the opportunity to articulate his vision of how his integrationist agenda could help not only the nations of the Western Hemisphere but also developing countries around the globe. During the planning process, the State Department also reported to the president that his trip could not come at a better time as "collectively and individually" the nations of Central America were "at somewhat of a crossroads." While the initial benefits of the CACM had resulted in widespread economic growth, this had recently begun to slow, undermined by falling prices of export commodities, and it was hoped that Johnson could renew enthusiasm for the integrationist agenda. The twin purposes of the trip—scheduled for the weekend of 6–7 July—were outlined as "dramatize the success of the Central American Common Market as an example . . . of what can be accomplished through regional cooperation" and "rally increased effort to expand the quantity and quality of education." El Salvador was identified as a nation pursuing both goals enthusiastically during what the CIA identified as a period of "relative political stability, both by general Latin American standards, and by the standards of its own previous history." In short, this would be an ideal setting for the president to reaffirm his commitment to regional development through integration.[52]

Johnson delivered several brief addresses during his stay, but the lengthiest and most significant followed the main presidential discussions at ODECA headquarters on 6 July. He began by praising the achievements of the Central American nations, including the creation of a common market, a regional bank, and a cooperative political body, and made sure to downplay the importance of the United States in the process, reminding the gathered politicians and journalists of the region: "This was—and this is—your vision." More than in previous speeches, however, Johnson also elaborated on the wider applicability of the integrationist model, declaring: "The world can find here a testament to regionalism . . . an abstract word—but its power is not abstract, nor its promise, nor its achievement." Similar projects around the world were then highlighted, including the recent creation of the East African Economic Community and the African Development Bank as well as the Asian Bank operating in "Free Asia." The model could even be of use in the Middle East, Johnson argued, where he hoped people could "find dignity and hope in working together on a regional basis." Finally, he highlighted the ongoing contributions the United States could make to supporting the process, noting that he had come bearing a $30 million loan to the Central American Fund for Economic Integration as well as having approved a range of smaller loans "totaling $35 million more to help you carry forward programs of social justice and economic progress." Nonetheless, he concluded, progress was now "built on a common understanding among the developing nations" that wealthier countries, "however enlightened or benevolent or rich, cannot solve their problems for them."[53]

Although the presidential discussions lasted little more than two hours, a joint declaration signed by all those present also provided a little more substance to the proceedings. The declaration celebrated recent achievements in regional integration, supported by US funds and technical assistance but driven by the determined efforts of those nations directly involved, and also made a series of pledges, including "the expansion and diversification of agricultural production," improvements in telecommunications and education in rural areas, and "staunch support of the formation of the Latin American Common Market." The declaration also celebrated recent Alliance for Progress initiatives related to health care and education, and Mann would have been gratified to see particular praise reserved for "efforts to give continuity to the International Coffee Agreement and to establish the Coffee Diversification Fund" as well as for Johnson's position "in favor of the establishment, by the industrialized nations, of a general system of unilateral and nondiscriminatory tariff preferences for the developing countries."[54]

A strong statement in support of recent economic policy secured, the remainder of Johnson's visit was spent demonstrating his long-held interest in education. The day after the ODECA discussions, Johnson—accompanied by his wife, Lady Bird, and daughter Luci—joined the other presidents for a picnic in a Salvadoran national park followed by the opening of a school named in his honor. Reminiscing about his own background—educated at a teacher-training college in Texas and briefly employed at an elementary school in Cotulla—the president informed his small audience during a brief address: "The Latin names . . . ring of those days in my own native south Texas when I was a schoolteacher in a Mexican school." He concluded that the reason he was committed to improving the educational resources of the region in order to address wider problems was that "most of the answers are here in these classrooms." As a final flourish, Air Force One dropped each president in turn back in their capital city, providing Johnson the opportunity for a brief address and photo opportunity at each stop.[55]

Temporarily buoyed by his experiences, Johnson offered on his return to Washington an assessment of the trip that was overwhelmingly positive. At a meeting with senior members of his foreign policy team, he declared not only that he was "convinced more than ever before that the road to peace and progress lies through regionalism and subregionalism in Central America" but also that the area could prove "a microcosm for this process which will be a challenge and stimulus for other areas to follow." Reports from the US embassy in San Salvador supported his assessment, describing his visit as "probably the greatest event this little country has ever experienced": "The President's demonstrated and expressed personal interest in Central American regionalism and integration cannot help but give a big shot in the arm to this concept." Condescending tone aside, the embassy report shared the president's view not only that the brief summit was a success in demonstrating positive progress in the Americas but that it could be utilized more widely as representative of the positive benefits of regional integration. Even the press was largely supportive, with the *Washington Post* praising Johnson's commitment to regional integration as "a vital way for a region to help itself achieve important self-sustaining growth." Coverage in Central America was also, according to one NSC report, "unstinting in its enthusiastic reaction." The reporting of Costa Rica's *La Prensa Libre* was particularly highlighted owing to its statement that the warm greeting given to Johnson at the airport was "particularly heartening as it did not result from anyone's orders, but was born of democratic sentiment."[56]

Taken in isolation, perhaps the small summit was worthy of such positive assessments. After all, the president had been able to demonstrate both the practical achievements of and widespread support for his reformulated vision of the Alliance for Progress and even had an opportunity to convincingly express his deep and abiding passion for education. Less openly acknowledged was that the other presidents attending the summit may have been less enamored with integration than they were with the opportunity to discuss a range of other issues, such as border disputes and bilateral trade. Nor did the joint presidential declaration acknowledge the deep-seated nature of many of the obstacles to development in the region, including a widespread and severe urban-rural divide and continued lack of diversification in national economic production. Of perhaps even greater relevance was that there was precious little of Johnson's presidency remaining to address these problems, given that he had announced in March that he would not seek reelection in November. Perhaps LBJ's most insightful comment on his return was that, despite his delight at many aspects of the trip, his "most vivid impression is that there is so much to do—and so little time to do it."[57]

The July summit also did less than was hoped to address the "growing Latin doubts" regarding the depth of US dedication to regional development. Although it may have provided a short-term boost in Central America, the more widespread view was that US commitment to the Alliance, in terms of both money and effort, was tenuous, and doubts remained over the feasibility of genuine integration. In part, those doubts were founded on tensions and disputes between Latin American nations. One particularly blunt but not wholly inaccurate CIA report on subregional organizations observed in July 1968 that "even in the embryonic stage" such schemes were undermined by "entrenched nationalist hostilities, jealousies, and fears, as well as practical economic problems that stand as serious obstacles to integration." More prosaic calculations also played a role, with those elites who were economically well-off and politically conservative happy to support the status quo and reject regional programs that might dilute their influence, just as they had other Alliance efforts that had threatened their position. On the other side of the political spectrum, much of the left remained suspicious of another scheme that seemingly sought to impose North American ideas and influence.[58]

Attempts by the Johnson administration to convince allies of their dedication to the Alliance were also continually undermined by funding cuts imposed by Congress and further weakened by the knowledge that 1968 would be the president's last year in office. As Johnson's political capital dwindled, Congress imposed even harsher cuts and abandoned multiyear appropriations, keeping an administration that many legislators viewed as deceitful and irresponsible on a shorter leash. The 1968 foreign aid bill was also attacked even more viciously than usual by Otto Passman's House Subcommittee on Appropriations, with a State Department report noting: "Latin America was singled out for especially insensitive, even hostile, treatment." Alliance loans requested at $515 million were reduced to $200 million, technical assistance funding was cut from $235 million to $150 million, and the Alliance contingency fund requested at $100 million was eliminated entirely. Overall, the subcommittee cut an aid budget request of over $2.5 billion to around $1.2 billion, although it was notable that financing for military assistance was only marginally affected, reduced from $420 million to $375 million.[59]

For many Latin Americans, this only confirmed long-held suspicions. *Expreso* of Lima asserted: "U.S. Congressmen take the easy way out by sacrificing Latin America while continuing to pour great sums into such an unpopular war as the one in Vietnam." Colombia's leading daily, *El Especta-dor*, accused the house of dealing "a coup de grace to the Alliance." *La Nacion* of Santiago simply observed that the cuts cast doubt on the "good faith of the U.S. to fulfill its promises." The Senate would slightly moderate the cuts made in the House, but a powerless and frustrated Johnson was still left publicly lamenting that "the richest nation in history" was "rejecting our part of the self-help bargain," with dangerous consequences for both the developing world and US national security.[60]

Despite these ongoing battles with Congress, the Punta del Este summit and subsequent efforts to implement its program reflect a genuine, if flawed, attempt by a beleaguered administration to breathe some life back into the Alliance for Progress. In recognizing that high levels of direct aid would not be sustainable, the vision of a more integrated and cooperative hemisphere offered a slightly more realistic path than the transformative rhetoric of early Alliance planning while also attempting to incorporate Latin American proposals and leadership into a more genuinely multilateral Alliance. Unfortunately, any progress made in the wake of a successful summit was hampered by the degree of antagonism from Congress, which was severely misjudged by Johnson even after the Senate had denied him any preconference funds. The administration also appeared to once again demonstrate the capacity of policy makers in Washington to underestimate the scale of the challenges that remained in Latin America, including the tensions that existed between many nations that shared long and often antagonistic histories, and the complex internal politics that not only made committing to long-term multilateral programs difficult but in many cases were also well on the way to prompting widespread political violence.[61] Johnson would be given a harsh reminder of this just one month after his successful visit to Central America when US ambassador John Mein was assassinated in the streets of Guatemala City. Indeed, the administration's struggles to convince allies of their commitment to a revitalized Alliance would be intensified by their continued failure to address the long-standing tension between US security and developmental goals that had been so starkly exposed in the Dominican Republic. Several other high-profile reminders of this would occur in the final years of the administration, culminating in an unwelcome but perhaps fitting coda to the Kennedy-Johnson era.

"We Don't Get Anywhere by Not Recognizing Them"

At an October 1967 celebration of the Chamizal border agreement with Mexico, President Johnson took the opportunity to address hemispheric security issues. Praising the principles of peace and cooperation on which the border dispute had been settled, he noted: "A generation ago, fascism threatened that principle. Today it is another doctrine." While the most prominent and immediately destructive combating of that threat would take place in Vietnam, Johnson's comments reflected the fact that the Cold War remained very much alive in Latin America as well. Despite an overall lessening of tensions with Fidel Castro during his presidency, in the post–Dominican intervention period, Cuban-sponsored subversion remained a significant concern. While advocating a reduction in military spending throughout the hemisphere, the administration continued to maintain close links with and provide substantial assistance to the armed forces of many nations in an effort to increase both their counterinsurgency capabilities and their commitment to Alliance-style development. As with the wider goals of the Alliance, the results would be distinctly mixed.[62]

In a June 1967 memo to the president, Walt Rostow provided a list of seven Latin American nations targeted by Cuba as ripe for subversive activities. While the majority of nations on the list could be found in Central America, the country identified as under the greatest threat from a Cuban-sponsored insurgency was Bolivia. Although the most dangerous group of insurgents identified there was relatively small—numbering only between sixty and one hundred—it was made all the more threatening by the fact that the hero of the Cuban Revolution, Ernesto "Che" Guevara, was among the fighters, "personally directing Bolivian guerrilla activities." The 1964 overthrow of Víctor Paz Estensorro had seen General René Barrientos come to power in La Paz, and there were mixed assessments of the menace that Guevara's group posed to his rule. One State Department intelligence report suggested that, while the guerrillas could certainly prove a problem, the relatively small-scale insurgency did not "constitute a serious threat to the government." Rostow and the CIA were less sanguine, worried by the "fragility of the political situation and the weakness of the armed forces," particularly the Barrientos regime's apparent "total inability to cope with the guerrillas." Indeed, the Bolivian military repeatedly came off second best in clashes with the enemy, often being captured and stripped of their weapons and equipment before being released. An unlikely but nevertheless alarming additional concern for the intelligence services was that, following the Six-Day War of June 1967, the Soviet Union would "recognize the possibilities of aggravating the situation in Bolivia as a means of drawing world attention away from [its] humiliating defeat in the Middle East."[63]

The Johnson administration's response to the threat was rapidly to increase the level of military assistance to a regime whose seizure of power it had opposed not even three years previously. The Defense Department dispatched a "17 man mobile training team" along with weapons and equipment to organize a "Ranger-type Battalion" tasked with counterinsurgency actions. Rostow also informed Johnson that the CIA had "increased its operations" and that, in short, the administration was "helping about as fast as the Bolivians are able to absorb our assistance." It was an approach that appeared to have paid dividends when reports emerged from the Bolivian military on 10 October that Guevara had been killed two days earlier in a firefight with the army unit trained, equipped, and guided by American advisers. The CIA reported a slightly different story, however, the new director, Richard Helms, informing Johnson that Che had in fact been captured alive and interrogated for a day before "the Second Ranger Battalion received direct orders from Bolivian Army Headquarters in La Paz to kill [him]." As Helms reported impassively: "[The] orders were carried out at 13.15 hours the same day with a burst of fire from an M-2 automatic rifle."[64]

Although there was some discomfort in Washington at the summary execution of such a prominent figure, assessments of events in Bolivia still bore a triumphalist tone. The CIA reported that Cuban leaders had hoped to "spark a movement of continental magnitude" through the removal of the Barrientos regime and that Guevara had admitted trying to "create a Viet Nam out of South America." His death, therefore, one State Department report opined, was "a crippling—perhaps fatal—blow to the Bolivian guerrilla movement" as well as a "serious setback" to Castro's plans for the hemisphere. After all, what potential rebel could help but be discouraged "by the defeat of the foremost tactician of the Cuban revolutionary strategy at the hands of one of the weakest armies in the hemisphere"? Media coverage in the United States tended to offer limited praise for Che but also to portray his death as symbolic of the decline of revolutionary appeal. Che was a "daring and dedicated yet fallible revolutionary," declared the *New York Times*, yet his death "should shatter the illusions of those who, like Fidel Castro, still think revolution is for export." The administration was also convinced that the destruction of Guevara's cadre was of positive benefit to the Bolivian people. Returning from a tour of the nation the following year, Covey Oliver reported: "Liquidation of the Guevara guerrillas has given the Bolivians pride and much needed self-confidence."[65]

The death of Che Guevara demonstrated the continued US commitment to combating Communist influence in the hemisphere as well as the close links that six years of the Alliance for Progress and related assistance had helped forge with many Latin American militaries. As had been the case in Argentina, the armed forces were often seen as a potential driver of modernization efforts, and this was tied to the administration's basic position—articulated clearly to the president by Walt Rostow—that the best way to deal with subversion was through the expansion of "rural police programs." In June 1967, Rostow had argued in favor of the "preventative medicine" of counterinsurgency training and cited the crackdowns of the military government of Colonel Alfredo Enrique Peralta Azurdia in Guatemala as an example of the "impressive results" that could be achieved with American help. Hence, while Rostow believed that the decision to execute Guevara was "stupid," he was also happy to report to Johnson that Che's death demonstrated "the soundness of our 'preventive medicine' assistance to countries facing incipient insurgency" as it was American-trained forces that "cornered him and got him." Indeed, by 1968, so many Latin American governments were either totally or partially dominated by the armed forces that Helms wrote to Rostow: "It is no longer useful to make broad generalizations as to the nature and value of the military's political role." He also argued that in some cases military governments were more likely than civilian to instigate positive change. Helms's argument might have been more convincing had he not cited the Brazilian regime as an example of such "responsible" governments, but nonetheless his views reflected how intertwined with US development efforts Latin American armed forces had become.[66]

Unfortunately, the results would not be so positive for the majority of the Bolivian people. Barrientos died in a helicopter crash in 1969, and his death sparked a series of coups and military dictatorships of increasing levels of brutality. A successful Cuban-led insurgency may not necessarily have resulted in a better lot for the average Bolivian, but it is nonetheless clear that the Alliance and related military assistance had once again strengthened the hand of forces of repression. US involvement in Bolivia also demonstrated

President Johnson meets with Walt Rostow in the Oval Office, 15 July 1967. The two became increasingly close during the remainder of Johnson's presidency. (Lyndon Baines Johnson Library photo by Kevin Smith.)

the enduring hostility toward Fidel Castro and the sheer determination of the administration to continue combating Cuban influence. When Thomas Mann contacted William Bowdler of the State Department in June 1968, concerned by reports that the administration was seeking "some kind of accommodation" with Castro's regime before Johnson left office, he was assured firmly that this was in no way the case.[67]

Aside from the death of Che Guevara, 1967 was notable as a year of relative political stability in the hemisphere. With no military coups or other unconstitutional changes of government in the Americas, this period of comparative calm was largely overlooked in the United States as the conflict in Vietnam and related domestic protest escalated and war erupted briefly in the Middle East. Such surface tranquility only masked deeply rooted problems, however, and 1968 would see both Fernando Belaúnde Terry of Peru and Arnulfo Arias of Panama ousted by their armed forces, starkly illustrating the continuing economic, social, and political problems faced by many nations of the hemisphere.

Developments in Peru in 1968 initially appeared to be positive for the Johnson administration when President Belaúnde announced in August that a deal had finally been reached to settle the long-running dispute with the American-based IPC via the Act of Talara. The situation became more complex, however, when Carlos Loret de Mola, the chief negotiator for the Peruvian government and the head of the state oil company, resigned and claimed publicly that a final page of the Act of Talara, which made the complicated compromise deal more favorable to the Peruvian government, was missing from the official document presented to the people. The Peruvian press and much of the public were infuriated at both Belaúnde and the IPC, believing the president to be kowtowing to a rapacious foreign corporation.[68]

Given that aid to Peru had been reduced to almost nothing during the IPC dispute, Belaúnde unsurprisingly looked to the United States for assistance once the dispute had been resolved, explaining to Ambassador John Wesley Jones that this would be evidence of American "appreciation of [his] government's courage in finally resolving this explosive problem." Jones strongly supported the request, and Rostow was soon advising Johnson to approve sales of rice and a new USAID loan of $25 million in order to "provide tangible political support for President Belaúnde at a key point in his administration, after he has taken several difficult development decisions." Rostow's recommendation came on 2 October, but by then it was already too late. Largely taking the Johnson administration by surprise, on 3 October, the military, led by Army chief of staff Juan Francisco Velasco Alvarado, seized power in Lima. Explaining the motivations of the military officers to Johnson, Rostow noted they feared that a "much hated" politician would likely win the next round of elections and resented Belaúnde's neglect of the armed forces but that anger at the terms of the IPC settlement was also an "obvious motive."[69]

As had been the case with the Argentine coup, the Peruvian coup was viewed as an unwelcome development in Washington. Diplomatic relations were suspended, and Covey Oliver cabled the embassy in Lima to deplore the "heavy-handed move," commenting: "My personal feeling is one of revulsion and that if it were otherwise feasible and in our interest, I would not want to deal with [the] Junta at all." To make matters worse, on 9 October, the new government under General Velasco tore up the Act of Talara and seized the remaining holdings of the IPC in Peru. While the administration was still deciding how to respond to events in Lima, reports emerged of more political turmoil in a country all too familiar to Lyndon Johnson; there was a new crisis in Panama.[70]

On 30 May 1968, Arnulfo Arias won a surprise victory in the Panamanian presidential election. The surprise was that, with the incumbent president and the immensely powerful national guard opposed to his election, widespread fraud had not been mobilized to deny him the victory. Certainly, the CIA had expected that would be the case, and analyses in Washington concluded that Arias's victory must have been so overwhelming that the national guard backed away from what would have been such a transparent case of vote tampering. Entering the presidential office for the third time in a long and controversial political career on 1 October 1968, Arias lasted less than two weeks before the national guard seized power, with Colonel Omar Torrijos soon installed as de facto president. Arias fled into the Canal Zone and appealed for assistance from the United States. Unfortunately for Arias, his popularity in Washington was little higher than it had been in 1964 when Thomas Mann had dismissed his attempts to secure US backing for his political maneuverings during the breakdown in US-Panamanian relations. With events in Panama coming so soon after the Peruvian coup, however, Johnson was reluctant to appear to be endorsing a military takeover. "What happens in Panama on [the] heels of Peru will also be relevant in terms encouraging or discouraging similar acts in other countries," Rostow reminded the president on 12 October, recommending pressuring the guard to form some kind of coalition with Arias.[71]

During a lunchtime meeting of key foreign policy advisers on 28 October, both Peru and Panama were discussed at some length, albeit with initially different outcomes. Peru was first on the agenda, and, despite Velasco's seizure of IPC holdings, Dean Rusk advised that recognition be extended. "This is the 62nd coup I've lived through since I've been Secretary of State," he noted wearily. "We don't get anywhere by not recognizing them, . . . [and] we can't impose our will over other countries." Making the decision a little more palatable, the IPC expropriation meant that the Hickenlooper Amendment would be invoked and therefore that aid to the Peruvian government would not be resumed. Johnson issued a "reluctant go-ahead to recognize." The situation in Panama was seen as somewhat more complex as, while Arias remained in the Canal Zone claiming to be still the president of Panama, US support for one side or the other could be pivotal. Overt support for Arias and denial of recognition could anger the de facto government of a strategically important nation, but rapid recognition would be taken by many throughout the Americas as evidence of US support for military governments and possible involvement in Arias's ouster. The issue was simplified somewhat by Arias's decision to seek asylum in the United States, effectively ending any realistic chance of his reinstatement. Johnson therefore felt comfortable delaying recognition, informing Rusk at the lunchtime meeting that he was "okay on that, holding off for a while."[72]

Initial assessments of Torrijos's nascent regime explain why Johnson was in no rush to extend recognition. CIA reports on the junta observed that the guard had acted "in order to protect its own position rather than to carry out any specific program for Panama" and that a return to democratic rule in the near future was unlikely, whatever actions the US government took. Having been asked to meet with Arias and offer his opinions in an unofficial capacity, Thomas Mann too warned against alienating the erstwhile president's supporters if the administration wanted "ever to get a canal treaty which can be ratified by Panama." The situation could not last, however, and it was eventually decided that, as was the case with Peru, there was little to be gained by an extended denial of relations. Once the Torrijos government had made a public commitment to holding elections "within a reasonable period of time" and relaxed some controls on press censorship, recognition was extended in November.[73]

The twin failures of democracy in Peru and Panama in 1968 were of course of greatest consequence for the citizens of those countries, who faced years of military rule, yet they also ensured a difficult end to Johnson's stewardship of his nation's Latin American policy as he made his preparations for departing the White House. Peru, like Argentina in 1966, demonstrated the damaging impact of drawn-out economic disputes with US-based corporations and the conflicting pressures they caused, undermining national governments, and encouraging ambitious plotters. Given that Belaúnde's ouster also led to the expropriation of IPC's holdings, it is difficult not to judge US policy on the matter a failure. Belaúnde had been, for the most part, the kind of progressive president that the Alliance proclaimed to support. Yet, in reducing aid and pressuring his government to reach a compromise with the oil company, Washington played a substantial role in his downfall. That is not to say that the Johnson administration desired his removal from office; quite the opposite. Nor would it have been realistic to expect it to have entirely ignored domestic pressure to protect IPC's interests. It clear, however, that both the Peruvian and the Panamanian cases served as reminders of the complex nature of those countries' relationship with Washington and the limits of US influence, unable to preserve, let alone further, the cause of democracy in the hemisphere. In his acceptance that "we don't get anywhere by not recognizing them," Dean Rusk was also acknowledging that recognition policy had little impact on political events elsewhere. The Brazilian case may have demonstrated that appearing too eager to welcome a regime that had come to power by force was inadvisable, but, after a decent interval, withholding recognition was ultimately only delaying the inevitable.

Policy makers were less willing to admit the ever more apparent consequences of the intimate ties built with the armed forces of the Americas. Nowhere was this clearer than in Panama, with Omar Torrijos a proud graduate of the School of the Americas, where Latin American officers were trained by US military instructors in the finer arts of counterinsurgency and internal security. While the murder of Che Guevara by US-trained allies was counted as a success, the more common outcome of these programs was seen in Lima and Panama City. Perhaps belatedly recognizing that fact, Johnson told Rostow in early December that he did not want to provide any military assistance to the Panamanian junta during the final few weeks of his administration, delaying all decisions until 20 January, when it would no longer be his problem. As it transpired, he was unable to maintain even that token gesture. Rostow informed him on 30 December that the national guard was growing resentful at the lack of new equipment, a dangerous situation with the anniversary of the 1964 riots approaching, and submitted a memo requesting the resumption of limited assistance. A weary Johnson simply ticked approve.[74]

The push for integration that marked the last years of the Alliance for Progress under Lyndon Johnson ultimately enjoyed limited success. Nevertheless, some praise is due for his administration's attempts to implement a potentially more sustainable policy framework, one that contradicted traditional US economic policy and envisioned a viable Latin American trading bloc capable of competing in the global marketplace and sustaining internal growth. Given the increasing skepticism of Congress regarding foreign aid specifically and the administration in general—something for which Johnson must of course bear substantial responsibility—combined with the general apathy of the American public toward the Alliance, efforts to devise a vision of development less reliant on the continued mass injection of aid appear eminently sensible. However, reductions in funding that occurred sooner and cut deeper than the administration had anticipated, the worsening of the situation in Vietnam, and continued instability and resistance to integration among the Latin American countries themselves all served to critically hamper the integration process, and evidence of long-term success is difficult to find. The CACM, for example, would be crippled by the 1969 "Soccer War" between El Salvador and Honduras, and key physical integration projects such as the closing of the Darien Gap, which intersects the Pan American Highway, remain incomplete as of today.[75]

If attempts to reinvigorate the Alliance struggled to gain traction, other events during the same period reflected wider challenges in inter-American relations, particularly the troubling intersection of economic, security, and development interests. The Alliance era as a whole witnessed more than its share of military takeovers, yet, as the decade progressed, it became increasingly clear that US policy was contributing to a certain form of coup. In some cases, political tensions were exacerbated by long-running economic disputes with US corporations, but, more pertinently, events in Argentina, Panama, and Peru reflected the inability of the Johnson administration to restrain armed forces that had been well trained in internal security, extensively equipped with the necessary tools to subdue their own populations, and told that they had a key role to play in the modernization of their nations. Subsequent decades would witness the full extent of such policies as forces that the United States had helped unleash—in the form of highly trained and well-armed modern military regimes and the resistance groups that opposed them—ravaged many of the countries of the hemisphere in brutal civil wars.

For Lyndon Johnson, then, Latin America had proved another frustrating foreign policy challenge. In the face of unrealistic development targets and "problems everywhere," he had largely remained committed to the programs and policies of his predecessor, seeking ways to streamline or refresh them, with mixed results. Ever sensitive to criticism, he would depart office feeling that, while he had received plenty of condemnation for his mistakes, there had been little credit given for his achievements. In the last weeks of his administration, the ever optimistic Rostow nonetheless encouraged the president to celebrate the accomplishments of his Latin American policy by attending ceremonies to mark the final completion of the Chamizal border adjustment with Mexico and to accept an award from the Pan American Society for his contributions to "inter-American friendship." Deliver a "valedictory speech on Latin America," Rostow urged, and "dramatize the contributions of your administration in this region." Johnson would attend the Chamizal ceremony, but he would limit his remarks to addressing positive gains made in the US-Mexican relationship. He would not even go that far with the Pan American Society, scrawling "no banquet" on a memo to Rostow, and quietly accepting the award from a small group of society members in the Oval Office. Exhausted, unpopular, and increasingly bitter, Johnson left the presidency on 20 January 1969 and retired to his beloved Texan ranch for good.[76]

Conclusion

If Lyndon Johnson's administration witnessed a dwindling of the energy and optimism of the early days of John F. Kennedy's Alliance for Progress, then his successor would preside over its disappearance. Johnson's attempts to promote regional integration were the last significant effort of an era characterized by the belief that the United States could further its own interests by encouraging Latin American modernization and economic development through various forms of aid and assistance. Johnson's successor, Richard Nixon, whose experiences during his ill-fated tour of 1958 had helped prompt the Eisenhower administration's belated interest in Latin America, would abandon the idea of hemispheric development almost entirely. Despite some claims to the contrary during the 1968 election campaign, the region did not play a significant role in the strategic vision of global affairs of Nixon and his chief foreign policy adviser, Henry Kissinger, and the Alliance was not part of their plans. As Nixon stated bluntly: "Latin America doesn't matter." To an even greater degree for the new administration than for its predecessors, stability was the key; few promises of economic assistance were forthcoming, and repressive governments would be embraced even more readily than in the Kennedy-Johnson era. "So unambitious as to be embarrassing," was the stark assessment of Nixon's regional agenda in the *Washington Post*.[1]

In tracing the evolution of US policy in the region, many historians have viewed Johnson's contributions as laying the groundwork for Nixon's disengagement. One overview of the literature by the historian Alan McPherson, for instance, describes the Johnson that emerges from most accounts as a "transitional president on Latin American policy, wedged between the reformist optimism of Kennedy and the realist cynicism of Nixon": "He slowly gave up on the Alliance for Progress. He wavered on democracy and tolerated authoritarianism. He reinforced fraudulent elections. His positive

214

achievements—Mexico comes to mind—were unimpressive." While such an assessment is not wholly unfair, it offers an ungenerous take on what was, as McPherson accurately identifies, a transitional period. With faith in the ability of modernization-influenced programs to engender economic development and democratization already waning during Kennedy's final year in office, it was left to Johnson and his experienced adviser Thomas Mann to fashion an alternative approach. Often hamstrung by domestic pressure from economic conservatives on the right and Kennedy loyalists on the left, the Johnson presidency nonetheless saw a new framework emerge that retained the modernizer's faith in economic development while embracing inter-American multilateralism to push an agenda of regional integration. Although regularly undermined by Cold War security concerns, this nonetheless offered an alternative vision for American engagement with the developing world even as congressional funding and enthusiasm waned. Nixon would retain the least successful aspects of Johnson's policies—the determination to contain any perceived Communist influence and combat economic nationalism—but rejected the vision of an integrated hemisphere. This progression from a focus on modernization driven by direct aid and technical assistance to gradual development through economic and physical integration projects and, ultimately, marginalization reveals as much about shifting American global and domestic priorities as it does about the relative merits of Johnson's policies in Latin America.[2]

This book has presented an account of US policy in Latin America during the 1960s that places the failings and the achievements of the Johnson administration within a balanced historical, political, and strategic context while remaining wary of swinging the pendulum too far and providing an overly positive assessment of a turbulent and troubled period. In considering policy toward a region as vast as the entirety of Latin America, it is also by necessity a partial account, and there remains much to be explored and understood about inter-American relations in the Johnson era. Nonetheless, the evidence presented here can provide the basis for a new understanding of the interrelated issues of Thomas Mann, Lyndon Johnson, and US policies in the Americas.

Central to understanding more about this period is Mann, whose reputation as a staunch conservative and enemy of the progressive forces of the hemisphere has driven much of the existing narrative regarding Johnson's policies. The foundation of this reputation was formed during clashes with the Kennedy loyalists in the early 1960s, something Mann himself was well aware of. In his view, the fact that he was willing to "question that not every hope would be realized, that there were certain limits to what just money and technical advice could do in a foreign country," resulted in his portrayal as an ideological enemy of the very program he was entrusted with administering, despite his progressive reputation during the later years of the Eisenhower administration and positive achievements while ambassador to Mexico. He was also convinced that the practical divergences between his own views and those of the Alliance true believers were distorted and exaggerated, arguing: "The differences on form rather than substance were dramatized. . . . [I]t became a burning question of who loved the poor the most rather than how does the U.S. go about helping the Latin American poor." Of course, Mann was not blameless in the rifts with the Kennedy loyalists, but his sense that his fundamental policy priorities were not so different from those of someone like Arthur Schlesinger would seemingly be confirmed years later, in 1983, when the two men both testified before the President's National Bipartisan Commission on Central America, chaired by Henry Kissinger. Informed by Kissinger that his and Mann's views on the potential challenge of Communist regimes, the need for economic integration, and the possibility of increased US aid were almost identical, Schlesinger noted in his journal: "I said that I was sure Tom Mann would be as much surprised by this as I am." Perhaps not.[3]

A fairer assessment of Mann, as of Johnson, highlights his faults and failures while also acknowledging the restrictions within which he was operating and recognizing his achievements. If we can be critical of the ill-judged and poorly timed Mann Doctrine speech and the reactionary anticommunism and blind support of his ambassador that drove his decision making during the Dominican Republic crisis, then we can also acknowledge that two of his nation's most notable postwar diplomatic achievements in the hemisphere— the Chamizal agreement and the renegotiation of the Panama Canal Treaty— owed much to his talents. His views on the exercising of US power were also more complex than his critics have allowed. The Dominican case certainly demonstrates that the specter of a Communist victory in the hemisphere— which he unconvincingly argued would essentially constitute an attack by a foreign power—was enough to prompt his support of military action, yet the blunt Texan reputed to deliver "a buck in the pocket and a kick in the ass" was far more aware of the dangers of American overreach than many of his contemporaries. His criticisms of the Bay of Pigs planning, position on the Panama crisis, and actions in his various ambassadorial posts all reflected his awareness of the potential repercussions of US interventionism and a reluctance "to impose our brand of democracy or capitalism or social justice on other American republics." Furthermore, it is clear that, rather than attempting to destroy the Alliance, as Schlesinger and others have suggested, he worked with Johnson to try and shape the program into something functional and practical while establishing a realistic appraisal of the limits of American power. In doing so, they lost some of the infectious idealism and enthusiasm that had accompanied the launch of the Alliance, but they were also able to administer it more efficiently, resulting in more tangible achievements than had been possible under their predecessors. Mann's final effort—continued by his successors—was to advocate for economic integration, which he hoped would provide self-sustaining growth for Latin America.[4]

Mann also deserves a more prominent place in the histories of the Johnson administration. To his mind, "the Foreign Service serves the President of the United States, whoever that President is," an ideal that he embraced throughout his career. Nonetheless, it was when working for Johnson, his fellow Texan, that his influence was at its peak. As LBJ's first significant appointee, he gained symbolic importance, but he also quickly earned the president's trust and enjoyed a level of access to the Oval Office that few others shared, was regularly consulted on crucial decisions such as senior staff appointments, and from his first day in the administration was given wide-ranging power to oversee Latin American policy. After his promotion to undersecretary of state for economic affairs in 1965, he remained most invested in the region of his specialty, but he also played a role in global economic policy, advocating increased trade links with the Communist nations of Eastern Europe, and consulting closely with Johnson on how best to handle congressional discontent. He also remained a consistent proponent of price-stabilization agreements for commodities such as coffee and sugar and regularly represented the United States at international economic conferences. For the first two and a half years of Johnson's presidency, he was an important and influential figure, more trusted, if not quite as powerful, than prominent policy makers such as McGeorge Bundy. Following his departure from office, he remained a regular source of counsel for the president, even as Walt Rostow took his place as the administration's most influential voice on Latin American issues.[5]

Such an adjusted view of Mann and his relative importance does not necessarily transform judgments of Lyndon Johnson. In the best accounts of various aspects of his presidency, the LBJ who emerges is a complex and often contradictory figure, a characterization not challenged here. Indeed, Johnson's record in Latin America is distinctly mixed and open to a variety of interpretations. William Bowdler, who worked in the State Department during Johnson's administration, has offered a particularly positive account of his efforts, arguing: "One of the ironies of the Johnson Administration is that if you go through the history of our relations with Latin America, I don't think that you will find a president who devoted more time, more energy, more effort, and more money to Latin America than President Johnson. And yet he didn't reap from that what he really should have." While Bowdler's view is colored by his own involvement in the administration, it is not wholly without foundation. In support of his case, one can to point to the successful resolution of the Panamanian crisis of 1964, the continued healthy relations with Mexico, or the 1967 presidential summit as evidence of Johnson's diplomatic skill and patience. Similarly, one could make the case that, statistically, aid levels and most other available measures of the Alliance were, on average, higher under Johnson than they had been under John F. Kennedy. Furthermore, Johnson's genuine desire to use the power of his office to aid those living in poverty—which was clear in his domestic programs—translated most easily in his foreign policy toward Latin America. Influenced by his experiences at the small school in Cotulla he taught at in his youth and his New Deal political education, he continued to push for new initiatives to sustain the Alliance, even as the impact of Vietnam began to be felt in terms of both domestic protests and congressional hostility. Only in the final tortuous months of his presidency did he appear to grow weary with inter-American issues, with endless battles with Congress and a series of coups undermining any chance of his stewardship ending on a positive note.[6]

Yet to characterize Johnson as a victim of circumstance would be erroneous, ignoring the fact that plenty of his problems stemmed from his own mistakes and misjudgments. While many of the policies he inherited were flawed, the quick endorsement of a military regime in Brazil and the panicked intervention in the Dominican Republic were, while not necessarily out of step with long-term US Cold War strategy, nevertheless handled in a manner that provoked congressional ire and enraged critics both in the United States and in the rest of the Americas. In these instances, Johnson demonstrated many of his worst traits as a leader, seeking, and often obtaining, complete consensus from his advisers, resorting to exaggeration and hyperbole in his public statements, and lashing out at critics who questioned his decision making. Similarly, the ongoing obsession with combating any form of Communist influence emboldened and in many cases trained and equipped the very forces that would undermine democratic progress in many nations. Ultimately, Johnson was unable to overcome the internal contradictions of US policy; in seeking an efficient and productive Alliance for Progress while desperately trying to keep the hemisphere free of Communist influence, he was unable to achieve either.

A fairer assessment of the period, then, would acknowledge that the Johnson administration inherited a Latin American policy that retained a traditional desire to influence political and economic developments for the benefit of the United States, intensified by the fear of another Cuba. The final years of Eisenhower's presidency had been characterized by a greater flexibility in economic assistance and aid policy, before the Kennedy administration embraced the goal of modernizing Latin America. The Alliance for Progress was still the most prominent element of US policy in the region when Johnson entered the Oval Office, but, throughout Kennedy's presidency, there had been a growing awareness of the limitations of this approach and an acceptance that the Alliance alone could not solve the social and political problems of the hemisphere, leading to some moderate policy adjustments. This readjustment process continued into the Johnson administration, where greater focus was initially placed on the efficiency of the Alliance bureaucracy and on raising the economic output of the hemisphere before a more sustainable solution was sought through increased economic integration and political cooperation. These changes were, however, readjustments, not a rejection of fundamental assumptions, and the goal of a functioning and effective Alliance for Progress remained an administration priority almost until the end.

Nonetheless, the commonly held view among historians that many of the efforts of this period—and particularly the Alliance—were a failure is difficult to dispute. Alliance targets were clearly not fulfilled, and, for both Kennedy and Johnson, traditional security concerns, enhanced by a degree of Cold War paranoia, continually undermined any chance of stable development. Even State Department reports recognized that security policy was "full of paradoxes" as the programs needed to encourage long-term prosperity and stability, such as widespread land and tax reform, were not vigorously pursued owing to the short-term instability they might provoke. Similarly, the overreliance on military partners to drive modernization efforts while ensuring domestic security opened the door for a succession of armed-forces dominated coups and governments that would in many cases be challenged by armed rebellions in brutal civil wars. The 1970s and 1980s witnessed horrific atrocities in several nations of Latin America, often perpetrated by regimes the United States had endorsed, such as those in El Salvador, Guatemala, Chile, and Brazil. The failures of the 1960s left a deeply troubling legacy.[7]

There does, however, remain room for acknowledgment of some of the positive aspects of the Alliance. An in-depth accounting of efforts in individual Latin American countries has not been possible in this book, but it should not be forgotten that programs sponsored through the Social Progress Trust Fund and the Alliance for Progress built schools, hospitals, roads, and sewage and drainage systems and helped establish agriculture and electric cooperatives. Results were uneven, but, for those who felt the benefits of such projects, increased US aid was surely not a complete failure. US policy was inevitably based largely on self-interest, but, for a few years at least, Washington considered development aid and a greater degree of political cooperation to be just as valid a set of policy tools as covert operations or support for repressive regimes. That in itself, however briefly it lasted, can be considered a minor success.

Within that brief period, Thomas Mann was an influential and controversial figure. Mr. Latin America often found himself out of step with dominant factions of both Republican and Democratic administrations yet played a role in many of the major policy developments of the era and remained remarkably consistent in his convictions, with results that were mixed for both his own career and hemispheric policy. He discovered his closest ally in Lyndon Johnson, a president who found Latin American policy a challenge, struggling to convince skeptics that his interest in the region reflected more than just lip service to his predecessor's legacy. Both Mann and Johnson made their share of mistakes and too often indulged their Cold War anxieties, but this book has argued that, driven by their own experiences and beliefs, they also both possessed a genuine desire to pursue a progressive agenda that sought alternative means of supporting Latin American development. Central to many of the positive and negative developments of inter-American relations during a period that Mann characterized as witnessing "problems everywhere," any fair accounting should acknowledge a record and a legacy that are as multifaceted and contradictory as the challenges they regularly faced.

Acknowledgments

Writing a book takes a long time, and the process with this project has been no exception. While my name is the only one that appears on the cover, I have been lucky enough to have been helped and supported along the way by countless brilliant and talented people, and I will do my best to give as many of them as I can the credit they deserve.

The original germ of an idea from which this project grew can be credited to David Milne, who as my supervisor during my early postgraduate work at the University of Nottingham suggested it might be worth looking into a guy called Thomas Mann and produced a pile of photocopied documents from the LBJ library for me to plough through. David, and later Bevan Sewell, who took over as my supervisor, were fantastically supportive advisers during my early attempts at research and patiently guided me to a point where I was able successfully to pursue my doctorate at the University of Cambridge. There I was supervised by Tony Badger and mentored by Andrew Preston, who both struck the perfect balance of leaving me to get on with things while always being available to offer advice and guide my development as a historian. I am immensely grateful to all my supervisors, who continue to mentor and support me, and I am delighted that one of the great pleasures of my subsequent career has turned out to be maintaining those relationships, now as friends and colleagues.

It would also be remiss of me not to mention the important role that the graduate workshop at Cambridge played in developing my writing, sharpening my arguments, and teaching me to articulate and defend my ideas and constructively critique others. Dan Matlin and Ellie Shermer were insightful and encouraging convenors, and the list of wonderful peers is too long to list exhaustively, but Hannah Higgin, James Cameron, Olivia Sohns, Johannes Kadura, Stephen Mawdsley, Adam Gilbert, Zach Fredman, Asa McKercher, and Stella Krepp were prominent among the friends who also made me a better historian. I am also immensely grateful to the generosity of Sidney Sussex College and the Fox International Fellowship program for providing me with a year's work in New Haven. Not only could I enjoy the benefits of the wonderful resources of Yale University, but the fellowship also enabled access to the multiple US-based archives that provided the core material for this book. Further archival work was enabled by generous grants from the British Association for American Studies, the Royal Historical Society, the University of Cambridge, and the Lyndon Baines Johnson Library.

Speaking of which, like most historians I owe a huge debt to the hard work and dedication of archivists at multiple locations. Countless staff at the US National Archives and the Eisenhower, Kennedy, and Johnson libraries all offered insight, advice, and suggestions that improved this project immeasurably. Special mention must also go to the staff at Baylor University's Texas Collection, home to both Thomas Mann's underused papers and brilliantly helpful archivists who even took pity on a poor carless Brit and drove him to the grocery store once the archive had closed. Additionally, parts of chapter 1 were published in the *Journal of Cold War Studies* as "The First Alliance for Progress? Reshaping the Eisenhower Administration's Policy toward Latin America," and elements of chapter 2 appeared in *Diplomatic History* as "Becoming 'Mr. Latin America': Thomas C. Mann Reconsidered." I am grateful to the editors of those journals for both publishing my work and for their permission to republish aspects of that research here.

Since 2013, I have been employed at the University of Manchester, where I have been lucky enough to find a community of collegial and hardworking colleagues and engaged, inspiring students. Particular thanks must go to Peter Gatrell for his mentoring and advice, but I am grateful to all my colleagues for creating an academic community that encourages and supports great research and teaching and to my students, who constantly surprise, challenge, entertain, and energize me. I am also fortunate to be part of an active and vibrant community of historians of the United States scattered throughout the United Kingdom and beyond, many of whom have read and critiqued portions of my work, commented on conference papers, or offered sage advice at important times. In addition to those mentioned above, in no particular order, and by no means exhaustively, these include Kaeten Mistry, Nick Witham, Tanya Harmer, Jeff Taffet, Robert McMahon, Richard Immerman, Odd Arne Westad, Thomas Field, Renata Keller, Matthew Jones, and many more. Thank you to all of you, and apologies and thanks to those I have forgotten. Finally, my thanks to the reviewers and my editors at the University Press of Kentucky for all their assistance and support in whipping the initial manuscript into the much improved book you hold today.

Most importantly, my thanks to all the family and friends whose love and support have made my career possible and worthwhile. All my parents—Kath and Keith, Chris and Ann—provided me with the foundation of a wonderful upbringing and constant emotional and financial support in pursuing a career that requires plenty of both for longer than is probably healthy. Keith's expert copyediting skills have been particularly useful, and mum has traveled to visit every odd place my academic career has taken me, encouraging me every step of the way. My sister Beth has provided important feedback on various stages of this work, and all my siblings provide love and friendship in their own unique ways, and my fantastic nieces and nephews are a constant source of joy. My aunt and uncle, Lesley and John, also need a special mention. They have followed and supported my academic career closely, and at times their generosity has enabled research trips and conference travel when more conventional funding attempts had failed. Finally, to Caitlin, whose decision to put an ocean between herself and her wonderful friends and family in order to be with me, inspires me more than I can put into words. I have gained the most generous, supportive partner I could wish for, one who makes me laugh every day and who is immensely proud of my work but also tells me when to take a break. I cannot imagine doing this without her.

Essentially, this book exists because I'm incredibly lucky and have a lot to be grateful for.

Notes

Introduction

1. Lyndon B. Johnson, "Remarks in Punta del Este at the Public Session of the Meeting of American Chiefs of State," 13 April 1967, American Presidency Project (APP), Public Papers of the President (PPP), http://www.presidency.ucsb.edu/ws/index.php?pid=28201.

2. United States Presidency Centre, UK Survey of US Presidents Results, 2010, http://community-languages.org.uk/US-presidency-survey/results.htm.

3. A detailed summary of the limited historiography related to Johnson's Latin American record can be found in Alan McPherson, "Latin America," in *A Companion to Lyndon B. Johnson,* ed. Mitchell Lerner (Malden, MA: Wiley-Blackwell, 2012), 387–406.

4. Arthur M. Schlesinger Jr., *Robert Kennedy and His Times* (London: Deutsch, 1978), 689.

5. Nicholas Evan Sarantakes refers to the small group of historians who focus on Johnson's record beyond Vietnam and provide more positive accounts of his handling of foreign affairs as the Longhorn school, a reference to their association with the University of Texas. Nicholas Evan Sarantakes, "Lyndon B. Johnson and the World," in Lerner, ed., *A Companion to Lyndon B. Johnson,* 487–504.

6. Prominent examples of this critical perspective can be found in Walter LaFeber, "Thomas C. Mann and the Devolution of Latin American Policy from the Good Neighbor to Military Intervention," in *Behind the Throne: Servants of Power to Imperial Presidents, 1898–1968,* ed. Walter LaFeber and Thomas J. McCormick (Madison: University of Wisconsin Press, 1993), 166–203; Schlesinger, *Robert Kennedy,* 630–92; and Richard Goodwin, *Remembering America: A Voice from the Sixties* (Boston: Perennial, 1988), 243–46.

7. Levels of aid reached anywhere near similar levels only during Ronald Reagan's administration, through support for Cold War allies in Central America during the 1980s. Detailed information on the level of US aid is available at "U.S. Overseas Loans and Grants: Obligations and Loan Authorizations, July 1, 1945–September 30, 2014," https://explorer.usaid.gov/reports-greenbook.html.

8. Transcript of Telephone Conversation, Johnson and Mann, 12 June 1964, Thomas Mann Papers, box 316, Texas Collection, Baylor University, Waco, TX (hereafter TC).

9. Quoted in LaFeber, "Thomas C. Mann," 198. For other examples of this view, see Gerard Colby and Charlotte Dennett, *Thy Will Be Done: The Conquest of the Amazon: Nelson Rockefeller and Evangelism in the Age of Oil* (New York: HarperCollins, 1995), 417–23; Federico G. Gil, "The Kennedy-Johnson Years," in *United States Policy in Latin America: A Quarter Century of Crisis and Challenge, 1961–1986,* ed. John D. Martz (Lincoln: University of Nebraska Press, 1998), 23–24; Goodwin, *Remembering America,* 243–46; Walter LaFeber, *Inevitable Revolutions: The United States in Central America* (New York: Norton, 1993), 157; Thomas M. Leonard, "Search for Security: The United States and Central America in the Twentieth Century," *The Americas* 47, no. 4 (April 1991): 477–90; Robert A. Packenham, *Liberal America and the Third World: Political Development Ideas in Foreign Aid and Social Science* (Princeton, NJ: Princeton University Press, 1973), 93–98; and Arthur Schlesinger Jr., "Myth and Reality," in *The Alliance for Progress: A Retrospective,* ed. L. Ronald Scheman (New York: Praeger, 1988), 67–72, and *Robert Kennedy,* 630–92.

10. For somewhat more balanced scholarly accounts of Mann, see Stephen Rabe, *The Most Dangerous Area in the World: John F. Kennedy Confronts Communist Revolution in Latin America* (Chapel Hill: University of North Carolina Press, 1999), 174–81; Alan McPherson, *Yankee No! Anti-Americanism in U.S.–Latin American Relations* (Cambridge, MA: Harvard University Press, 2003), 101–2; Jeffrey F. Taffet, *Foreign Aid as Foreign Policy: The Alliance for Progress in Latin America* (New York: Routledge, 2007), 59–62; and Randall B. Woods, *LBJ: Architect of American Ambition* (Cambridge, MA: Harvard University Press, 2006), 494–96. For positive views expressed by his contemporaries, see Adolf Berle, *Navigating the Rapids, 1918–1971* (New York: Harcourt Brace Jovanovich, 1973), 785–86; Richard M. Bissell, *Reflections of a Cold Warrior: From Yalta to the Bay of Pigs* (New Haven, CT: Yale University Press, 1996), 158–97; and Edwin M. Martin, *Kennedy and Latin America* (Lanham, MD: University Press of America, 1994), 156–57. Nonetheless, in less specialized texts such as overviews of US foreign policy, biographies of Kennedy and Johnson, and historical dictionaries, Mann is characterized as a hard-line and divisive figure, most notable for his hostility to Kennedy's aid programs. In his account of the history of US foreign policy, George Herring describes Mann as "deeply conservative." In the latest volume of his biography of Lyndon Johnson, Robert Caro views the appointment of the "controversial" Mann as a means by which Johnson humiliated a faction of Kennedy supporters. Finally, an entry in a recent historical dictionary describes Mann's "reversal" of Kennedy's idealistic policies. George C. Herring, *From Colony to Superpower: U.S. Foreign Relations since 1776* (New York: Oxford University Press, 2008), 732; Robert A. Caro, *The Years of Lyndon Johnson: The Passage of Power* (London: Knopf, 2012), 581–88; David W. Dent, *Historical Dictionary of U.S.–Latin American Relations* (Westport, CT: Greenwood, 2005), 286.

11. For recent explorations of the foreign policy developments of the 1970s, see Barbara Keys, *Reclaiming American Virtue: The Human Rights Revolution of the 1970s* (Cambridge, MA: Harvard University Press, 2014); and Daniel Sargent, *A Superpower Transformed: The Remaking of American Foreign Relations in the 1970s* (Oxford: Oxford University Press, 2015).

12. Paul Geyelin, *Lyndon Johnson and the World* (New York: Praeger, 1966), 50. For further examples, see Larry Berman, *Planning a Tragedy* (New York: Norton, 1983); Irving Bernstein, *Guns or Butter: The Presidency of Lyndon Johnson* (Oxford: Oxford University Press, 1996); David Fromkin, "Review Essay: Lyndon Johnson and Foreign Policy: What the New Documents Show," *Foreign Affairs* 74, no. 1 (January 1995): 161–70; Eric Goldman, *The Tragedy of Lyndon Johnson* (New York: Macdonald, 1969); Waldo Heinrichs, "Lyndon B. Johnson: Change and Continuity," in *Lyndon Johnson Confronts the World: American Foreign Policy, 1963–1968,* ed. Warren I. Cohen and Nancy Bernkopf Tucker (Cambridge: Cambridge University Press, 1994), 9–30; Fredrik Logevall, *Choosing War: The Lost Chance for Peace and the Escalation of War in Vietnam* (Berkeley and Los Angeles: University of California Press, 1999); and Nancy Bernkopf Tucker, "Lyndon Johnson: A Final Reckoning," in Cohen and Bernkopf Tucker, eds., *Lyndon Johnson Confronts the World,* 311–20.

13. In addition to McPherson, "Latin America," see Gil, "The Kennedy-Johnson Years"; Thomas J. McCormick, *America's Half-Century: United States Foreign Policy in the Cold War and After,* 2nd ed. (Baltimore: Johns Hopkins University Press, 1995), 146; Tony Smith, "The Alliance for Progress: The 1960s," in *Exporting Democracy: The United States and Latin America: Themes and Issues,* ed. Abraham F. Lowenthal (Baltimore: Johns Hopkins University Press, 1991), 71–89; Taffet, *Foreign Aid as Foreign Policy;* Joseph S. Tulchin, "The Promise of Progress: U.S. Relations with Latin America during the Administration of Lyndon B. Johnson," in Cohen and Bernkopf Tucker, eds., *Lyndon Johnson Confronts the World,* 211–44; and William O. Walker III, "Mixing the Sweet with the Sour: Kennedy, Johnson, and Latin America," in *The Diplomacy of the Crucial Decade: American Foreign Relations during the 1960s,* ed. Diane B. Kunz (New York, Columbia University Press, 1994), 42–79.

14. See David C. Engerman, Nils Gilman, Mark Haefele, and Michael E. Latham, eds., *Staging Growth: Modernization, Development, and the Global Cold War* (Amherst: University of Massachusetts Press, 2003); Nils Gilman, *Mandarins of the Future: Modernization Theory in Cold War America* (Baltimore: Johns Hopkins University Press 2004); Michael Latham, *Modernization as Ideology: American Social Science and "Nation Building" in the Kennedy Era* (Chapel Hill: University of North Carolina Press, 2000); and David Milne, *America's Rasputin: Walt Rostow and the Vietnam War* (New York: Hill & Wang, 2008).

15. For details of the global applications of New Deal liberalism, see Elizabeth Borgwardt, *A New Deal for the World: America's Vision for Human Rights* (Cambridge, MA: Harvard University Press, 2005). For more on the intellectual roots of modernization theory, see Michael Adas, "Modernization Theory and the American

Revival of the Scientific and Technological Standards of Social Achievement and Human Worth," in Engerman, Gilman, Haefele, and Latham, eds., *Staging Growth*, 25–46; Nils Gilman, "Modernization Theory: The Highest Stage of American Intellectual History," in ibid., 47–80; and Gilman, *Mandarins of the Future*, 19–20.

16. Gilman, *Mandarins of the Future*, 203–40; Charles Kimber Pearce, *Rostow, Kennedy, and the Rhetoric of Foreign Aid* (East Lansing: Michigan State University Press, 2001), 108–15.

17. Thomas Schwartz, e.g., has dismissed the idea of Johnson as "the quintessential provincial," using relations with Europe to demonstrate that he not only cared about foreign policy but also could be skillful and effective and learned from his mistakes. H. W. Brands has offered a much broader interpretation, suggesting that Johnson inherited an overstretched and unsustainable approach to world affairs and was moderately successful in managing a tumultuous period of readjustment. Thomas Alan Schwartz, *Lyndon Johnson and Europe: In the Shadow of Vietnam* (Cambridge, MA: Harvard University Press, 2003); H. W. Brands, *The Wages of Globalism: Lyndon Johnson and the Limits of American Power* (New York: Oxford University Press, 1995). See also Mitchell Lerner, ed., *Looking Back at LBJ: White House Politics in a New Light* (Lawrence: University Press of Kansas, 2005); and Michael Lumbers, *Piercing the Bamboo Curtain: Tentative Bridge-Building to China during the Johnson Years* (Manchester: University of Manchester Press, 2008).

18. Taffet, *Foreign Aid as Foreign Policy*, 10; Enrique Lerdau, "The Alliance for Progress: The Learning Experience," in Scheman, ed., *The Alliance for Progress*, 165–84, 169.

19. For a survey of these developments, see Max Paul Friedman, "Retiring the Puppets, Bringing Latin America Back In: Recent Scholarship on United States–Latin American Relations," *Diplomatic History* 27, no. 5 (November 2003): 621–36. For examples of this work, see Virginia Garrard-Burnett, Mark Atwood Lawrence, and Julio E. Moreno, eds., *Beyond the Eagle's Shadow: New Histories of Latin America's Cold War* (Albuquerque: University of New Mexico Press, 2013); Greg Grandin and Gilbert M. Joseph, eds., *A Century of Revolution: Insurgent and Counterinsurgent Violence during Latin America's Long Cold War* (Durham, NC: Duke University Press, 2010); Thomas C. Field Jr., *From Development to Dictatorship: Bolivia and the Alliance for Progress in the Kennedy Era* (Ithaca, NY: Cornell University Press, 2014); Tanya Harmer, *Allende's Chile and the Inter-American Cold War* (Chapel Hill: University of North Carolina Press, 2011); Gilbert M. Joseph and Daniela Spenser, eds., *In from the Cold: Latin America's New Encounter with the Cold War* (Durham, NC: Duke University Press, 2007); and Renata Keller, *Mexico's Cold War: Cuba, the United States, and the Legacy of the Mexican Revolution* (Cambridge: Cambridge University Press, 2015).

20. See, e.g., Greg Grandin, *Empire's Workshop: Latin America, the United States, and the Rise of the New Imperialism* (New York: Metropolitan, 2006). For the classic "benevolent United States" view, see Samuel Flagg Bemis, *The Latin American Policy of the United States: An Historical Analysis* (New York: Harcourt, Brace, 1943).

21. Transcript, Thomas C. Mann Oral History Interview, 17 December 1975, by Maclyn P. Burg, Dwight D. Eisenhower Library, Abilene, KS (hereafter DDEL) (TC copy).

22. For details of Johnson's early life, see Robert A. Caro, *The Years of Lyndon Johnson: The Path to Power* (New York: Knopf, 1982); Robert Dallek, *Lone Star Rising: Lyndon Johnson and His Times, 1908–1960* (New York: Oxford University Press, 1991); and Woods, *LBJ.*

1. Trade, Aid, and the Cold War in the Americas

1. Transcript, Thomas C. Mann Oral History Interview, 13 March 1968, by Larry J. Hackman, John F. Kennedy Library, Boston (hereafter JFKL) (TC copy); Mann Oral History Interview, DDEL; Department of State Press Release, 9 November 1950, Thomas Mann Papers, box 325, TC; "One Mann & 20 Problems," *Time,* 31 January 1964; LaFeber, "Thomas C. Mann," 167–69; Woods, *LBJ,* 495.

2. Transcript, Thomas Mann Oral History Interview, 12 June 1972, by Richard D. McKinzie, Harry S. Truman Library (hereafter HSTL) (TC copy).

3. Ibid.; Telegram, Embassy Buenos Aires to the Secretary of State, 9 May 1947, *Foreign Relations of the United States (FRUS), 1947,* vol. 8, *The American Republics* (Washington, DC: US Government Printing Office, 1972), doc. 236; Department of State Press Release, 9 November 1950, Thomas Mann Papers, box 325, TC; "Interest of the United States in Venezuelan Oil Production and Other Extractive Industries; Concern of the United States over Possible Communist Sabotage in the Oil Fields," March–October 1948, *FRUS, 1948,* vol. 9, *The Western Hemisphere* (Washington, DC: US Government Printing Office, 1972), docs. 531–41; Telegram, State Department to Embassy Guatemala City, 13 October 1955, Thomas Mann Papers, box 325, TC.

4. Franklin D. Roosevelt, "Address on the Occasion of the Celebration of Pan-American Day, Washington," 12 April 1933, APP, PPP, http://www.presidency.ucsb.edu/ws/index.php?pid=14615; Transcript, Covey Oliver Oral History Interview I, 12 February 1968, by Paige E. Mulhollan, Lyndon Baines Johnson Library, Austin, TX (hereafter LBJL). See also Irwin F. Gellman, *Good Neighbor Diplomacy: United States Policies in Latin America, 1933–1945* (Baltimore: Johns Hopkins University Press, 1980); David Green, *The Containment of Latin America: A History of the Myths and Realities of the Good Neighbor Policy* (Chicago: Quadrangle, 1971); and Fredrick B. Pike, *FDR's Good Neighbor Policy: Sixty Years of Generally Gentle Chaos* (Austin: University of Texas Press, 1995).

5. Quoted in John H. Coatsworth, *Central America and the United States: The Clients and the Colossus* (New York: Twayne, 1994), 54.

6. Transcript, Adolf A. Berle Jr. Oral History, 6 July 1967, by Joseph E. O'Connor, Oral History Program, JFKL. For more details on the structure of executive branch bureaucracy as it relates to Latin American policy, see Gabriel Marcella, "The Presidential Advisory System," in *U.S.–Latin American Policymaking: A Reference Handbook,* ed. David W. Dent (Westport, CT: Greenwood, 1995), 275–306.

7. Memo, Battle to Bundy, "Language Proficiency of Foreign Service Officers at Latin American Posts," National Security File (hereafter NSF), Regional Security, box 215A, JFKL.

8. Mann observed: "Our program of economic aid to Latin America is . . . so small, in fact, that it could almost be financed by Export-Import Bank profits from loans to Latin America alone." Quoted in LaFeber, *Inevitable Revolutions,* 106. In December 1952, he also supported the rights of a Brazilian company to sell small amounts of iron ore to Poland, arguing that Latin American nations should not be treated differently than European ones and that such small-scale trade was not worth risking Brazilian resentment. Memo, Mann to Atwood, 11 December 1952, Record Group 59, General Records of the Department of State (hereafter RG 59), Records of Deputy Assistant Secretaries of State for Inter-American Affairs, 1945–1956, Subject File, box 1, National Archives, College Park, MD (hereafter NAMD).

9. Memo, Mann to Smith, "Ambassador Wiley's Proposal for a $50 Million Agricultural Grant for Panama," 13 February 1953, RG 59, Records of Deputy Assistant Secretaries of State for Inter-American Affairs, 1945–1956, Subject File, box 5, NAMD.

10. Michael Adamson, e.g., has written: "By 1953, the World Bank had become a conservative institution, conditioning its lending on the development of approved infrastructure projects, the settlement of outstanding private debts in default, and the adoption of 'policies and attitudes conducive to sound economic growth.'" Michael R. Adamson, "'The Most Important Single Aspect of Our Foreign Policy'? The Eisenhower Administration, Foreign Aid, and the Third World," in *The Eisenhower Administration the Third World, and the Globalization of the Cold War,* ed. Kathryn Statler. and Andrew Johns (Lanham, MD: Rowman & Littlefield, 2006), 47–74, 50. However, Mann had also shown himself more than willing to turn down requests for financial assistance when he thought it in his government's best interests to do so, successfully blocking a loan to Mexico in 1950 due to the nationalization of their oil industry. James F. Siekmeier, *Aid, Nationalism and Inter-American Relations: Guatemala, Bolivia, and the United States, 1945–1961* (Lewiston, NY: Edwin Mellen, 1999), 120.

11. For a detailed consideration of the influence of this group, see Thomas Tunstall Allcock, "The First Alliance for Progress? Reshaping the Eisenhower Administration's Latin American Policy," *Journal of Cold War Studies* 16, no. 1 (Winter 2014): 85–110.

12. Stephen Rabe, *Eisenhower and Latin America: The Foreign Policy of Anticommunism* (Chapel Hill: University of North Carolina Press, 1988), 31, quoted in LaFeber, *Inevitable Revolutions,* 109.

13. The economic component of Eisenhower's Latin American policy was summarized in the 1954 Randall Commission Report on Foreign Economic Policy, overseen by Clarence Randall of the Inland Steel Co. State Department Report, "Latin America: A Study of US Problems and Policy," 14 October 1953, Commission on Foreign Economic Policy Records, 1953–1954, Randall Commission, box 59, DDEL.

14. Quoted in Lars Schoultz, *Beneath the United States: A History of U.S. Policy toward Latin America* (Cambridge, MA: Harvard University Press, 1998), 347. See also Piero Gleijeses, *Shattered Hope: The Guatemalan Revolution and the United States, 1944–1954* (Princeton, NJ: Princeton University Press, 1991), 236.

15. Memo of Conversation, Dulles and Eisenhower, "Brazilian Loan," 20 February 1953, Papers of John Foster Dulles, Telephone Calls Series—White House Conversations, box 10, DDEL; Memo, Mann to Dulles, 20 February 1953, *FRUS, 1952–1954,* vol. 4, *The American Republics* (Washington, DC: US Government Printing Office, 1984), doc. 192.

16. The political sections of key policy documents focused almost exclusively on the problem. NSC 144/1, "United States Objectives and Courses of Action with Respect to Latin America," White House Office Files (hereafter WHO), Office of the Special Assistant for National Security Affairs, Records 1952–1961, NSC Series Policy Papers, box 4, DDEL.

17. Memo, Eisenhower to Dulles, 12 January 1954, Papers of John Foster Dulles, Subject Files, box 5—Milton Eisenhower Trip, DDEL; Rabe, *Eisenhower and Latin America,* 77–81; James F. Siekmeier, "Persistent Condor and Predatory Eagle: The Bolivian Revolution and the United States, 1952–1964," in Statler and Johns, eds., *The Eisenhower Administration,* 197–224, and *Aid, Nationalism, and Inter-American Relations.*

18. Telegram, Peurifoy to Department of State, 17 December 1953, *FRUS, 1952–1954,* vol. 4, *The American Republics,* doc. 427. For more detailed explorations of the circumstances surrounding the coup, see Nick Cullather, *Secret History: The CIA's Classified Account of Its Operations in Guatemala, 1952–1954* (Stanford, CA: Stanford University Press, 1999); Gleijeses, *Shattered Hope;* Richard H. Immerman, *The CIA in Guatemala: The Foreign Policy of Intervention* (Austin: University of Texas Press, 1982); Zachary Karabell, *Architects of Intervention: The United States, the Third World, and the Cold War, 1946–1962* (Baton Rouge: Louisiana State University Press, 1999), 93–195; and Rabe, *Eisenhower and Latin America,* 41–62.

19. Mann believed that military aid could "drive a wedge" between elements of the government. Memo, Mann to Miller, 31 July 1951, RG 59, Records of Deputy Assistant Secretaries of State for Inter-American Affairs, 1945–1956, Subject File, box 3, NAMD. However, he also rejected would-be plotters from the Guatemalan military who made "a number of ill-concealed allusions" during diplomatic meetings. Memo of Conversation, "Arms for Guatemala," 29 December 1950, RG 59, Bureau of Inter-American Affairs, Office of Middle American Affairs, Subject Files 1947–1956, box 3, NAMD.

20. Memo of Conversation, "United Fruit Company in Guatemala," 26 September 1951, RG 59, Bureau of Inter-American Affairs, Office of Middle American Affairs, Subject Files 1947–1956, box 3, NAMD.

21. Memo of Conversation, "United Fruit Company Negotiations with the Guatemalan Government," 14 November 1951, RG 59, Bureau of Inter-American Affairs, Office of Middle American Affairs, Subject Files 1947–1956, box 3, NAMD.

22. Memo of Conversation, "Call of Mr Jorge Toriello," 21 May 1952, RG 59, Bureau of Inter-American Affairs, Office of Middle American Affairs, Subject Files 1947–1956, box 4, NAMD; Cullather, *Secret History*, 17; David McKean, *Peddling Influence: Thomas "Tommy the Cork" Corcoran and the Birth of Modern Lobbying* (Hanover, NH: Steerforth, 2004), 220; Gleijeses, *Shattered Hope*, 231; Memo for the Record, "Central American Situation," 8 October 1952, *FRUS, 1952–1954*, vol. 4, *The American Republics*, doc. 24.

23. Memo, Mann to Matthews, "U.S. Policy toward Guatemala," 20 February 1953, RG 59, Records of Deputy Assistant Secretaries of State for Inter-American Affairs, 1945–1956, Subject File, box 1, NAMD; Memo, Mann to Charles Murphy, "Latin America and U.S. Policy," 11 December 1952, President's Special File, box 182, HSTL.

24. Memo for the Record, "PBFORTUNE—Meeting with DD/P," 19 August 1953, *FRUS, 1952–1954*, vol. 4, *The American Republics*, doc. 42; Transcript, Thomas C. Mann Oral History Interview, 23 February 1968, by Ed Edwin, Eisenhower Administration Project, Columbia University (hereafter EAP).

25. Transcript of Telephone Conversation, Dulles and McCardle, 28 June 1954, Papers of John Foster Dulles, Telephone Calls Series, box 2, DDEL; Report of the Subcommittee to Investigate Communist Aggression in Latin America, WHO, OCB Central File Series, box 73, DDEL.

26. Memo of Conversation, "Current Situation in Guatemala and Projected Aid Program," 29 April 1955, *FRUS, 1955–1957*, vol. 7, *American Republics: Central and South America* (Washington, DC: US Government Printing Office, 1987), doc. 27; Memo, "Grant Aid to Guatemala," ca. July 1955, WHO, OCB Central File Series, box 73, DDEL; Rabe, *Eisenhower and Latin America*, 62.

27. Foreign Service Dispatch, San Salvador, 14 October 1955, Record Group 84, Records of the Foreign Service Posts of the Department of State (hereafter RG 84), El Salvador, U.S. Legation and U.S. Embassy, San Salvador General Records 1936–1961, box 137, NAMD.

28. Memo, Mann to Hackney, 15 February 1956, RG 84, El Salvador, U.S. Legation and U.S. Embassy, San Salvador General Records 1936–1961, box 141, NAMD; Editorial Note, *FRUS, 1950*, vol. 2, *The United Nations; The Western Hemisphere* (Washington, DC: US Government Printing Office, 1976), n. 452.

29. Foreign Service Dispatch, San Salvador, "Economic Summary April–September 1955," 31 October 1955, RG 84, El Salvador, U.S. Legation and U.S. Embassy, San Salvador General Records 1936–1961, box 137, NAMD; Department of State Instruction, "Encouragement of Free Enterprise in Latin America," 18 January 1957, RG 84, El Salvador, U.S. Legation and U.S. Embassy, San Salvador General Records 1936–1961, box 140, NAMD; Mann Oral History, EAP.

30. NSC Progress Report, "U.S. Policy on Latin America," 28 March 1956, WHO, Office of the Special Assistant for National Security Affairs, Records 1952–1961, NSC Series Policy Papers, box 13, DDEL; NSC 5613/1, "U.S. Policy toward Latin America," 25 September 1956, WHO, Office of the Special Assistant

for National Security Affairs, Records 1952–1961, NSC Series Policy Papers, box 18, DDEL.

31. Foreign Service Dispatch, San Salvador, "Assertions That United States Latin American Policy Supports Dictatorial Governments," 5 September 1957, RG 84, El Salvador, U.S. Legation and U.S. Embassy, San Salvador General Records 1936–1961, box 140, NAMD.

32. For instance, Mann would deliver an only slightly edited version of the article as a speech at his alma mater, Baylor University, in 1960 and in a later interview argued: "The [Monroe] Doctrine is an awful thing, nobody ought to defend the Monroe Doctrine." Address by Thomas C. Mann at Baylor University, Waco, TX, "The Democratic Ideal in the Latin American Policy of the United States," 11 November 1960, Thomas Mann Papers, box 303, TC; Mann Oral History, HSTL.

33. Transcript, Clarence Douglas Dillon Oral History Interview, 2 May 1972, by John Luter, Oral History Research Office, Columbia University.

34. Dillon believed that Humphrey had effectively established a system whereby every State Department memo and telegram that so much as mentioned monetary affairs required clearance from the Treasury Department. Dillon Oral History.

35. "Those top two had never been to Latin America before, and I think they learned a lesson," Rubottom later recalled. "They got their eyes opened while they were there." Transcript, Roy Rubottom Oral History Interview, 22 December 1969, by John Luter, EAP.

36. Thomas C. Mann Unpublished Memoirs, Thomas Mann Papers, box 2, DDEL; Mann Oral History, EAP; Rubottom Oral History, EAP.

37. Rubottom Oral History, EAP; Memo, Mann to Rubottom, "Practices of American Business Concerns in Foreign Countries," 7 October 1957, Thomas Mann Papers, box 299, TC.

38. Draft, "Economic Cooperation in United States Foreign Relations," ca. December 1957, Thomas Mann Papers, box 299, TC; "Off-the-Record Comments of Thomas C. Mann on the Economic Situation in Latin America Made before Dinner Meeting of the Council on Foreign Relations," 19 January 1958, Thomas Mann Papers, box 303, TC.

39. Raúl Prebisch, *The Economic Development of Latin America* (New York: UN Department of Economic Affairs, 1950), and "A New Economic Model for Latin America," in *Latin America and the United States: A Documentary History*, ed. Robert H. Holden and Eric Zolov (New York: Oxford University Press, 2000), 198–200, 189–92. For explorations of Prebisch's career and the impact of dependency theory, see Edgar J. Dosman, *The Life and Times of Raúl Prebisch, 1901–1986* (Montreal: McGill-Queen's University Press, 2008); John S. Gitlitz and Henry A. Landsberger, "The Inter-American Political Economy: How Dependable Is Dependency Theory?" in *Latin America, the United States, and the Inter-American System*, ed. John D. Martz and Lars Schoultz (Boulder, CO: Westview, 1980), 45–70; and Robert A. Packenham, *The Dependency Movement: Scholarship and Politics in Development Studies* (Cambridge, MA: Harvard University Press, 1992).

40. "Americas Study Set," *New York Times,* 27 October 1958.

41. Juscelino Kubitschek, "Operation Pan America," in Holden and Zolov, eds., *Latin America and the United States,* 214–15; Address by Senate Democratic Leader Lyndon B. Johnson at the El Paso Chamber of Commerce, 6 November 1958, Office Files of George Reedy, box 23, LBJL.

42. Dwight D. Eisenhower, "Letter to President Kubitschek of Brazil on the Occasion of Secretary Dulles' Visit," 5 August 1958, APP, PPP, http://www.presidency .ucsb.edu/ws/?pid=11159; Rabe, *Eisenhower and Latin America,* 105. Kubitschek had hoped that the initial capitalization of the IADB would be as high as $5 billion; Eisenhower agreed to $1 billion. Walker, "Mixing the Sweet with the Sour," 45.

43. Schoultz, *Beneath the United States,* 356.

44. Memo, Mann to Secretary of State, "Proposal for OAS Action on Cuba Problem," 22 November 1960, RG 59, Bureau of Inter-American Affairs, Subject Files of the Assistant Secretary 1959–1962, box 2, NAMD. For details of Mann and Rubottom's initial assessments of Castro, see Lars Schoultz, *That Infernal Little Cuban Republic: The United States and the Cuban Revolution* (Chapel Hill: University of North Carolina Press, 2009), 90–92.

45. Memo of Conversation, "Properties of the American and Foreign Power Company in Latin America," 3 May 1960, and Memo, Herter to Eisenhower, "Assistance to Guatemala, Costa Rica, and Nicaragua," 15 November 1960, both RG 59, Bureau of Inter-American Affairs, Subject Files of the Assistant Secretary 1959–1962, box 2, NAMD; Memo, Mann to Donnelly, 4 February 1960, Thomas Mann Papers, box 299, TC.

46. The Act of Bogota can be found online at http://avalon.law.yale.edu/20th _century/intam08.asp. For more on the early influence of modernization theory, see Engerman, Gilman, Haefele, and Latham, eds., *Staging Growth;* Gilman, *Mandarins of the Future;* and Bevan Sewell, "Early Modernisation Theory? The Eisenhower Administration and the Foreign Policy of Development in Brazil," *English Historical Review* 125, no. 517 (December 2010): 1449–80.

47. Mann Oral History, DDEL; Notes on CFEP Meeting, 12 October 1960, WHO, NSC Staff Papers, Special Staff File Series, box 5, DDEL.

48. "Rubottom Is Out of Top Latin Post," *New York Times,* 29 July 1960; Thomas C. Mann, "Paper Prepared for the New Secretary," ca. November 1960, RG 59, Bureau of Inter-American Affairs, Subject Files of the Assistant Secretary 1959–1962, box 2, NAMD.

49. Mann, "Paper Prepared for the New Secretary"; Rabe, *Eisenhower and Latin America,* 141.

50. Broadly speaking, some argue that Eisenhower's programs laid the foundation for Kennedy's aid initiatives, while others view them as too limited in scope and ambition to compare to the Alliance for Progress. For examples of the first school of thought, see Rabe, *Eisenhower and Latin America,* 148–50; Kenneth A. Rodman, *Sanctity versus Sovereignty: The United States and the Nationalization of Natural Resource Investments* (New York: Columbia University Press, 1988), 9; Schoultz,

Beneath the United States, 356; and James M. Hagen and Vernon W. Ruttan, "Development Policy under Eisenhower and Kennedy," *Journal of Developing Areas* 23, no. 1 (October 1988): 1–30, 9. For examples of the second, see Adamson, "The Most Important Single Aspect," 66; LaFeber, *Inevitable Revolutions,* 141–48; and William D. Rogers, *The Twilight Struggle: The Alliance for Progress and the Politics of Development in Latin America* (New York: Random House, 1967), 32–33.

51. Henry Raymont, "Mann Is Urged for Latin Job," *Washington Daily News,* 4 October 1958, Thomas Mann Papers, box 325, TC; Tad Szulc, "U.S.-Latin Relations Take on 'New Look,'" *New York Times,* 17 May 1959, quoted in McPherson, *Yankee No!* 123.

52. Thomas Mann, "Comments on Inter-American Relations," 26 February 1959, reel 8, frames 676–86, *Minutes and Documents of the Cabinet Meetings of President Eisenhower (1953–1961).*

53. Rabe, *Most Dangerous Area,* 1–3; Editorial Note, *FRUS, 1961–1963,* vol. 12, *American Republics* (Washington, DC: US Government Printing Office, 1996), doc. 1.

54. For details of the formulation of the Alliance for Progress, see Goodwin, *Remembering America,* 149–66; and Rogers, *The Twilight Struggle,* 29–34. For relevant portions of the debate, see Richard M. Nixon and John F. Kennedy, "Debating Cuba and Castro," in Holden and Zolov, eds., *Latin America and the United States,* 215–18.

55. Memo, Mann to Fitzgerald, "Latin American Program," 25 January 1961, RG 59, Bureau of Inter-American Affairs, Subject Files of the Assistant Secretary 1959–1962, box 3, NAMD; Memo, Bowles to Kennedy, 5 December 1960, Chester Bowles Papers, box 210, Yale University Library, New Haven, CT (hereafter YUL).

56. Mann Oral History, DDEL; Mann Oral History, JFKL; Letter, Mann to Rubottom, 31 January 1961, RG 59, Bureau of Inter-American Affairs, Subject Files of the Assistant Secretary 1959–1962, box 2, NAMD.

57. Report from the Task Force on Immediate Latin American Problems to President-Elect Kennedy, 4 January 1961, *FRUS, 1961–1963,* vol. 12, *American Republics,* doc. 2; Goodwin, *Remembering America,* 151.

58. Draft Memo, Gordon to Goodwin, 6 March 1961, NSF, Subjects, Alliance for Progress, box 290A, JFKL; Memo, Schlesinger to Goodwin, "Latin America Speech," 8 March 1961, *FRUS, 1961–1963,* vol. 12, *American Republics,* doc. 6.

59. John F. Kennedy, "Address at a White House Reception for Members of Congress and for the Diplomatic Corps of the Latin American Republics," 13 March 1961, APP, PPP, http://www.presidency.ucsb.edu/ws/?pid=8531.

60. "Statement by Secretary Dillon," *Department of State Bulletin* 44, no. 355 (28 August 1961): 356–60.

61. Goodwin, *Remembering America,* 149; Rogers, *Twilight Struggle,* 31–33; Mann Oral History, DDEL.

62. For key texts of modernization theory, see Walt W. Rostow, *The Stages of Economic Growth: A Non-Communist Manifesto* (Cambridge: Cambridge University Press, 1960); and Max F. Millikan and Donald L. M. Blackmer, eds., *The Emerging Nations:*

Their Growth and United States Policy (Boston: Little, Brown, 1961). For explorations of its impact, see Engerman, Gilman, Haefele, and Latham, eds., *Staging Growth;* Latham, *Modernization as Ideology;* and Taffet, *Foreign Aid as Foreign Policy.*

63. Lars Schoultz compares the appeal of modernization theory to that of Huntington Wilson's dollar diplomacy hypothesis, which argued: "Prosperity means contentment and contentment means repose." Schoultz, *Beneath the United States,* 357.

64. Memo, Rostow to Kennedy, "The Idea of an Economic Development Decade," 2 March 1963, NSF, Regional Security, box 215, JFKL. For details of Rostow's career, see Milne, *America's Rasputin* (Kennedy quote on 99). For Rostow's contributions to the Alliance charter, see Pearce, *Rostow,* 107.

65. Mann Oral History, DDEL. For more on the intellectual connections between the New Deal and modernization theory, see Gilman, *Mandarins of the Future,* 12–20.

66. Memo, Berle to Kennedy, "Hemispheric Policy," 25 April 1961, *FRUS, 1961–1963,* vol. 12, *American Republics,* doc. 10. The historian Joseph Tulchin, e.g., has argued that, through the Alliance for Progress, the United States "deliberately manipulated its Wilsonian past . . . in return for support in the campaign to neutralize the influence of Fidel Castro in the hemisphere." Joseph S. Tulchin, "The United States and Latin America in the 1960s," *Journal of Interamerican Studies and World Affairs* 30, no. 1 (Spring 1988): 1–36, 13.

67. Memo, Robert Kennedy to John Kennedy, 11 September 1961, NSF, Regional Security, box 215A, JFKL; "Moscow Blames U.S. for Attack," *New York Times,* 18 March 1961. USAID figures on foreign aid are available at https://explorer.usaid .gov/aid-trends.html.

68. Arthur M. Schlesinger Jr., *A Thousand Days: John F. Kennedy in the White House* (London: Deutsch, 1965), 681–82. The obvious flaws in the plan and the failure of multiple officials to acknowledge them are well covered elsewhere. For good examples, see James Blight and Peter Kornbluh, eds., *Politics of Illusion: The Bay of Pigs Invasion Reexamined* (Boulder, CO: Lynne Rienner, 1999); Piero Gleijeses, "Ships in the Night: The CIA, the White House and the Bay of Pigs," *Journal of Latin American Studies* 27, no. 1 (February 1995): 1–42; and Howard Jones, *The Bay of Pigs* (Oxford: Oxford University Press, 2008).

69. Memo, Mann to Rusk, 15 February 1961, *FRUS, 1961–1963,* vol. 10, *Cuba, January 1961–September 1962* (Washington, DC: US Government Printing Office, 1997), doc. 45.

70. Gleijeses, "Ships in the Night," 28; Mann Oral History, JFKL.

71. Observations regarding Mann's absolute loyalty can be found in Transcript, Pat Holt Oral History Interview VI: The Dominican Republic and Gulf of Tonkin Affairs, 10 November 1980, by Donald A. Ritchie, US Senate Oral History Project, https://www.senate.gov/artandhistory/history/resources/pdf/Holt_interview_6 .pdf. "In retrospect, I would never again vote for any large clandestine operation," Mann would claim in a later interview. Mann Oral History, JFKL.

72. Memo, Schlesinger to Kennedy, 10 March 1961, NSF, Regional Security, box 215, JFKL.

73. Transcript, Richard T. Davies Oral History Interview, 11 December 1980, by Peter Jessup, Columbia University Oral History Project, New York; Transcript, Wymberly Coerr Oral History Interview, 22 November 1967, by Larry J. Hackman, JFKL.

74. Martin, *Kennedy and Latin America,* 154–55; Report, "Mexico and the Alliance for Progress," 13 June 1962, Papers of Arthur Schlesinger Jr., White House Files, Classified Subject Files, box WH41, JFKL; CIA Report on Lopez Mateos, 22 June 1962, and Commerce Department Report, "Mexico's Commercial Policy," 15 June 1962, both President's Office Files, Countries, box 122, JFKL. For a detailed exploration of Mexico's role in the Cold War, see Keller, *Mexico's Cold War.*

75. Memo, "The President's State Visit to Mexico," 4 June 1962, President's Office Files, Countries, box 122, JFKL; Memo, Battle to Bundy, "Dollar Financial Assistance to Mexico," 25 March 1962, NSF, Country File (hereafter CF), Mexico, box 141A, JFKL. USAID figures on foreign aid are available at https://explorer.usaid.gov/aid-trends.html.

76. Sarah McLendon, "Mann, Telles Leave Soon for Vital Jobs," *Waco Herald Tribune,* 30 April 1961, and Special Report, *Mexican American Review,* May 1961, both Thomas Mann Papers, box 326, TC.

77. Telegram, Mann to Secretary of State, 6 December 1961, Papers of Arthur Schlesinger Jr., White House Files, Classified Subject Files, box WH41, JFKL; Telegram, Mann to Secretary of State, 16 April 1963, NSF, Countries, box 141A, JFKL. For a more critical assessment of Mann's handling of the Cuban issue, see Keller, *Mexico's Cold War,* 130–35.

78. Mann Oral History, JFKL; Telegram, Mann to Secretary of State, 16 April 1963, NSF, Countries, box 141A, JFKL.

79. David Weber, "Mann Scores Hit with Mexicans," *Dallas Morning News,* 15 May 1961, David Weber, "Mann a New Image in Mexico," *Houston Post,* 19 July 1961, Walter Trohan, "Report from Washington," *Chicago Daily Tribune,* 25 November 1961, and Jules Dubois, "Our Diplomats South of the Border: Thomas Clifton Mann Is a Career Envoy Who Commands Respect," *Chicago Daily Tribune,* 12 December 1961, all Thomas Mann Papers, box 326, TC.

80. Paul Kennedy, "Mexico Acclaims Kennedy on Visit; 1,000,000 Cheer," *New York Times,* 30 June 1962; Carroll Kilpatrick, "Kennedy Welcomed in Mexico," *Washington Post,* 30 June 1962.

81. Message of Congratulations from Kennedy to Mann, 1 July 1962, Letter, Mann to Kennedy, 10 July 1962, and Letter, Tello to Kennedy, 7 July 1962, all President's Office Files, Countries, box 122, JFKL; Mann Oral History, JFKL.

82. Joint Communiqué from Presidents Kennedy and Lopez Mateos, 30 June 1962, President's Office Files, Countries, box 122, JFKL.

83. Mann Oral History, JFKL; Martin, *Kennedy and Latin America,* 413.

84. The 1944 agreement guaranteed that an annual quantity of 1.5 million acrefeet of water from the Colorado River would flow south over the border. In 1961, the

salinity of the water Mexico was receiving jumped from an annual average of about eight hundred parts of salt per million to nearly fifteen hundred parts per million. Herbert Brownell and Samuel D. Eaton, "The Colorado River Salinity Problem with Mexico," *American Journal of International Law* 69, no. 2 (April, 1975): 255–71.

85. Telegram, Mann to Secretary of State, 8 March 1962, Press Release, "1944 Water Treaty with Mexico," 16 March 1962, Telegram, Mann to Secretary of State, 18 June 1962, and Telegram, Mann to Martin, 22 August 1963, all NSF, Countries, box 141A, JFKL. Kennedy had not helped matters when he derailed a discussion of the dispute with the Mexican ambassador by delivering a lengthy lecture on the dangers of communism. Memo of Conversation, Kennedy and Ambassador Flores, 28 February 1963, NSF, Countries, box 141A, JFKL.

86. Memo of Conversation, "Colorado River Salinity Problem," 11 October 1963, and Telegram, Mann to Secretary of State, 24 October 1963, both NSF, Countries, box 141A, JFKL.

87. James E. Hill Jr., "El Chamizal: A Century-Old Boundary Dispute," *Geographical Review* 55, no. 4 (October 1965): 510–22; Martin, *Kennedy and Latin America*, 157; Transcript, Thomas C. Mann Oral History Interview I, 4 November 1968, by Joe B. Frantz, LBJL.

88. Airgram, State Department to Mann and Enclosed Note for Tello, 6 August 1962, Memo, Brubeck to Dungan, "Status Report on Chamizal Negotiations," 27 February 1963, Airgram, Mann to State Department, "Draft Text of Proposed Joint US-Mexican Memorandum," 9 March 1963, Telegram, Mann to Secretary of State, 25 April 1963, Telegram, Mann to Secretary of State and Translation of Lopez Mateos Statement, 19 July 1963, and Memo, Read to Bundy, "Full Power for Ambassador Thomas Mann to Sign a Convention with Mexico," 27 August 1963, all NSF, Countries, box 141A, JFKL.

89. Mann Oral History, JFKL; Letter, Mayfield to Mann, 23 July 1962, Record of Meeting, El Paso Chamber of Commerce, 21 February 1963, and Records of Meetings, El Paso International City Association, 19 July 1962 and 19 February 1963, all White House Staff Files, Papers of Ralph A. Dungan, box 2, JFKL; Mann Oral History, LBJL.

90. Report, "U.S. Relations with Mexico," NSF, CF, Latin America, box 59, LBJL; Keller, *Mexico's Cold War*, esp. chap. 4.

91. Mann Oral History, JFKL.

2. A New Deal for the New Frontier

1. Mann Oral History, JFKL.

2. The most critical accounts come from former Kennedy aides, but historians' accounts have also endorsed the view that there was a substantial reorientation of policy. For examples, see Dent, *Historical Dictionary*, 286; Leonard, "Search for Security"; and Schlesinger, *Robert Kennedy*, 689, and "Myth and Reality." Alternatively, Joseph Tulchin has argued: "There is no evidence that a systematic re-evaluation of

policy had occurred." He has also noted: "A great deal of valuable work was done to ameliorate the conditions of underdevelopment because of Johnson's policies, . . . [but] the detailed history of this good work has yet to be written." Tulchin, "The Promise of Progress," 230. Jeffrey Taffet, Stephen Rabe, and Tony Smith have also emphasized the gap between the Kennedy administration's rhetoric and the reality of its policies and downplayed the idea of a radical change in policy between administrations, but they are still largely critical of Johnson and Mann. See Smith, "The Alliance for Progress"; Rabe, *Most Dangerous Area;* and Taffet, *Foreign Aid as Foreign Policy.*

3. Memo, Bundy to Kennedy, "White House Organization," 16 May 1961, *FRUS, 1961–1963,* vol. 25, *Organization of Foreign Policy; Information Policy; United Nations; Scientific Matters* (Washington, DC: Government Printing Office, 2001), doc. 13.

4. His success had led to Puerto Rico being christened "the economic miracle of the Caribbean." See A. W. Maldonado, *Teodoro Moscoso and Puerto Rico's Operation Bootstrap* (Gainesville: University of Florida Press, 1997).

5. Taffet, *Foreign Aid as Foreign Policy,* 38.

6. Rostow, *The Stages of Economic Growth.*

7. Journal Entry, 2 February 1961, Papers of Arthur Schlesinger Jr., Journals, box 311, New York Public Library, Manuscripts and Archives, New York (hereafter NYPL); Memo, Bundy to Johnson, "The White House Staff," 23 November 1963, NSF, Agency File, AID & Alliance for Progress (hereafter AF), box 1, LBJL. For further details, see John Dumbrell, "The Action Intellectuals," in *A Companion to John F. Kennedy,* ed. Marc Selverstone (Hoboken, NJ: Wiley-Blackwell, 2014), 133–51.

8. Memo, Schlesinger to Kennedy, "Bureau of Inter-American Affairs," 27 June 1961, Papers of Arthur Schlesinger Jr., White House Files, Subject Files, box WH2, JFKL.

9. Arthur M. Schlesinger Jr., *Journals, 1952–2000* (New York: Penguin, 2007), 164; Memo, Bundy to Kennedy, "White House Organization," 16 May 1961, *FRUS, 1961–1963,* vol. 25, *Organization of Foreign Policy; Information Policy; United Nations; Scientific Matters,* doc. 13; Goodwin, *Remembering America,* 205–15. Ralph Dungan was apparently told by his fellow Kennedy aide Kenny O'Donnell "to keep an eye on that 'Goddamned Goodwin and Schlesinger, crazy nuts on Latin America.'" Quoted in Woods, *LBJ,* 494.

10. Memo, Morales-Carrion to Martin, "US Mexican Relations," 24 April 1963, Papers of Arthur Schlesinger Jr., White House Files, Subject Files, box WH15, JFKL.

11. Telegram, Mann to Woodward, 17 November 1961, RG 59, Bureau of Inter-American Affairs, Subject Files of the Assistant Secretary 1959–1962, box 3, NAMD; LaFeber, "Thomas C. Mann," 185.

12. Telegram, Mann to State Department, 28 September 1962, Airgram, Mann to State Department, 2 October 1963, and Telegram, Mann to State Department, 27 April 1962, all Papers of Arthur Schlesinger Jr., White House Files, Subject Files, box WH15, JFKL.

13. Quoted in Rabe, *Most Dangerous Area,* 156.

14. Taffet, *Foreign Aid as Foreign Policy,* 27–31; Morales-Carrion, "The Alliance for Progress: A Political and Ideological Force in the Hemisphere," 9 April 1962, NSF, Departments and Agencies, box 290A, JFKL.

15. Joseph Grunwald, "The Alliance for Progress," *Proceedings of the Academy of Political Science* 27, no. 4 (May 1964): 386–401; Robert David Johnson, "Constitutionalism Abroad and at Home: The United States Senate and the Alliance for Progress, 1961–1967," *International History Review* 21, no. 2 (June 1999): 414–42, 417.

16. Bruce Kuklick, *Blind Oracles: Intellectuals and War from Kennan to Kissinger* (Princeton, NJ: Princeton University Press, 2006), 1; Memo, Bowdler to Rostow, 24 June 1966, NSF, AF, box 8, LBJL; Taffet, *Foreign Aid as Foreign Policy,* 38–39.

17. Research Memo, Roger Hilsman, "Dictatorial Acts and Attitudes of Selected Latin American Regimes," 17 September 1962, Papers of Arthur Schlesinger Jr., White House Files, Classified Subject Files, box WH-40, JFKL; Rogers, *The Twilight Struggle,* 122; State Department Intelligence Memo, 24 December 1963, NSF, CF, Latin America, box 1, LBJL.

18. L. Ronald Scheman, "The Alliance for Progress: Concept and Creativity," in Scheman, ed., *The Alliance for Progress,* 3–62, 14; Rabe, *Most Dangerous Area,* 162.

19. Editorial, "One Down, Nine to Go," *Vision,* 14 August 1962, Papers of Arthur Schlesinger Jr., Writings, box W-1, JFKL; "A Year of the Alliance," *New York Times,* 17 August 1962.

20. Memo, Brubeck to Bundy, "Survey of Economic Growth, Trade and Investment in Latin America—1962," 6 February 1963, NSF, Regional Security, box 216, JFKL; Taffet, *Foreign Aid as Foreign Policy,* 41 (table of foreign aid appropriations); OAS Report, "The Alliance for Progress: Its Second Year, 1962–1963," NSF, AF, box 4, LBJL.

21. Tad Szulc, "U.S. Closes Rifts on Latin Policy," *New York Times,* 28 April 1962; Goodwin, *Remembering America,* 215.

22. Rodman, *Sanctity versus Sovereignty,* 169; Jerome Levinson and Juan de Onis, *The Alliance That Lost Its Way: A Critical Report on the Alliance for Progress* (Chicago: Quadrangle, 1970), 72.

23. Rodman, *Sanctity versus Sovereignty,* 171–74; Memo, Schlesinger to Dungan, "Alliance for Progress," 15 October 1962, and Memo, Schlesinger to Dungan, "Alliance for Progress II," 18 October 1962, both Papers of Arthur Schlesinger Jr., White House Files, Subject Files, box WH-2, JFKL.

24. "Special Message to the Congress on Free World Defense and Assistance Programs," 2 April 1963, APP, PPP, http://www.presidency.ucsb.edu/ws/index .php?pid=9136; Memo, Bell to Bundy, 21 September 1963, and Memo, Dungan to Bundy, 24 September 1963, both NSF, Regional Security, box 216, JFKL.

25. James D. Cochrane, "U.S. Policy toward Recognition of Governments and Promotion of Democracy in Latin America since 1963," *Journal of Latin American Studies* 4, no. 2 (November 1972): 275–91, 275–76; Circular to All ARA Posts, "The Martin Doctrine," 5 October 1963, NSF, Regional Security File, box 216, JFKL.

26. Memo, Schlesinger to Kennedy, "The Martin Doctrine," 8 October 1963, and Circular to All ARA Posts, "The Martin Doctrine," 5 October 1963, both NSF, Regional Security File, box 216, JFKL.

27. President's Press Conference, 31 October 1963, NSF, Departments and Agencies, box 287, JFKL. Following the assassination of the Dominican dictator Rafael Trujillo in May 1961, Kennedy is said to have remarked: "There are three possibilities in descending order of preference: a decent democratic regime, a continuation of the Trujillo regime, or a Castro regime. We ought to aim at the first but we really cannot renounce the second until we are sure that we can avoid the third." Quoted in Schlesinger, *A Thousand Days*, 769.

28. Memo, Fishburn to Martin, "The Alliance for Progress—a Shift in Emphasis," 4 December 1963, RG 59, Bureau of Inter-American Affairs, Assistant Secretary and US Coordinator Alliance for Progress, Subject and Country Files 1962–1975, box 2, NAMD.

29. Memo, Schlesinger to Kennedy and Rusk, 28 October 1963, Papers of Arthur Schlesinger Jr., White House Files, Classified Subject Files, box WH-40, JFKL; Memo, Bundy to Kennedy, 25 May 1963, and Memo, Bundy to Mann et al., 21 February 1964, both NSF, Regional Security, box 216, JFKL; "Address in Miami before the Inter-American Press Association," 18 November 1963, APP, PPP, http://www.presidency.ucsb.edu/ws/?pid=9529.

30. Dallek, *Lone Star Rising;* Robert A. Caro, *The Years of Lyndon Johnson: Master of the Senate* (New York: Vintage, 2002); Woods, *LBJ;* "George A. Smathers, United States Senator, 1951–1969," Oral History Interviews, Senate Historical Office, Washington, DC.

31. Article quoted in Mitchell Lerner, "'A Big Tree of Peace and Justice': The Vice Presidential Travels of Lyndon Johnson," *Diplomatic History* 34, no. 2 (March 2010): 357–93, 357; Transcript, Ralph Dungan Oral History Interview, 18 April 1969, by Paige Mulhollan, LBJL.

32. For details of Johnson's early life, see Caro, *The Path to Power;* Dallek, *Lone Star Rising;* and Woods, *LBJ.*

33. Quoted in Randall B. Woods, *Fulbright: A Biography* (Cambridge: Cambridge University Press, 1995), 411. See also Jeff Shesol, *Mutual Contempt: Lyndon Johnson, Robert Kennedy, and the Feud That Defined a Decade* (New York: Norton, 1997).

34. Senate Papers, Subject Files 1958, box 602, LBJL; Senate Papers, Subject Files 1960—Latin America, LBJL; Dungan Oral History, LBJL.

35. Address by Senate Democratic Leader Lyndon B. Johnson at the El Paso Chamber of Commerce, 6 November 1958, and Remarks by Senate Democratic Leader Lyndon B. Johnson on the Senate Floor, 19 August 1960, both Office Files of George Reedy, box 23, LBJL; "Meets Mexico's President," *New York Times,* 19 October 1959; Martin, *Kennedy and Latin America,* 157. See also Julie Leininger Pycior, *LBJ and Mexican Americans: The Paradox of Power* (Austin: University of Texas Press, 1997).

36. Transcript of Telephone Conversation, Johnson and Donald Cook, 30 November 1963, Michael R. Beschloss, *Taking Charge: The Johnson White House*

Tapes, 1963–1964 (New York: Simon & Schuster, 1997), 74; Roger Hilsman, *To Move a Nation: The Politics of Foreign Policy in the Administration of John F. Kennedy* (New York: Doubleday, 1967), 44–47.

37. Memo for the Record, 2 December 1963, McCone Memoranda, Meetings with the President, box 1, LBJL.

38. Memo, McCone to Johnson, 3 December 1963, NSF, AF, box 4, LBJL; Memo for the Record, 9 December 1963, McCone Memoranda, Meetings with the President, box 1, LBJL.

39. The journalist Paul Geyelin wrote in 1966: "What a lot of the liberal, left-of-center critics in Washington and Latin America were quick to conclude was that because Tom Mann was a Texan, he must be an old Johnson crony, that he must also be a Johnson Trojan horse." Geyelin, *Johnson and the World*, 96. For examples in the literature, see LaFeber, *Inevitable Revolutions*, 156; and Walker, "Mixing the Sweet with the Sour," 60.

40. Mann Oral History, LBJL.

41. Memo, Battle to Bundy, "Language Proficiency of Foreign Service Officers at Latin American Posts," NSF, Regional Security, box 215A, JFKL; Woods, *LBJ,* 496.

42. Mann Oral History, JFKL; Lyndon Johnson, "Letter to Thomas C. Mann upon His Assuming New Responsibilities for Latin American Affairs," 15 December 1963, APP, PPP, http://www.presidency.ucsb.edu/ws/index.php?pid=26376.

43. "Johnson's Inter-American Policy," *Excelsior,* 17 December 1963, "An American Community," *Novedades,* 17 December 1963, UPI Report, Morris W. Rosenberg, "Outlook on Mann in His New Post," ca. December 1963, and "Thomas C. Mann, Amigo Sincero de Mexico," *El Universal,* 23 December 1963, all Thomas Mann Papers, box 328, TC.

44. Lyndon Johnson, "Remarks on the Alliance for Progress to Representatives of the Countries of Latin America," 26 November 1963, APP, PPP, http://www.presidency.ucsb.edu/ws/?pid=26785.

45. Dungan Oral History, LBJL; Transcript, Arthur M. Schlesinger Jr. Oral History Interview, 4 November 1971, by Joe B. Frantz, LBJL; Goodwin, *Remembering America,* 243–44.

46. Theodore C. Sorensen, *The Kennedy Legacy* (London: Macmillan, 1969), 93.

47. Letter, Mann to Braden, 19 December 1963, Thomas Mann Papers, box 303, TC; Mann Oral History, JFKL; Schlesinger, *Journals,* 213; "High Latin Post Seen for Mann," *Mexico City Times,* 13 December 1963, Thomas Mann Papers, box 328, TC.

48. Memo, Dungan to Johnson, December 10, 1963, White House Central Files (hereafter WHCF), Name File, box M67, LBJL; Memo, Schlesinger to Johnson, 14 December 1963, Papers of Arthur M. Schlesinger Jr., White House Files, Subject Files, box WH-2, JFKL.

49. Schlesinger, *Robert Kennedy,* 631; Goodwin, *Remembering America,* 245.

50. Mann Oral History, HSTL; Schlesinger Oral History, LBJL.

51. Johnson, "Constitutionalism Abroad and at Home," 433–35; Transcript, Lincoln Gordon Oral History Interview I, 10 July 1969, by Paige E. Mulhollan, LBJL, https://www.adst.org/OH%20TOCs/Gordon,%20A.%20Lincoln.LBJ.pdf; Transcript of Telephone Conversation, Ball and Heller, 17 December 1963, Papers of George W. Ball, box 3, LBJL; Memo, Dungan to Johnson, December 10, 1963, Letter, Milton Eisenhower to Dungan, 20 December 1963, and Letter, Leslie Cogbill to Johnson, 21 January 1964, all WHCF, Name File, box M67, LBJL.

52. Woods, *LBJ*, 496; Transcript of Telephone Conversation, Johnson and Fulbright, 14 December 1963, Beschloss, *Taking Charge*, 101.

53. Quoted in Rabe, *Most Dangerous Area*, 174.

54. Mann Oral History, HSTL.

55. For more on New Deal–era foreign policy, particularly in Latin America, see Robert Dallek, *Franklin D. Roosevelt and American Foreign Policy, 1932–1945* (Oxford: Oxford University Press, 1995); Lloyd Gardner, *Economic Aspects of New Deal Diplomacy* (Madison: University of Wisconsin Press, 1964); Gellman, *Good Neighbor Diplomacy;* Kiran Klaus Patel, *The New Deal: A Global History* (Princeton, NJ: Princeton University Press, 2016), 147–66; and Sarah T. Phillips, *This Land, This Nation: Conservation, Rural America, and the New Deal* (Cambridge: Cambridge University Press, 2007), 242–85.

56. Transcript of Telephone Conversation, Ball and Bundy, 16 April 1964, Papers of George W. Ball, box 2, LBJL; Details of the Fabian Society's history and activities can be found at http://www.fabians.org.uk. See also Edward R. Pease, *The History of the Fabian Society*, 3rd ed. (London: F. Cass, 1963); and Deirdre Terrins and Phillip Whitehead, eds., *100 Years of Fabian Socialism: 1884–1984* (London: Fabian Society, 1984).

57. Address by Senate Democratic Leader Lyndon B. Johnson at the El Paso Chamber of Commerce, 6 November 1958, Office Files of George Reedy, box 23, LBJL; Memo, Bowdler to Rostow, "Research Projects: The OAS Summit," 17 October 1968, NSF, International Meetings and Travel File, box 19, LBJL.

58. Memo, Schlesinger to Dungan, "Alliance for Progress," 15 October 1962, Papers of Arthur Schlesinger Jr., White House Files, Subject Files, box WH-2, JFKL; Memo, Goodwin to Kennedy, 14 March 1962, Papers of Arthur Schlesinger Jr., Writings, box W1, JFKL.

59. *Liberal internationalism* in a US context is most often associated with Woodrow Wilson's attempts to build a democratic world order from the ashes of World War I. Drawing on Kant's theory of democratic peace, it refers to the idea that liberal nations should actively attempt to spread democracy in order to achieve a lasting world peace. This can involve humanitarian aid, economic pressure, or, in some cases, military intervention. For explorations of the history and impact of liberal internationalism, see John D. Martz, "Democracy and the Imposition of Values: Definitions and Diplomacy," in Martz and Schoultz, eds., *The Inter-American System*, 145–72; Michael H. Hunt, *Ideology and U.S. Foreign Policy* (New Haven, CT: Yale University Press, 1987); Tony Smith, *America's Mission: The United States*

and the Worldwide Struggle for Democracy in the Twentieth Century (Princeton, NJ: Princeton University Press, 1994); Mark Peceny, *Democracy at the Point of Bayonets* (University Park: Pennsylvania State University Press, 1999), 1–48; and Michael Cox, G. John Ikenberry, and Takashi Inoguchi, eds., *American Democracy Promotion: Impulses, Strategies, and Impacts* (Oxford: Oxford University Press, 2000).

60. John F. Kennedy Inaugural Address, 20 January 1961, APP, PPP, http://www.presidency.ucsb.edu/ws/index.php?pid=8032.

61. Mann would later demonstrate his lack of attention to the finer points of internal politics, commenting: "The main thing is what are the issues and what really should we be doing about them. That's the ball game, and the rest of the stuff I never paid much attention to." Mann Oral History, JFKL.

62. Recording of Telephone Conversation, Johnson and Mann, 9 December 1963, Recording 6312.06, Miller Center, Charlottesville, VA; Notes, 10 December 1963, Thomas Mann Papers, box 303, TC.

63. Transcript of Telephone Conversation, Mann and Bullett, 17 October 1964, Thomas Mann Papers, box 309, TC; Warren I. Cohen, *Dean Rusk* (Totowa, NJ: Cooper Square, 1980), 227.

64. UPI Report on Mann's Appointment, 15 December 1963, Thomas Mann Papers, box 328, TC; Pat Holt Oral History Interview; Robert Jones, "State Department Aides Block Mann's Policies," *Indianapolis Star,* 10 January 1964, Thomas Mann Papers, box 329, TC; Airgram to All ARA Posts, 21 March 1964, NSF, CF, Latin America, box 1, LBJL.

65. "Remarks by the Honorable Thomas C. Mann, Assistant Secretary of State for Inter-American Affairs, at the Regional Chambers of Commerce Annual Meeting, Brownsville, Texas," 17 September 1964, Thomas Mann Papers, box 303, TC; Rogers, *Twilight Struggle,* 226.

66. Tad Szulc, "Latin Aid Set Up Is Revised by U.S.," *New York Times,* 8 March 1964; Martin, *Kennedy and Latin America,* 458.

67. Transcript of Telephone Conversation, Mann and Reedy, 11 February 1964, Thomas Mann Papers, box 309, TC.

68. Transcript of Telephone Conversations, Mann and Johnson, 17 February 1964 and 19 February 1964, both Thomas Mann Papers, box 316, TC.

69. Transcript of Telephone Conversation, Mann and Bundy, 7 March 1964, Thomas Mann Papers, box 309, TC; Tad Szulc, "Johnson Renews Pledge to Latins; Sees a Bright Era," *New York Times,* 17 March 1964.

70. Tad Szulc, "U.S. May Abandon Efforts to Deter Dictators," *New York Times,* 19 March 1964.

71. Editorial Notes, *FRUS, 1964–1968,* vol. 31, *South and Central America; Mexico* (Washington, DC: US Government Printing Office, 2004), doc. 10; Transcript of Telephone Conversation, Mann and Manning, 19 March 1964, Thomas Mann Papers, box 309, TC; Transcript of Telephone Conversation, Mann and Morse, 19 March 1964, and Transcript of Telephone Conversation, Mann and Gruening, 19 March 1964, both Thomas Mann Papers, box 309, TC.

72. "Latin America in Politics," *New York Times,* 14 October 1963; Tad Szulc, "U.S. Denies Switch in Its Latin Policy," *New York Times,* 20 March 1964; Drew Pearson, "U.S. Mistakes in Latin America," *Washington Post,* 23 March 1964.

73. "A Welcome Reappraisal," *Newsday,* 20 March 1964, and John McMullan, "Who Stuck the Knife in Latin Chief Mann?" *Miami Herald,* 20 March 1964, both Thomas Mann Papers, box 329, TC.

74. Transcript of Telephone Conversation, Mann and Hensley, 19 March 1964, Transcript of Telephone Conversation, Mann and Reston, 20 March 1964, and Transcript of Telephone Conversation, Mann and McCloy, 9 April 1964, all Thomas Mann Papers, box 309, TC.

75. Memo, Bundy to Johnson, 13 January 1966, NSF, AF, box 14, LBJL; Memo, Chase to Bundy, 27 August 1964, NSF, CF, Latin America, box 2, LBJL; Transcript of Telephone Conversation, Mann and Johnson, 5 May 1964, Thomas Mann Papers, box 316, TC.

76. Memo, Chase to Bundy, 19 March 1964, NSF, CF, Latin America, LBJL; Rogers, *The Twilight Struggle,* 226.

77. Memo, Bundy to Mann, 25 March 1964, and Memo, Bundy to Johnson, "Speech by Tom Mann," 4 May 1964, both NSF, AF, box 4, LBJL.

78. For examples, see Gil, "The Kennedy-Johnson Years," 23–24; LaFeber, "Thomas C. Mann," 185–89; and Levinson and de Onis, *The Alliance That Lost Its Way,* 87.

79. Martin, *Kennedy and Latin America,* 457–58; Department of State Press Release, 17 April 1963, NSF, Departments and Agencies, box 287, JFKL; Rabe, *Most Dangerous Area,* 74–77.

80. Quoted in LaFeber, *Inevitable Revolutions,* 180.

81. Memo, "U.S. Military Sales in Latin America," ca. May 1963, Papers of Arthur Schlesinger Jr., White House Files, Classified Subject Files, box WH-40, JFKL. For a case study of the role of the military in the modernization process, see Field, *From Development to Dictatorship.*

82. Circular to All ARA Posts, ca. February 1963, NSF, Regional Security, box 216, JFKL; Summary of State Department Report on Military Assistance Program, 8 October 1964, NSF, CF, Latin America, box 1, LBJL.

83. Remarks of the President to the Committee for International Alliance for Progress, 27 October 1964, NSF, AF, box 5, LBJL; Memo, Mann to Johnson, "United States Alliance for Progress Program," 27 June 1964, NSF, AF, box 4, LBJL; Scheman, "Concept and Creativity," 10. Detailed figures on foreign aid are available at https://explorer.usaid.gov/aid-trends.html.

3. *The Good Neighbor Returns?*

1. Transcript of Telephone Conversation, Johnson and Reedy, 8 April 1964, Beschloss, *Taking Charge,* 301; Drew Pearson, "U.S. Mistakes in Latin America," *Washington Post,* 23 March 1964, Thomas Mann Papers, box 329, TC.

2. USIA Report, "Foreign Reaction to Panama Situation," 13 January 1964, NSF, CF, Panama, box 64, LBJL.

3. Extract from Theodore Roosevelt, "Theodore Roosevelt: An Autobiography with Illustrations," in Holden and Zolov, eds., *Latin America and the United States,* 92–94, 93. See also Richard H. Collin, *Theodore Roosevelt's Caribbean: The Panama Canal, the Monroe Doctrine, and the Latin American Context* (Baton Rouge: Louisiana State University Press, 1990); and Ovidio Diaz Espino, *How Wall Street Created a Nation: J. P. Morgan, Teddy Roosevelt, and the Panama Canal* (New York: Four Walls Eight Windows, 2001).

4. "Hay-Bunau-Varilla Treaty," in Holden and Zolov, eds., *Latin America and the United States,* 90–91, 90.

5. Most North American employees were on the "gold rolls," which resulted in much higher wages than the "silver rolls," which accounted for most Panamanians. Walter LaFeber, *The Panama Canal: The Crisis in Historical Perspective* (New York: Oxford University Press, 1978), 106. For a detailed account of the tensions between Zonians and Panamanians, see Michael Donoghue, *Borderland on the Isthmus: Race, Culture and the Struggle for the Canal Zone* (Durham, NC: Duke University Press, 2014).

6. LaFeber, *Panama Canal,* 118–29; McPherson, *Yankee No!,* 92.

7. LaFeber, *Panama Canal,* 143.

8. Ibid., 136; Special National Intelligence Estimate, "The Short Run Outlook in Panama," 11 March 1964, NSF, National Intelligence Estimates, box 9, LBJL; Joint Communiqué from Presidents Kennedy and Chiari, 13 June 1962, NSF, CF, Panama, box 64, LBJL.

9. "Summary of Communications from Ambassador Farland on Developing Crisis," 16 January 1964, and Latin American Policy Committee Memo, "Panama: Plan of Action for Period from Present to October 1964," 26 December 1963, both NSF, CF, Panama, box 63, LBJL.

10. "Chronology of Events Relating to Flag Controversy," and Translation of Solis Message to Rusk, 10 January 1964, both NSF, CF, Panama, box 64, LBJL.

11. "Info Received Washington 13.40 by State," 10 January 1964, NSF, CF, Panama, box 64, LBJL; Transcript of Telephone Conversation, Mann, Abraham, and Johnston, 10 January 1964, Thomas Mann Papers, box 309, TC; Transcript of Telephone Conversation, Johnson and Chiari, 10 January 1964, NSF, CF, Panama, box 64, LBJL.

12. "Text (Not Precise) of Mann's Arrival Statement in the Zone," WHCF, Name File, box M67, LBJL; Telegram, Rusk to Mann, 11 January 1964, NSF, CF, Panama, box 63, LBJL.

13. Telegram, Mann to Rusk, 11 January 1964, NSF, CF, Panama, box 63, LBJL; Mann Oral History, LBJL.

14. Telegram, Mann to Rusk, 11 January 1964, NSF, CF, Panama, box 63, LBJL.

15. Telegram, Mann to State Department, 11 January 1964, NSF, CF, Panama, box 63, LBJL; Transcript of Telephone Conversation, Johnson and Russell,

15 January 1964, Beschloss, *Taking Charge,* 163; Telegram, Mann to Rusk, 11 January 1964, NSF, CF, Panama, box 63, LBJL.

16. Telegram, Mann to Rusk and McNamara, 12 January 1964, NSF, CF, Panama, box 63, LBJL; Memo of Conversation, Mann, Vance, Dungan, Chiari, and Solis, 13 January 1964, Thomas Mann Papers, box 309, TC.

17. Memo of Conversation, "White House Meeting on Panamanian Crisis," 13 January 1964, John McCone Memoranda, Meetings with the President, box 1, LBJL.

18. Transcript of Telephone Conversation, Johnson and Mann, 14 January 1964, Thomas Mann Papers, box 316, TC.

19. Woods, *LBJ,* 498; LaFeber, *Panama Canal,* 143.

20. State Department Public Opinion Summary, 13 January 1964, NSF, CF, Panama, box 63, LBJL; Copy of President's Statement on Panama Crisis, 23 January 1964, Office Files of Bill Moyers, box 105, LBJL; State Department Public Opinion Summary, 24 January 1964, NSF, CF, Panama, box 63, LBJL.

21. "Panama: Semantics, Politics & Passion," *Time,* 24 January 1964; Transcript of Telephone Conversation, Mann and Rockefeller, 4 March 1964, Thomas Mann Papers, box 309, TC; Telegram, Embassy Panama City to State Department, 23 January 1964, NSF, CF, Panama, box 64, LBJL.

22. Telegram, Martin to Mann and Attached Response, 14 January 1964, NSF, CF, Panama, box 63, LBJL; McPherson, *Yankee No!,* 112; Telegram, Mann to Martin, 8 February 1964, NSF, CF, Panama, box 65, LBJL.

23. Quoted in McPherson, *Yankee, No!,* 108; Transcript of Telephone Conversation, Mann and Dungan, 28 January 1964, and Transcript of Telephone Conversation, Mann and Moyers, 21 January 1964, both Thomas Mann Papers, box 309, TC.

24. Mark A. Lawrence, "Exception to the Rule? The Johnson Administration and the Panama Canal," in Lerner, ed., *Looking Back at LBJ,* 20–52, 44–51; Transcript of Telephone Conversation, Mann and Dungan, 30 January 1964, Thomas Mann Papers, box 309, TC; McPherson, *Yankee No!,* 111.

25. Copy of President's Statement on Panama Crisis, 21 March 1964, Office Files of Bill Moyers, box 105, LBJL.

26. Johnson rarely convened the full NSC, preferring to discuss foreign policy at the more informal "Tuesday Lunches."

27. Memo of Conversation, "NSC Meeting with Congressional Leaders," 3 April 1964, Transcript of Telephone Conversation, Johnson and Chiari, 3 April 1964, and "Senator Morse Reports," all NSF, NSC Meetings File, box 1, LBJL.

28. McPherson, *Yankee No!,* 114; Copy of President's Statement on Panama Crisis, 18 December 1964, Office Files of Bill Moyers, box 105, LBJL; LaFeber, *Panama Canal,* 146.

29. Dungan Oral History, LBJL.

30. See, e.g., Transcript of Telephone Conversations, Johnson and Mann, 23 January 1964 and 25 January 1964, Thomas Mann Papers, box 316, TC.

31. Transcript of Telephone Conversation, Johnson and Mann, 23 January 1964, Thomas Mann Papers, box 316, TC; LaFeber, "Thomas C. Mann," 192; Lyndon B.

Johnson, *The Vantage Point: Perspectives of the Presidency, 1963–1969* (New York: Holt, Rinehart & Winston, 1971), 184.

32. Transcript of Telephone Conversation, Mann and Vance, 21 January 1964, Thomas Mann Papers, box 309, TC; Memo, McNamara to Johnson, "Contingency Planning for U.S. Military Intervention in Panama," 31 January 1964, NSF, CF, Panama, box 65, LBJL.

33. Transcript of Telephone Conversation, Mann and Dungan, 31 January 1964, Thomas Mann Papers, box 309, TC; Memo, Chase to Bundy, 18 February 1964, NSF, CF, Panama, box 65, LBJL; Memo, Bundy to Johnson, "Staff Assistance in Latin America," 16 June 1964, NSF, Memos to the President, box 3, LBJL.

34. Transcript of Telephone Conversation, Johnson and Mann, 17 February 1964, Thomas Mann Papers, box 316, TC; "Mann's Role Disputed in Confusion on Canal," *Evening Star*, 19 March 1964, Thomas Mann Papers, box 329, TC.

35. Note, Papers of Arthur Schlesinger Jr., Subject Files, box 366, NYPL; National Intelligence Estimate, "Situation and Prospects in Brazil," 10 July 1963, NSF, National Intelligence Estimates, box 9, LBJL.

36. For Walter LaFeber, the coup provided "the opportunity to implement the Mann Doctrine announced just two weeks before: destroy restraints on economic growth through private help by recognizing the new military regime." Jeffrey Taffet has argued that it demonstrated "how the Alliance for Progress lost its reformist goals and moral compass." LaFeber, "Thomas C. Mann," 190; Taffet, *Foreign Aid as Foreign Policy*, 8. See also Stephen Rabe, *The Killing Zone: The United States Wages Cold War in Latin America* (New York: Oxford University Press, 2011), 86–119; and Joseph Smith, *Brazil and the United States: Convergence and Divergence* (Athens: University of Georgia Press, 2010), 161.

37. Broadly similar conclusions regarding the irrelevance of the Mann Doctrine can be found in Ruth Leacock, *Requiem for Revolution: The United States and Brazil, 1961–1969* (Kent, OH: Kent State University Press, 1990), 200. David F. Schmitz has stated that the Mann Doctrine was "immediately applied" to Brazil but also acknowledged the consistencies between the Kennedy and the Johnson administrations' Brazilian policies. David F. Schmitz, *Thank God They're on Our Side: The United States and Right Wing Dictatorships, 1921–1965* (Chapel Hill: University of North Carolina Press, 1999), 264–82.

38. Jan Knippers Black, "Lincoln Gordon and Brazil's Military Counterrevolution," in *Ambassadors in Foreign Policy: The Influence of Individuals on U.S. Latin American Policy*, ed. C. Neale Ronning and Albert P. Vannucci (New York: Praeger, 1987), 95–113, 100; Smith, *Brazil and the United States*, 158.

39. Journal Entry, 3 April 1961, Papers of Arthur Schlesinger Jr., Journals, box 311, NYPL. The Brazilian historian Luiz Alberto Moniz Bandeira has observed that Gordon often acted "as if he were running the country." Quoted in Black, "Lincoln Gordon," 104.

40. Notes Taken by Mann during Meeting with Gordon, 22 January 1964, RG 59, Bureau of Inter-American Affairs, Assistant Secretary and U.S. Coordinator

Alliance for Progress, Subject and CFs 1962–1975, box 1, NAMD; Airgram, Gordon to State Department, 30 December 1963, NSF, CF, Brazil, box 9, LBJL; Schmitz, *Thank God They're on Our Side*, 272; Telegram, Gordon to State Department, 30 December 1963, and Airgram, Gordon to State Department, 20 January 1964, both NSF, CF, Brazil, box 9, LBJL.

41. Transcript of Telephone Conversation, Johnson and Mann, 19 February 1964, Thomas Mann Papers, box 316, TC; Telegram and Attached Article, Martin to Gordon, 28 December 1963, and Telegram, Gordon to Mann, 4 March 1964, both NSF, CF, Brazil, box 9, LBJL.

42. During the crisis of leadership that followed Quadros's resignation, the military had acted as something of a "stabilizing and moderating factor," allowing Vice President Goulart to assume the presidency but with some powers ceded to Congress. Thomas E. Skidmore, *Politics in Brazil, 1930–1964: An Experiment in Democracy* (New York: Oxford University Press, 1967), 8.

43. Tad Szulc, "Brazil Prepares to Seize Farms and Refineries," *New York Times*, 10 March 1964, Telegram, Gordon to State Department, 17 March 1964, and Telegrams, Embassy Brazil to State Department, 18 April 1964 and 19 April 1964, all NSF, CF, Brazil, box 9, LBJL.

44. Telegram, Gordon to State Department, 24 March 1964, NSF, CF, Brazil, box 9, LBJL.

45. Brizola was thought to be of the extreme left and highly ambitious and had a difficult relationship with Lincoln Gordon. Skidmore, *Politics in Brazil*, 304; Telegram, Gordon to State Department, 25 March 1964, NSF, CF, Brazil, box 9, LBJL.

46. Telegram, Gordon to Bundy, Mann, Rusk, McNamara, et al., 29 March 1964, NSF, CF, Brazil, box 9, LBJL.

47. Telegram Gordon to Bundy, Mann, Rusk, McNamara, et al., 27 March 1964, NSF, CF, Brazil, box 9, LBJL.

48. "Brazil at the Brink Again," *New York Times*, 31 March 1964.

49. Memo, Bundy to Johnson, 28 March 1964, Memo of Conversation, Bundy, Goodpaster, Helms, et al., 28 March 1964, and Telegram, Rusk to Gordon, 30 March 1964, all NSF, CF, Brazil, box 9, LBJL.

50. Memo, Chase to Bundy, 30 March 1964, Telegram, Gordon to State Department, 31 March 1964, CIA Intelligence Cable, 30 March 1964, and Telegram, Consulate Belo Horizonte to State Department, 31 March 1964, all NSF, CF, Brazil, box 9, LBJL.

51. Teleconference, Gordon, Ball, Mann, and Dungan, 31 March 1964, and JCS Orders to Carrier Fleet, 31 March 1964, both NSF, CF, Brazil, box 9, LBJL.

52. LBJ Message to Mazzilli, 2 April 1964, NSF, Special Head of State Correspondence, box 5, Brazil, LBJL; Leacock, *Requiem for Revolution*, 221; JCS Orders to Carrier Fleet, 3 April 1964, NSF, CF, Brazil, box 9, LBJL; Transcript of Telephone Conversation, Johnson and Mann, 3 April 1964, Beschloss, *Taking Charge*, 306.

53. William O. Walker III, "The Struggle for the Americas: The Johnson Administration and Cuba," in *The Foreign Policies of Lyndon Johnson: Beyond Vietnam*, ed.

H. W. Brands (College Station: Texas A&M University Press, 1999), 61–97, 73; Telegram, Embassy Santiago to State Department, 4 April 1964, Telegram, Embassy Lima to State Department, 4 April 1964, and Telegram, Embassy Montevideo to State Department, 3 April 1964, all RG 59, Central Foreign Policy Files 1964–1966, Political and Defense Subject Numeric File, box 1943, NAMD; Teleconference, Gordon and Ball, 2 April 1964, NSF, CF, Brazil, box 9, LBJL.

54. Telegram, Gordon to State Department, 10 April 1964, NSF, CF, Brazil, box 10, LBJL; Edward C. Burks, "Thousands Held in Brazil's Drive to Root Out Reds," *New York Times,* 6 April 1964; Tad Szulc, "Washington Concern Grows," *New York Times,* 10 April 1964.

55. Telegram, Mann to Gordon, 6 April 1964, NSF, CF, Brazil, box 10, LBJL; Transcript of Telephone Conversation, Mann and Bundy, 9 April 1964, and Transcript of Telephone Conversation, Mann and McCloy, 9 April 1964, both Thomas Mann Papers, box 309, TC; Transcript of Telephone Conversation, LBJ and Bundy, 14 April 1964, Beschloss, *Taking Charge,* 318.

56. Memo, Mann to Rusk, 7 May 1964, Thomas Mann Papers, box 322, TC; CIA Intelligence Cable, 8 May 1964, NSF, CF, Brazil, box 10, LBJL; Memo, Mann to Rusk, 10 June 1964, and Summary of Latin American Progress, 12 June 1964, both Thomas Mann Papers, box 322, TC.

57. Memo, Rostow to Mann, 23 April 1964, RG 59, Bureau of Inter-American Affairs, Assistant Secretary and U.S. Coordinator Alliance for Progress, Subject and CFs 1962–1975, box 1, NAMD; Memo, Mann to Bell, 8 June 1964, Thomas Mann Papers, box 322, TC; "Summary of Major Events in ARA since September," 4 January 1965, Thomas Mann Papers, box 323, TC. Detailed figures on foreign aid are available at https://explorer.usaid.gov/aid-trends.html.

58. Airgram, Schlesinger to Department of State, "Notes on the Italian Situation," 23 April 1964, NSF, AF, box 2, LBJL.

59. Although a letter drafted by Bundy stating, "If one is reporting through official channels, one ought not to engage in sarcasm about Administration policy," remained unsent, he did suggest that he would "make the same point to Arthur by conversation." Memo and Attached Letter, Bundy to Johnson, 12 May 1964, NSF, AF, box 2, LBJL.

60. Dan Kurzman, "Brazil Caught in Grip of Army Dictatorship," *Washington Post,* 3 May 1964; "Brazil's New Regime," *New York Times,* 16 April 1964.

61. Memo, Mann to Rusk, 30 April 1964, Thomas Mann Papers, box 322, TC; Telegram, Gordon to State Department and Attached Notes from Sayre and Bundy, 11 June 1964, NSF, CF, Brazil, box 10, LBJL; Message, Branco to Johnson, ca. August 1964, and Message, Branco to Johnson, 10 August 1965, both NSF, Special Head of State Correspondence, box 5, Brazil, LBJL.

62. Telegram, Gordon to State Department and Attached Notes from Sayre and Bundy, 11 June 1964, NSF, CF, Brazil, box 10, LBJL; Memo, Mann to Bell, 8 June 1964, Thomas Mann Papers, box 322, TC; Schmitz, *Thank God They're on Our Side,* 277.

63. Smith, *Brazil and the United States*, 156–58; Telegram, Gordon to Bundy, Mann, Rusk, McNamara, et al., 27 March 1964, NSF, CF, Brazil, box 9, LBJL.

64. Memo, Mann to Rostow, 10 April 1964, Thomas Mann Papers, box 322, TC. For an excellent exploration of ties between the Alliance and Latin American militaries, see Field, *From Development to Dictatorship*.

65. Bundy quoted in Schmitz, *Thank God They're on Our Side*, 279.

66. Memo, Vaughn to Bell, "Performance of Latin American Countries in Relation to Aid," 20 October 1965, NSF, AF, box 5, LBJL; Memo, Read to Bundy, "The Political Performance of Latin American Countries," 10 November 1965, RG 59, Central Foreign Policy Files 1964–1966, Political and Defense Subject Numeric File, box 2410, NAMD; Memo, Freeman to Johnson, 27 April 1966, NSF, CF, Latin America, box 2, 2 of 2, LBJL.

67. Stephen Rabe makes the case most explicitly that US actions during the Brazilian coup signaled to the rest of the hemisphere that military repression would now be tolerated. See Rabe, *Killing Zone*, esp. chap. 5.

68. AID Report, "Use of Foreign Aid Funds," 7 May 1964, and AID Report and Attached Note from Bundy, 23 May 1964, both NSF, AF, box 3, LBJL; Memo, Mann to Johnson, "Alliance for Progress Program," 27 June 1964, NSF, AF, box 4, LBJL.

69. On the sheer amount of often contradictory statistics produced over the course of the Alliance, Enrique Lerdau has observed: "I doubt that any one person in the world has read them all, and if such a person existed he would probably have even greater difficulties in deriving valid generalizations than do the rest of us." Lerdau, "The Alliance for Progress," 169.

70. Chase, "Summary and Talking Points: Alliance for Progress," ca. January 1965, and Alliance for Progress Report on FY64, both NSF, AF, box 5, LBJL.

71. ARA Circular, "U.S. Policies toward CIAP," 21 May 1964, NSF, AF, box 4, LBJL; Rostow, Report on CIAP Meeting, ca. July 1964, NSF, AF, box 5, LBJL.

72. Emmett John Hughes, "A Mann for LBJ's Season," *Newsweek,* 18 May 1964, Thomas Mann Papers, box 340, TC; Transcript of Telephone Conversation, Johnson and Mann, 11 May 1964, Thomas Mann Papers, box 316, TC.

73. Memo and speech draft, Mann to Bundy, 27 April 1964, and Memo, Bundy to Mann, 10 April 1964, both NSF, AF, box 4, LBJL; Memo, Bundy to Johnson, "Speech by Tom Mann," 4 May 1964, NSF, Memos to the President, box 4, LBJL.

74. Speech by Thomas Mann at Notre Dame University, "The Democratic Ideal in Our Policy toward Latin America," 7 June 1964, Thomas Mann Papers, box 303, TC.

75. "U.S. Pliancy Urged in Notre Dame Talk," *New York Times,* 8 June 1964; "Policy on Latin Coups Set Forth by Mann," *Washington Post,* 8 June 1964; Schmitz, *Thank God They're on Our Side,* 267; Memo, Vallimarescu to Mann, "Reaction Report on Your Notre Dame Speech," 18 June 1964, Thomas Mann Papers, box 305, TC.

76. For instance, by January 1964, sections of the press were already reporting that Johnson lacked "an effective technique for the day-to-day running of foreign affairs." Robert Dallek, *Flawed Giant: Lyndon Johnson and His Times, 1961–1973* (New York: Oxford University Press, 1998), 84–85.

77. Memo and Attached Copy of Speech, Chase to Bundy, 10 May 1964, and "Memorandum of Conversation in the Cabinet Room," 11 May 1964, both NSF, AF, box 4, LBJL.

78. Memo, Chase to Bundy, "Alliance for Progress Ceremonies," 12 May 1964, NSF, AF, box 4, LBJL.

79. The charges related to a cache of arms discovered in Venezuela in November 1963 alleged to have been transported from Cuba and intended for use by Venezuelan rebels. Although the Venezuelan government subsequently spearheaded the campaign through the OAS, its actions were fully supported every step of the way behind the scenes by the United States. Memo for the Record, "Cuba Meeting," 21 February 1964, *FRUS, 1964–1968*, vol. 31, *South and Central America; Mexico,* doc. 4.

80. "Statement of Rep. Armistead Selden, U.S. House of Representatives," 27 July 1964, WHCF, Countries 1–8, Latin America, box 10, LBJL; Memo and Attachments, Mann to Harriman, "Statements of Cuban Policy," 16 April 1964, Thomas Mann Papers, box 322, TC.

81. Memo for the Record, "Meeting with the President on Cuba," 19 December 1963, and Memo for the Record, "Review of Covert Program Directed against Cuba," 7 April 1964, both McCone Memoranda, Meetings with the President, box 1, LBJL; Robert Dallek, *John F. Kennedy: An Unfinished Life, 1917–1963* (London: Little, Brown, 2003), 657–59.

82. Jonathan Colman, *The Foreign Policy of Lyndon Johnson: The United States and the World, 1963–1969* (Edinburgh: Edinburgh University Press, 2010), 16; Memo for the Record, "Review of Covert Program Directed against Cuba," 7 April 1964, McCone Memoranda, Meetings with the President, box 1, LBJL. Mann later commented that he opposed an invasion as he "never thought that it would be in our interests to spill that much blood." Mann Oral History, JFKL.

83. Transcript of Telephone Conversation, Mann and Bell, 27 March 1964, Thomas Mann Papers, box 309, TC.

84. Pat Holt Oral History Interview; Milan J. Kubic, "Frei's Election Victory Based on Reform Program and the Clergy," *Washington Post,* 6 August 1964.

85. Memorandum, King to McCone, 3 January 1964, and Editorial Note, both *FRUS, 1964–1968*, vol. 31, *South and Central America; Mexico,* 245, 269.

86. Transcript of Telephone Conversation, Johnson and Mann, 12 June 1964, Thomas Mann Papers, box 316, TC; Editorial Note, *FRUS, 1964–1968*, vol. 31, *South and Central America; Mexico,* 273.

87. For studies of the Allende presidency and coup, see Harmer, *Allende's Chile;* and Jonathan Haslam, *The Nixon Administration and the Death of Allende's Chile: A Case of Assisted Suicide* (New York: Verso, 2005).

88. Transcript of Telephone Conversation, Johnson and Mann, 5 May 1964, Thomas Mann Papers, box 316, TC.

89. Rodman, *Sanctity versus Sovereignty*, 192; Transcript of Telephone Conversation, Mann and Orrick, 27 January 1964, Thomas Mann Papers, box 309, TC.

90. Memo, Mann to Johnson, "Aid to Peru and the IPC Problem," 21 February 1966, Thomas Mann Papers, box 324, TC.

91. Telegram, Martin to Mann, 10 December 1963, RG 59, Bureau of Inter-American Affairs, Assistant Secretary and U.S. Coordinator Alliance for Progress, Subject and CFs 1962–1975, box 1, NAMD; Rodman, *Sanctity versus Sovereignty*, 74; Memo, Mann to Rusk, "Oil Contract Problem in Argentina," 25 November 1964, Thomas Mann Papers, box 322, TC; Memo, Mann to Johnson, "Aid to Peru and the IPC Problem," 21 February 1966, Thomas Mann Papers, box 324, TC.

92. "Text of the Speech Delivered by Assistant Secretary of State Thomas C. Mann at the IA-ECOSOC Conference in Lima, Peru," 8 December 1964, Thomas Mann Papers, box 303, TC; Mann Oral History, HSTL; CIA Intelligence Memo, "Some Political and Economic Problems Arising from State Enterprise in Latin America," 15 January 1965, NSF, CF, Latin America, box 2, LBJL.

93. Mann Oral History, HSTL.

94. Transcript of Telephone Conversation, Johnson and Various Congressmen, 20 December 1963, Beschloss, *Taking Charge*, 124; Memo, Mann to Rusk, "Coffee," 4 August 1964, Thomas Mann Papers, box 322, TC; "Text of the Speech Delivered by Assistant Secretary of State Thomas C. Mann at the IA-ECOSOC Conference in Lima, Peru," 8 December 1964, Thomas Mann Papers, box 303, TC.

95. Telegram, Mann to Gordon, 11 August 1964, and Outline Used for Briefing of Senators, 24 November 1964, both Thomas Mann Papers, box 322, TC.

96. Carl M. Marcy, Chief of Staff, Foreign Relations Committee, 1955–1973, Oral History Interviews, Senate Historical Office, Washington, DC.

97. Speech at Planned Parenthood Annual Banquet, "Population Growth and the Alliance for Progress," 9 November 1964, Thomas Mann Papers, box 303, TC; Levinson and de Onis, *The Alliance That Lost Its Way*, 221.

98. Field, *From Development to Dictatorship;* Rabe, *Eisenhower and Latin America*, 77–81; James F. Siekmeier, "Persistent Condor and Predatory Eagle: The Bolivian Revolution and the United States, 1952–1964," in Statler and Johns, eds., *The Eisenhower Administration*, 197–224.

99. Memo, Chase to Bundy, 28 October 1964, *FRUS, 1964–1968*, vol. 31, *South and Central America; Mexico*, doc. 150; Telegram, Mann to Embassy La Paz, 29 October 1964, RG 59, Bureau of Inter-American Affairs, Assistant Secretary and U.S. Coordinator Alliance for Progress, Subject and CFs 1962–1975, box 1, NAMD; Telegram from the Department of State to All American Republic Posts, 4 November 1964, *FRUS, 1964–1968*, vol. 31, *South and Central America; Mexico*, doc. 151.

100. Memo, Mann to Rusk, 21 November 1964, and Memo, Mann to Ball, 2 December 1964, both Thomas Mann Papers, box 322, TC.

101. Transcripts of Telephone Conversations, Johnson and Mann, 5 May 1964 and 12 June 1964, both Thomas Mann Papers, box 316, TC.

4. No More Cubas

1. Most accounts of the US intervention are highly critical, portraying Johnson's actions as rushed, reactionary, and overly supportive of a corrupt military elite. See Piero Gleijeses, *The Dominican Crisis: The 1965 Constitutionalist Revolt and American Intervention*, trans. Lawrence Lipson (Baltimore: Johns Hopkins University Press, 1978), and "Hope Denied: The US Defeat of the 1965 Revolt in the Dominican Republic," Cold War International History Project Working Paper Series, no. 72 (Washington, DC: Wilson Center, November 2014); Michael Grow, *US Presidents and Latin American Interventions: Pursuing Regime Change in the Cold War* (Lawrence: University Press of Kansas, 2008); and Alan McPherson, "Misled by Himself: What the Johnson Tapes Reveal about the Dominican Intervention of 1965," *Latin American Research Review* 38, no. 2 (June 2003): 127–46, and *Yankee No!* Eric Chester makes a similar argument and is also particularly critical of Mann's role. See Eric Thomas Chester, *Rag-Tags, Scum, Riff-Raff, and Commies: The U.S. Intervention in the Dominican Republic, 1965–1966* (New York: Monthly Review Press, 2001). There are more sympathetic accounts, and they often focus on the relatively successful execution of the intervention, the prevention of further bloodshed, and the holding of elections the following year. See G. Pope Atkins and Larman C. Wilson, *The Dominican Republic and the United States: From Imperialism to Transnationalism* (Athens: University of Georgia Press, 1998); Colman, *The Foreign Policy of Lyndon Johnson;* Russell Crandall, *Gunboat Democracy: U.S. Interventions in the Dominican Republic, Grenada, and Panama* (Lanham, MD: Rowman & Littlefield, 2006); Lawrence M. Greenberg, "The US Dominican Intervention: Success Story," U.S. Army War College Report (1987), http://www.dtic.mil/cgi-bin/GetTRDoc?AD=ADA516121; and Jerome Slater, *Intervention and Negotiation: The United States and the Dominican Revolution* (New York: Harper & Row, 1970).

2. Lyndon B. Johnson, "The President's Inaugural Address," 20 January 1965, APP, PPP, http://www.presidency.ucsb.edu/ws/index.php?pid=26985.

3. Transcript of Telephone Conversation, Johnson and Mann, 19 February 1965, Thomas Mann Papers, box 316, TC; Memo, Valenti to Johnson, 21 April 1965, WHCF, Federal Government Files 105—State Department, box 133, LBJL; Transcript of Telephone Conversation, Ball and Bundy, 16 April 1964, Papers of George W. Ball, box 2, LBJL.

4. Transcript of Telephone Conversation, Johnson and Mann, 25 January 1965, Thomas Mann Papers, box 316, TC.

5. The two titles were effectively used interchangeably, denoting the number three position in the State Department after the secretary and the undersecretary.

6. Transcript of Telephone Conversation, Johnson and Mann, 26 January 1965, Thomas Mann Papers, box 316, TC.

7. "Confers with Mann," *New York Times,* 4 February 1965; Tom Wicker, "Mann Is Appointed to Harriman Post as No. 2 Rusk Aide," *New York Times,* 13 February 1965; Memo, Bundy to Johnson, 8 September 1965, NSF, Memos to the President, box 11, LBJL.

8. Memo, Read to Bundy, "Rates of Economic Growth in Latin America in 1964 and 1965," 20 November 1965, and Memo, Mann to Watson, 10 February 1965, both NSF, CF, Latin America, box 2, LBJL.

9. Mann's son, Clifton, would later recall: "He was perceived to be a political figure when he was, in fact, a diplomat." Obituary, Thomas C. Mann, *New York Times,* 30 January 1999.

10. Joseph Pincus, "The Central American Common Market," USAID Report (September 1962), http://pdf.usaid.gov/pdf_docs/PNABI422.pdf; Memo, Mann to Rusk, 12 February 1965, Thomas Mann Papers, box 323, TC.

11. Statement by the Honorable Thomas C. Mann before the House Committee on Ways and Means, 13 April 1965, Thomas Mann Papers, box 323, TC; "President Signs Coffee Pact Bill," *Washington Post,* 25 May 1965.

12. Memo, Valenti to Johnson, 5 March 1965, WHCF, Countries 1–8, Latin America, box 10, LBJL.

13. Memo, Sayre to Bundy, 2 March 1965, NSF, CF, Latin America, box 2, LBJL, Memo, Mann to Bundy, "The President's Proposed Visit to South America," 23 February 1965, Memo, Mann to Valenti, "President's Trip to Latin America," February 8 1965, and Memo, Mann to Bundy, "The President's Proposed Visit to South America," 23 February 1965, all NSF, International Meetings and Travel, box 1, LBJL.

14. Circular Telegram, Mann to ARA Embassies, 5 March 1965, and Memo of Conversation, "Presidential Visits," 28 February 1965, both NSF, International Meetings and Travel, box 1, LBJL.

15. Circular Telegram, Mann to ARA Posts, 11 January 1965, NSF, CF, Latin America, box 2, LBJL.

16. Richard Lawrence, "Latin Nation Aid Project Held Success," *Journal of Commerce,* 22 April 1965, Thomas Mann Papers, box 335, TC; Tad Szulc, "U.S. Aides Predict Latin Gains in '65," *New York Times,* 23 April 1965; "Big Latin Outlay for Progress Due," *New York Times,* 24 April 1965.

17. Memo, Bradford to Office Directors of ARA, "Cuernavaca Meeting," 27 April 1965, NSF, CF, Latin America, box 2, LBJL.

18. Memo, Mann to Bundy, "The President's Proposed Visit to South America," 23 February 1965, NSF, International Meetings and Travel, box 1, LBJL.

19. National Intelligence Estimate, "Instability and the Insurgent Threat in the Dominican Republic," 17 January 1964, NSF, National Intelligence Estimates, box 9, LBJL; Atkins and Wilson, *The Dominican Republic and the United States,* 86–126. USAID figures are available at https://explorer.usaid.gov/aid-trends.html.

20. Memo, Martin to Johnson, RG 59, Bureau of Inter-American Affairs, Assistant Secretary and US Coordinator Alliance for Progress, Subject and CFs 1962–1975, box 2, NAMD; Brands, *The Wages of Globalism,* 50; McPherson, *Yankee No!,* 129.

21. Gleijeses, "Hope Denied," 8; Memo, Read to Bundy, "United States Policy in the Aftermath of the Dominican Military Coup," 4 October 1963, RG 59, Bureau

of Inter-American Affairs, Assistant Secretary and US Coordinator Alliance for Progress, Subject and CFs 1962–1975, box 2, NAMD.

22. Memo, Mann to Rusk, "The Situation in the Dominican Republic," 24 June 1964, Thomas Mann Papers, box 322, TC; National Intelligence Estimate, "Opportunities for Communist Exploitation in Latin America," 7 April 1964, NSF, CF, Latin America, box 1, LBJL; Telegram, Mann to Bennett, 26 June 1964, Thomas Mann Papers, box 322, TC.

23. Telegram, Connett to State Department, 24 April 1965, NSF, NSC Histories: Dominican Crisis, box 4 1°f 2, LBJL; Gleijeses, "Hope Denied," 17; Telegram, Connett to State Department, 26 April 1965, NSF, NSC Histories: Dominican Crisis, box 4, 1 of 2, LBJL.

24. Telegram, Mann to Connett, 26 April 1965, NSF, NSC Histories: Dominican Crisis, box 5, LBJL; Transcript of Telephone Conversation, Mann, Connett, Sayre, and Crockett, 27 April 1965, and Transcript of Telephone Conversation, Mann, Vaughn, and Moyers, 27 April 1965, both Thomas Mann Papers, box 311, TC.

25. State Department Biography of Ambassador William Tapley Bennett, 18 June 1964, Thomas Mann Papers, box 322, TC; Memo, Barber to Mann, "Inter-American Highway," 21 June 1950, RG 59, Bureau of Inter-American Affairs, Office of Middle American Affairs Subject Files 1947–1956, box 3, NAMD; Letter, Bennett to Mann, 12 November 1964, and Letter, Mann to Bennett, 16 November 1964, both RG 59, Bureau of Inter-American Affairs, Assistant Secretary and US Coordinator Alliance for Progress, Subject and CFs 1962–1975, box 1, NAMD.

26. McPherson, *Yankee No!*, 133. See also Grow, *US Presidents and Latin American Interventions*, 83; and Letter, Bennett to Mann, 21 May 1965, RG 59, Bureau of Inter-American Affairs, Assistant Secretary and US Coordinator Alliance for Progress, Subject and CFs 1962–1975, box 1, NAMD.

27. Transcript of Telephone Conversation, Mann and Vaughn, 27 April 1965, Thomas Mann Papers, box 311, TC; Chester, *Rag-Tags*, 65; Gleijeses, "Hope Denied," 20–22.

28. Chester, *Rag-Tags*, 75.

29. Transcript of Telephone Conversation, Mann and Johnson, 26 April 1965, and Transcript of Telephone Conversation, Mann and Johnson, 28 April 1965, both Thomas Mann Papers, box 316, TC; Transcript of Telephone Conversation, Mann, Vaughn, and Sayre, 28 April 1965, and Transcript of Telephone Conversation, Mann and Hightower, 28 April 1965, both Thomas Mann Papers, box 311, TC.

30. Transcript of Telephone Conversation, Mann and Bundy, 28 April 1965, Thomas Mann Papers, box 311, TC; "Text of Request by Newly Formed Junta for U.S. Military Assistance," 28 April 1965, RG 59, Records of the Undersecretary of State for Economic Affairs, Records Relating to the Dominican Republic, box 2, NAMD.

31. Telegram, Bennett to State Department, 28 April 1965, RG 59, Records of the Undersecretary of State for Economic Affairs, Records Relating to the Dominican Republic, box 2, NAMD.

32. Transcript of Telephone Conversation, Mann and Bundy, 28 April 1965, and Transcript of Telephone Conversation, Mann and Vance, 28 April 1965, both Thomas Mann Papers, box 311, TC.

33. Transcript of Telephone Conversation, Mann, Johnson, Rusk, and Bundy, 28 April 1965, Thomas Mann Papers, box 316, TC; Transcript of Telephone Conversation, Mann and Bennett, 29 April 1965, Thomas Mann Papers, box 311, TC.

34. Minutes of Meeting with Congressional Leadership on the Dominican Republic, 28 April 1965, Meeting Notes File, box 1, LBJL; Transcript of Telephone Conversation, Mann and Johnson, 28 April 1965, Thomas Mann Papers, box 316, TC.

35. Transcript of Telephone Conversation, Mann and Johnson, 28 April 1965, Thomas Mann Papers, box 316, TC.

36. Quoted in Editorial Note, *FRUS, 1964–1968*, vol. 32, *Dominican Republic; Cuba; Haiti; Guyana* (Washington, DC: US Government Printing Office, 2005), doc. 43.

37. Randall Woods has argued: "LBJ pursued a policy of double containment; containment of communism abroad and anticommunism at home." Michael Grow makes a similar argument but also emphasizes the pervasiveness of the "Cuba Syndrome" and the desire to convince allies of US resolve. Woods, *LBJ*, 624; Grow, *US Presidents and Latin American Interventions,* 75–89. See also Brands, *The Wages of Globalism,* 55–59; McPherson, "Misled by Himself"; and Randall B. Woods, "Conflicted Hegemon: LBJ and the Dominican Republic," *Diplomatic History* 32, no. 5 (November 2008): 749–66.

38. Brands, *The Wages of Globalism,* 58; Memo, Valenti to Johnson, 30 April 1965, WHCF, Countries 1–8, Latin America, box 10, LBJL; Woods, *Fulbright,* 377.

39. Gleijeses, "Hope Denied," 25; Transcript of Telephone Conversation, Mann and Johnson, 28 April 1965, Thomas Mann Papers, box 316, TC. See also Transcript of Telephone Conversation, Johnson and Raborn, 29 April, 1965, *FRUS, 1964–1968,* vol. 32, *Dominican Republic; Cuba; Haiti; Guyana,* doc. 39.

40. Memo, Hoover to Watson, 28 April 1965, Office Files of Mildred Stegall, box 65A, LBJL.

41. Bundy informed Johnson that Kennedy had intended to dedicate a stand-alone speech to his doctrine of no more Cubas but had managed only to make a brief mention of it before the doctrine was "blanketed almost immediately by his death." Memo, Bundy to Mann et al., 21 February 1964, NSF, Regional Security, box 216, JFKL.

42. Mann Oral History, HSTL.

43. Thomas Mann, "Memorandum," 18 July 1964, Thomas Mann Papers, box 322, TC.

44. Transcript of Telephone Conversation, Mann and Johnson, 28 April 1965, Thomas Mann Papers, box 316, TC. Bennett has admitted as much in interviews. See Grow, *US Presidents and Latin American Interventions,* 82.

45. For more detailed analysis of the landing and subsequent operations, see Atkins and Wilson, *The Dominican Republic and the United States,* 135–40; Chester, *Rag-Tags,* 86–92; and Greenberg, "The US Dominican Intervention."

46. McPherson, *Yankee No!*, 139.

47. Gleijeses, "Hope Denied," 29; Memo of Conversation, Mann, Vaughn, Betancourt, and Sayre, 1 May 1965, RG 59, Records of the Undersecretary of State for Economic Affairs, Records Relating to the Dominican Republic, box 1, NAMD.

48. Schlesinger had initially been asked to act as liaison to some contacts in Latin America but soon, according to the president, became openly critical of Johnson's actions. Transcript of Telephone Conversation, Mann and Johnson, 2 May 1965, Thomas Mann Papers, box 316, TC.

49. Transcript of Telephone Conversation, Mann and Johnson, 4 May 1965, Thomas Mann Papers, box 316, TC.

50. Transcript of Telephone Conversation, Mann and Bundy, 2 May 1965, and Transcript of Telephone Conversation, Mann and Valenti, 2 May 1965, both Thomas Mann Papers, box 311, TC; Transcript of Telephone Conversation, Mann, Johnson, and Valenti, 5 May 1965, Thomas Mann Papers, box 316, TC.

51. Transcript of Telephone Conversation, Mann and Bundy, 7 May 1965, and Transcript of Telephone Conversation, Mann and Bunker, 7 May 1965, both Thomas Mann Papers, box 311, TC; Transcript of Telephone Conversation, Mann and Johnson, 7 May 1965, Transcript of Telephone Conversation, Mann, Johnson, and Valenti, 5 May 1965, and Transcript of Telephone Conversation, Mann and Johnson, 11 May 1965, all Thomas Mann Papers, box 316, TC.

52. State Department Circular Telegram, "Sitrep—Dominican Republic," 10 May 1965, NSF, NSC Histories: Dominican Crisis, box 5, LBJL.

53. Center for Strategic Studies Committee Report on the Dominican Republic Intervention, 17 June 1966, Eleanor Lansing Dulles Papers, box 47, DDEL.

54. Lyndon Johnson, "Statement by the President upon Ordering Troops into the Dominican Republic," 28 April 1965, APP, PPP, http://www.presidency.ucsb.edu/ws/?pid=26922; Lyndon Johnson, "Statement by the President on the Situation in the Dominican Republic," 30 April 1965, APP, PPP, http://www.presidency.ucsb.edu/ws/index.php?pid=26926; Lyndon Johnson, "Radio and Television Report to the American People on the Situation in the Dominican Republic," 2 May 1965, APP, PPP, http://www.presidency.ucsb.edu/ws/?pid=26932.

55. Transcript of Telephone Conversation, Mann, Johnson, and Ball, 28 May 1965, Thomas Mann Papers, box 316, TC; Transcript of Telephone Conversation, Johnson and McNamara, 30 April 1965, Michael Beschloss, ed., *Reaching for Glory: Lyndon Johnson's Secret White House Tapes, 1964–1965* (New York: Simon & Schuster, 2001), 302; Memo, Valenti to Johnson, 30 April 1965, WHCF, Countries 1–8, Latin America, box 10, LBJL.

56. Raborn had little experience of the intelligence services and was seemingly cowed by the force of Johnson's personality. LBJ had little respect for the new CIA chief, once dismissing him with: "If I want to see you, Raborn, I'll telephone you." Quoted in Colman, *The Foreign Policy of Lyndon Johnson*, 18.

57. Transcript of Telephone Conversation, Johnson and Raborn, 29 April 1965, National Security Archive Electronic Briefing Book no. 513, "Lyndon Johnson

and the Dominican Intervention of 1965," http://nsarchive.gwu.edu/NSAEBB /NSAEBB513 (hereafter NSAEBB 513); Woods, *Fulbright*, 382; Memo, Hoover to Watson, "Demonstrations Protesting United States Intervention in the Dominican Republic," 7 May 1965, Office Files of Mildred Stegall, box 65, LBJL; Transcript of Telephone Conversation, Johnson and Raborn, 29 April 1965, NSAEBB 513.

58. Transcript of Telephone Conversation, Mann and Valenti, 4 May 1965, Thomas Mann Papers, box 311, TC; Memo for the Record, "Meeting on the Dominican Republic," 3 May 1965, NSF, NSC Histories, Dominican Crisis, box 7, 1 of 2, LBJL; Transcript of Telephone Conversation, Mann and Johnson, 10 May 1965, Thomas Mann Papers, box 316, TC; Mann Oral History, DDEL.

59. "The Johnson Doctrine," *Evening Star,* 6 May 1965, Thomas Mann Papers, box 335, TC. See also Stephen Rabe, "The Johnson (Eisenhower?) Doctrine for Latin America," *Diplomatic History* 9, no. 1 (January 1985): 95–100.

60. Transcript of Interview, Thomas Mann, *The Today Show,* 4 May 1965, Thomas Mann Papers, box 340, TC; Transcript of Interview, Cyrus Vance, *Issues and Answers,* 9 May 1965, Cyrus Vance Papers, Group 1664, series no. 1, box 5, YUL; "Safety First in the Caribbean," *The Economist,* 8 May 1965, Thomas Mann Papers, box 340, TC.

61. Telegram, Embassy Santo Domingo to State Department, 7 May 1965, NSF, NSC Histories, Dominican Crisis, box 4, 2 of 2, LBJL; Woods, *Fulbright,* 380; Transcript of Telephone Conversation, Mann and Johnson, 8 May 1965, Thomas Mann Papers, box 316, TC.

62. McPherson, *Yankee No!,* 150; Memo, Rowan to Mann, "Daily Reaction Report," 1 May 1965, RG 59, Records of the Undersecretary of State for Economic Affairs, Records Relating to the Dominican Republic, box 1, NAMD; Transcript of Juan Bosch Interview, 7 May 1965, Abe Fortas Papers, Group no. 858, Series no. 4, box 154, YUL.

63. Quoted in Woods, "Conflicted Hegemon," 762.

64. Memo for the Record, Mann, 11 May 1965, Thomas Mann Papers, box 323, TC; Memo for the Record, Mann, "The Bundy-Mann Mission," 12 July 1965, RG 59, Records of the Undersecretary of State for Economic Affairs, Records Relating to the Dominican Republic, box 1, NAMD.

65. Telegram, Bundy to Johnson, 17 May 1965, NSF, NSC Histories, Dominican Crisis, box 7, 1 of 2, LBJL; Transcript, William G. Bowdler Oral History Interview, 30 May 1969, by Joe B. Frantz, LBJL.

66. Chester, *Rag-Tags,* 188; McPherson, "Misled by Himself," 133; Woods, "Conflicted Hegemon," 763.

67. McPherson, "Misled by Himself," 134; Andrew Preston, *The War Council: McGeorge Bundy, the NSC, and Vietnam* (Cambridge, MA: Harvard University Press, 2006), 200.

68. Memo of Conversation, Mann and Loyalist Generals, 15 May 1965, RG 59, Records of the Undersecretary of State for Economic Affairs, Records Relating to the Dominican Republic, box 1, NAMD.

69. Chronology of Bundy-Mann Mission, 24 September 1965, NSF, NSC Histories, Dominican Crisis, box 7, 1 of 2, LBJL.

70. Transcript of Mann and Vance Senate Committee Hearings, 14 July 1965–15 July 1965, RG 59, Records of the Undersecretary of State for Economic Affairs, Records Relating to the Dominican Republic, box 1, NAMD.

71. Gleijeses, "Hope Denied," 35–36.

72. Memo, Thomas Mann, "Recommendations," 19 May 1965, and Memo, "The Secretary's Points," 22 May 1965, both Thomas Mann Papers, box 323, TC; Transcript of Telephone Conversation, Mann and Johnson, 24 May 1965, Thomas Mann Papers, box 316, TC; Chester, *Rag-Tags*, 188.

73. Bowdler Oral History, LBJL; Telegram from the Embassy in the Dominican Republic to the Department of State, 10 June 1965, *FRUS, 1964–1968*, vol. 32, *Dominican Republic; Cuba; Haiti; Guyana*, doc. 103.

74. Atkins and Wilson, *The Dominican Republic and the United States*, 141.

75. Speech by Senator Robert F. Kennedy, "Vietnam and the Dominican Republic," 6 May 1965, Papers of Arthur Schlesinger Jr., Private Files, box P-2, JFKL; Transcript of Telephone Conversation, Mann and Harriman, 9 May 1965, Thomas Mann Papers, box 311, TC; Transcript of Telephone Conversation, Mann and Johnson, 12 July 1965, Thomas Mann Papers, box 316, TC.

76. Transcript of Mann and Vance Senate Committee Hearings, 14 July 1965–29 July 1965, RG 59, Records of the Undersecretary of State for Economic Affairs, Records Relating to the Dominican Republic, box 1, NAMD.

77. Recording of Telephone Conversation, Johnson and Bennett, 2 May 1965, Recording WH6505.02, Miller Center, https://nsarchive2.gwu.edu/NSAEBB/NSAEBB513/docs/Tape%2008%20transcript.pdf; Statement by Ambassador Bennett to the Senate Foreign Relations Committee, 16 July 1965, RG 59, Records of the Undersecretary of State for Economic Affairs, Records Relating to the Dominican Republic, box 2, NAMD.

78. Woods, *Fulbright*, 381; Transcript of Mann and Vance Senate Committee Hearings, 14 July 1965–29 July 1965, RG 59, Records of the Undersecretary of State for Economic Affairs, Records Relating to the Dominican Republic, box 1, NAMD; Transcript of Telephone Conversation, Mann and Ball, 29 July 1965, Papers of George W. Ball, box 1, LBJL; Pat Holt Oral History Interview.

79. Marcy Oral History; Memo, Bowdler to Bundy, "Fulbright Trip to Brazil," 2 August 1965, NSF, CF, Brazil, box 9, LBJL; Woods, *Fulbright*, 383–84; Transcript of Speech by Senator Fulbright, 15 September 1965, Eleanor Lansing Dulles Papers, box 47, DDEL.

80. Memo, Bundy to Johnson, 17 September 1965, NSF, Memos to the President, box 11, LBJL; Woods, *Fulbright*, 385.

81. Memo, Bowdler to Moyers, "Selden Resolution," 20 September 1965, NSF, CF, Latin America, box 2, 2 of 2, LBJL. Selden's actions were so unpopular that even the Nicaraguan Congress, still firmly controlled by the Somoza family, attacked the "unfriendly resolution that deeply wounds our sovereignty and dignity." Airgram,

Nicaraguan Embassy to State Department, 5 October 1965, RG 59, Central Foreign Policy Files 1964–1966, Political and Defense Subject Numeric File, box 2411, NAMD; Research Memo, "Latin American Reaction to the Selden Resolution," 30 September 1965, NSF, CF, Latin America, box 2, 2 of 2, LBJL; Memo, Bundy to Johnson, "Developments in Latin America," 29 September 1965, NSF, Memos to the President, box 19, LBJL.

82. Transcript of Telephone Conversation, Mann and Johnson, 6 January 1966, Thomas Mann Papers, box 316, TC; Chester, *Rag-Tags,* 226; Draft Press Release, ca. March 1966, Press Guidance, ca. March 1966, and Memo, Bowdler to Johnson, "Assignment of Ambassador Bennett," 17 March 1966, all NSF, CF, Dominican Republic, box 46, LBJL.

83. Johnson, *The Vantage Point,* 203. For the first viewpoint, see Colman, *The Foreign Policy of Lyndon Johnson,* 181; Walker, "Mixing the Sweet with the Sour," 63; and Atkins and Wilson, *The Dominican Republic and the United States,* 142–44. For the second, see Chester, *Rag-Tags,* 220.

84. Report, "Post-Election Latin American Views on the Dominican Crisis Experience," ca. June 1966, NSF, CF, Dominican Republic, box 47, LBJL; Memo, Rostow to Johnson, "Latin American Press Reaction to the Dominican Election," 14 June 1966, NSF, AF, box 8, LBJL; Memo, Bowdler to Rostow, ca. May 1966, and Memo, Moyers to Bowdler, 16 May 1966, both NSF, Intelligence File, box 10, LBJL.

85. Memo, Helms to Fitzgerald, 29 December 1965, *FRUS, 1964–1868,* vol. 32, *Dominican Republic; Cuba; Haiti; Guyana,* doc. 151; Memo, Raborn to Johnson, 31 March 1966, and Memo, Bowdler to Komer, "Elections in the DR," 14 March 1966, both NSF, CF, Dominican Republic, box 46, LBJL; "Message from Ambassador Bunker in Santo Domingo," 15 May 1965, NSF, Intelligence File, box 10, LBJL.

86. Gleijeses, "Hope Denied," 45.

87. Quoted in Tulchin, "The United States and Latin America in the 1960s," 28.

88. LaFeber, "Thomas C. Mann," 167; Walker, "Mixing the Sweet with the Sour," 63; Transcript of Telephone Conversation, Johnson, Bennett, Martin, and Bundy, 2 May 1965, and Transcript of Telephone Conversation, Johnson, Fortas, and McNamara, 23 May 1965, both NSAEBB 513.

89. Transcript of Telephone Conversation, Johnson and Bundy, 29 April 1965, NSAEBB 513.

90. Transcript of Telephone Conversation, Johnson, Fortas, and McNamara, 23 May 1965, NSAEBB 513.

5. New Alliances

1. LaFeber, *Inevitable Revolutions,* 159; Tulchin, "The Promise of Progress," 236.

2. Transcript of Telephone Conversation, Mann and Johnson, 4 June 1965, Thomas Mann Papers, box 316, TC.

3. Quoted in Schwartz, *Lyndon Johnson and Europe,* 143.

4. Peter Lisagor, "LBJ Aide Answers Latin Policy Critics," *Chicago News,* 13 October 1965, Richard Eder, "Firm Latin Policy Outlined by Mann," *New York Times,* 14 October 1965, and Memo, "Latin American Media Reaction to International Issues," 14 October 1965, all Thomas Mann Papers, box 305, TC.

5. Memo, Vaughn to Rusk, 3 August 1965, NSF, AF, box 5, LBJL; Lyndon Johnson, "Remarks at a Ceremony Commemorating the Fourth Anniversary of the Alliance for Progress," 17 August 1965, APP, PPP, http://www.presidency.ucsb.edu/ws/index.php?pid=27162.

6. Memo, Read to Bundy, "Reactions in Latin America to President's Alliance for Progress Speech," 21 August 1965, NSF, AF, box 5, LBJL; "Support for the Alliance," *New York Times,* 18 August 1965; Richard Eder, "Johnson Mission Woos Latins by Aiding Progress," *New York Times,* 21 August 1965.

7. Memo, Rostow to Johnson, "Alliance for Progress at Rio," 29 November 1965, NSF, AF, box 5, LBJL; "Official Documents of the Second Special Inter-American Conference," *American Journal of International Law* 60, no. 2 (April 1966): 445–61; Memo, Rostow to Johnson, "Alliance for Progress at Rio," 29 November 1965, NSF, AF, box 5, LBJL.

8. Transcripts of Telephone Conversations, Mann and Johnson, 13 November 1965 and 17 January 1966, both Thomas Mann Papers, box 316, TC. Regarding Mann's declining influence, Max Frankel, e.g., wrote: "The 'one voice' with which President Johnson has wanted to speak to Latin America will no longer be the controversial voice of Thomas C. Mann." Max Frankel, "New Link to Latins," *New York Times,* 24 January 1966.

9. Annotated Transcript of Audio Diary, Lady Bird Johnson, 23 January 1966 (Sunday), Lady Bird Johnson's White House Diary Collection, LBJ Presidential Library, http://discoverlbj.org/item/ctjd-19660123.

10. Transcript of Telephone Conversation, Mann and Johnson, 15 July 1965, and Transcript of Telephone Conversation, Mann and Johnson, 13 November 1965, both Thomas Mann Papers, box 316, TC.

11. Transcript of Telephone Conversation, Mann and Johnson, 13 November 1965, Thomas Mann Papers, box 316, TC.

12. Memo, Rostow to Johnson, 10 February 1966, *FRUS, 1964–1968,* vol. 31, *South and Central America; Mexico,* doc. 476; Transcript of Telephone Conversation, Mann and Johnson, 13 November 1965, Thomas Mann Papers, box 316, TC.

13. Milne, *America's Rasputin;* Transcript of Telephone Conversation, Mann and. Johnson, 2 June 1966, Thomas Mann Papers, box 316, TC; US Department of State, Office of the Historian, "Principal Officers by Title," http://history.state.gov/departmenthistory/people/principalofficers.

14. Letter, Johnson to Mann, 25 April 1966, WHCF, Name File, box M67, LBJL; Transcript of Telephone Conversation, Mann and Johnson, 2 June 1966, Thomas Mann Papers, box 316, TC.

15. "Johnson Accepts Mann's Resignation from State Department," *New York Times,* 29 April 1966; "The World: Johnson and Critics," *New York Times,* 1 May 1966.

16. William S. White, "The Mann Who Insisted on Respect for US," *Washington Post,* 3 May 1966, and "Johnsons Bid Mann Goodbye," *Evening Star,* 26 May 1966, both Thomas Mann Papers, box 340, TC.

17. Transcript of Telephone Conversation, Johnson and Mann, 2 June 1966, Thomas Mann Papers, box 316, TC; Memo, Watson to Johnson, 2 August 1966, WHCF, Name File, box M67, LBJL; Thomas Mann Statement to Subcommittee on Foreign Economic Policy, 18 July 1967, box 304, Thomas Mann Papers, TC; Thomas Mann Statement before House Foreign Affairs Committee, 25 July 1967, box 305, Thomas Mann Papers, TC.

18. Memo, Sayre to Bundy, 24 June 1964, Telegram, Martin to State Department, 24 February 1965, and Telegram, Solomon to Embassy Buenos Aires, 12 March 1965, all NSF, CF, Argentina, box 6, LBJL.

19. Guillermo O'Donnell, *Bureaucratic Authoritarianism: Argentina, 1966–1973, in Comparative Perspective,* trans. James McGuire and Rae Flory (Berkeley and Los Angeles: University of California Press, 1988), 46–60; CIA Intelligence Information Cable, 29 May 1965, and CIA Intelligence Information Cable, "Remarks of General Julio Alsogaray," 2 June 1966, both NSF, CF, Argentina, box 6, LBJL.

20. Editorial Note, *FRUS, 1964–1968,* vol. 31, *South and Central America; Mexico,* doc. 130; Telegram, Gordon to Martin, 6 June 1966, NSF, CF, Argentina, box 6, LBJL.

21. María José Moyano, *Argentina's Lost Patrol: Armed Struggle, 1969–1979* (New Haven, CT: Yale University Press, 2012), 17; William Michael Schmidli, *The Fate of Freedom Elsewhere: Human Rights and U.S. Cold War Policy toward Argentina* (Ithaca, NY: Cornell University Press, 2013), 39.

22. State Department Intelligence Report, "Latin American Reaction to the Argentine Coup," 1 July 1966, NSF, CF, Argentina, box 6, LBJL; Memo, Rostow to Johnson, "Argentine Situation," 28 June 1966, NSF, Memos to the President, box 8, LBJL.

23. Memo, Gordon to Rusk, "Argentina—Diplomatic Recognition of New Government," 1 August 1966, NSF, CF, Argentina, box 6, LBJL; Jose Moyano, *Argentina's Lost Patrol,* 19; Schmidli, *The Fate of Freedom Elsewhere,* 40. *Bureaucratic-authoritarian state* is a term coined by the Argentine political scientist Guillermo O'Donnell and refers to a certain type of authoritarian state that emerged in Latin America during this period, one characterized by the dominance of modern technocrats and a professionalized military. See O'Donnell, *Bureaucratic Authoritarianism.*

24. Telegram, Martin to State Department, "Private Conversation with General Alsogaray," 30 June 1966, NSF, CF, Argentina, box 6, LBJL.

25. For a detailed exploration, see Field, *From Development to Dictatorship.*

26. Airgram, Martin to State Department, "Political-Economic Assessment," 27 April 1966, NSF, CF, Argentina, box 6, LBJL; Schmidli, *The Fate of Freedom Elsewhere,* 40.

27. Schmidli, *The Fate of Freedom Elsewhere,* 41; Airgram, Martin to State Department, "Political-Economic Assessment," 27 April 1966, NSF, CF, Argentina, box 6, LBJL.

28. Report, "Major Gains under the Alliance for Progress since 1964," ca. September 1968, NSF, Memos to the President, box 14, LBJL; Table, "Physical Accomplishments of the Alliance for Progress," 13 January 1965, NSF, AF, box 5, LBJL; Memo, Fowler to Bowdler, "U.S. Non-Public and Non-Profit Assistance to Latin America, 1961–1966," 3 October 1967, NSF, CF, Latin America, box 3, LBJL.

29. Memo, Rostow to Johnson, 29 November 1966, NSF, International Meetings and Travel File, box 15, LBJL; Memo, Gordon to Johnson, "Funding Availabilities for the Alliance for Progress, Latin America FY1967," 3 October 1966, NSF, AF, box 5, LBJL.

30. For examples, see Gabriel Kolko, *Confronting the Third World: United States Foreign Policy, 1945–1980* (New York: Pantheon, 1988), 168; LaFeber, *Inevitable Revolutions,* 159; and Abraham F. Lowenthal, "Alliance Rhetoric versus Latin American Reality," *Foreign Affairs* 48, no. 3 (April 1970): 494–508, 505.

31. Lyndon B. Johnson, "Remarks at a Ceremony Marking the Fifth Anniversary of the Alliance for Progress," August 17, 1966, APP, PPP, http://www.presidency.ucsb.edu/ws/index.php?pid=27777; Memo, Mann to Rusk, 12 February 1965, Thomas Mann Papers, box 323, TC; Pincus, "The Central American Common Market."

32. LaFeber, *Inevitable Revolutions,* 189; Salvador Rivera, *Latin American Unification: A History of Political and Economic Integration Efforts* (Jefferson, NC: McFarland, 2014); Taffet, *Foreign Aid as Foreign Policy,* 182; Mann Oral History, LBJL.

33. Pearce, *Rostow,* 110.

34. Memorandum from the President's Special Assistant (Rostow) to President Johnson, 27 May 1966, *FRUS, 1964–1968,* vol. 31, *South and Central America; Mexico,* doc. 40; National Security Action Memorandum no. 349, "Development of the Frontiers of South America," 31 May 1966, NSAMs, LBJL, https://www.discoverlbj.org/item/nsf-nsam349.

35. Pearce, *Rostow,* 113; Walker, "Mixing the Sweet with the Sour," 68.

36. Memo, Bowdler to Moyers, 31 March 1966, NSF, CF, Argentina, box 6, LBJL; Memo, Rostow to Johnson, "Inter-American Summit Meeting," 31 May 1966, NSF, Memos to the President, box 8, LBJL; Memo, Rostow to Johnson, "Meeting with Latin American Experts on the Summit," 6 March 1967, NSF, Memos to the President, box 14, LBJL; Memo, Bowdler to Rostow, 17 January 1967, and Telegram from the Embassy in Argentina to the Department of State, 19 February 1967, both *FRUS, 1964–1968,* vol. 31, *South and Central America; Mexico,* doc. 43, 46.

37. Memo, Rostow to Johnson, "Program for the OAS Summit," 27 January 1967, NSF, International Meetings and Travel File, box 15, LBJL; Memo, Rostow to Johnson, "Meeting the Latin American Experts on the Summit," 6 March 1967, and Memo, Rostow to Johnson, 10 February 1967, both *FRUS, 1964–1968,* vol. 31,

South and Central America; Mexico, docs. 47, 44; Memo, Rostow to Johnson, "Proposed Ideas for the Summit," 8 March 1967, NSF, Memos to the President, box 14, LBJL.

38. Memo, Mann to Johnson, "Comments on the Proposed Inter-American Summit Meeting," 20 January 1967, NSF, International Meetings and Travel File, box 37.

39. Memo, Bowdler to Rostow, "Research Projects: the OAS Summit," 17 October 1968, NSF, International Meetings and Travel File, box 19, LBJL; Lyndon B. Johnson, "Special Message to the Congress on the Latin American Summit Meeting," 13 March 1967, APP, PPP, http://www.presidency.ucsb.edu/ws/?pid=28129.

40. Max Frankel, "Fulbright Group Rebuffs Johnson on Latin Policy," *New York Times,* 4 April 1967.

41. Benjamin Welles, "GOP Senators Hunt a Latin Plan," *New York Times,* 6 April 1967; Walter Lippmann, "Today and Tomorrow: Prospects at Punta del Este," *Washington Post,* 13 April 1967.

42. Memo, Rostow to Johnson, 16 March 1967, NSF, CF Latin America, box 5, LBJL; Lyndon B. Johnson, "Statement by the President at an Informal Meeting with the American Chiefs of State at Punta del Este, Uruguay," 12 April 1967, APP, PPP, http://www.presidency.ucsb.edu/ws/index.php?pid=28200; Lyndon B. Johnson, "Remarks in Punta del Este at the Public Session of the Meeting of American Chiefs of State," 13 April 1967, APP, PPP, http://www.presidency.ucsb.edu/ws/index .php?pid=28201.

43. Draft, "Charter of the Presidents of American Republics for the Peoples of Americas," 7 March 1967, NSF, CF Latin America, box 3, LBJL; Circular Telegram from the Department of State to All American Republic Posts, 17 April 1967, *FRUS, 1964–1968,* vol. 31, *South and Central America; Mexico,* doc. 52; Memo, Rostow to Johnson, 22 April 1967, NSF, Memos to the President, box 15, LBJL; Memo, Read to Rostow, "Official Latin American Reaction to the Summit," 22 April 1967, NSF, CF Latin America, box 3, LBJL.

44. Richard J. Walter, *Peru and the United States, 1960–1975: How Their Ambassadors Managed Foreign Relations in a Turbulent Era* (University Park: Pennsylvania State University Press, 2010), 98; Memo, Mann to Johnson, "Comments on the Proposed Inter-American Summit Meeting," 20 January 1967, NSF, International Meetings and Travel File, box 37, LBJL; James Reston, "Parley within a Parley: Behind Ceremonies at Punta del Este, Johnson Dominates a Series of Talks," *New York Times,* 13 April 1967.

45. Memo, Rostow to Johnson, 22 April 1967, NSF, Memos to the President, box 15, LBJL; CIA Intelligence Memo, "Latin American Governmental Views of the Summit Meeting," 1 May 1967, NSF, CF, Latin America, box 3, LBJL; Dungan Oral History, LBJL.

46. Memo, Rostow to Johnson, "List of OAS Summit Follow Up Actions," 19 April 1967, NSF, CF Latin America, box 3, LBJL; "Statement by the President on the Summit Conference," NSF, International Meetings and Travel File, box 19,

LBJL; Memo Rostow to Johnson, "Talking Points," 13 July 1967, Memo, Gaud to Johnson, "Status of the Aid Bill," 2 June 1967, Memo, Bator to Johnson, 5 June 1967, and Memo, Oliver to the Undersecretary, "Weekly Report—Inter-American Affairs," 25 August 1967, all NSF, CF Latin America, box 3, LBJL.

47. Memo, Rusk to Johnson, "Second Progress Report on Implementation of the Inter-American Summit Decisions," 15 July 1967, Memo, Katzenbach to Johnson, 18 October 1967, Inter-American Development Bank Press Release, 9 November 1967, Memo, Rusk to Johnson, "Second Progress Report on Implementation of the Inter-American Summit Decisions," 15 July 1967, and Memo, Bowdler to Johnson, "Covey Oliver's Trip to Venezuela, Bolivia, Peru and Colombia," 1 March 1968, all NSF, CF Latin America, box 3, LBJL.

48. Letter, Johnson to Oliver, 30 June 1967, NSF, CF Latin America, box 3, LBJL; Covey Oliver Oral History, LBJL; Tulchin, "The Promise of Progress," 239; Address by Covey T. Oliver at the Latin American Forum, Georgetown University, "The Alliance Moves On," 14 November 1967, Covey T. Oliver Papers, LBJL.

49. Memo, Rostow to Johnson, "Measures to Invigorate the Form and Substance of Our Activities in Latin America," 5 February 1968, NSF, CF Latin America, box 4, LBJL; Memo, Oliver to Johnson, "Report on My Trip to Venezuela, Bolivia, Peru and Colombia," 4 March 1968, Memo, Bowdler to Johnson, "Covey Oliver's Trip to Venezuela, Bolivia, Peru and Colombia," 1 March 1968, and Memo, Rostow to Johnson, "Ceremony on Latin America," 10 April 1968, all NSF, CF Latin America, box 3, LBJL.

50. "First Anniversary Progress Report on Implementation of the Inter-American Summit Decisions," 22 April 1968, NSF, CF Latin America, box 4, LBJL.

51. Thomas M. Leonard, "Meeting in San Salvador: President Lyndon B. Johnson and the 1968 Central American Summit Conference," *Journal of Third World Studies* 23, no. 2 (Fall 2006): 119–46; Editorial Note, *FRUS, 1964–1968,* vol. 31, *South and Central America; Mexico,* doc. 111.

52. State Department Scope Paper, "President's Trip to El Salvador," 29 June 1968, NSF, International Meetings and Travel File, box 22, LBJL; Minutes of Cabinet Meeting and Attachments, 10 July 1968, *FRUS, 1964–1968,* vol. 31, *South and Central America; Mexico,* doc. 112; Special National Intelligence Estimate, "The President's Trip to Central America," 3 June 1968, CIA Records, Freedom of Information Act Electronic Reading Room. For more on Salvadoran education programs, see Héctor Lindo-Fuentes and Erik Ching, *Modernizing Minds in El Salvador: Education Reform and the Cold War, 1960–1980* (Albuquerque: University of New Mexico Press, 2012).

53. Lyndon B. Johnson, "Remarks at the Working Session of the Presidents of the Central American Republics in San Salvador," 6 July 1968, APP, PPP, http://www.presidency.ucsb.edu/ws/index.php?pid=28988.

54. "Joint Declaration of the Presidents Following Their Meeting in San Salvador," 6 July 1968, APP, PPP, http://www.presidency.ucsb.edu/ws/index.php?pid=28989.

55. Lyndon B. Johnson, "Remarks at the Lyndon B. Johnson School in San Salvador," 7 July 1968, APP, PPP, http://www.presidency.ucsb.edu/ws/index.php?pid =28992; Schedule, "The President's Trip to Central America," 2 July 1968, NSF, International Meetings and Travel File, box 22, LBJL.

56. Minutes of Cabinet Meeting and Attachments, 10 July 1968, and Editorial Note, both *FRUS, 1964–1968,* vol. 31, *South and Central America; Mexico,* docs. 112, 111; Memo, Rostow to Johnson, "US Media Reaction to President Johnson's Central American Trip," 26 July 1968, and Memo, Read to Rostow, "Latin American Media Coverage of the President's Trip," July 18 1968, both NSF, International Meetings and Travel File, box 23, LBJL; Leonard, "Meeting in San Salvador," 137.

57. Minutes of Cabinet Meeting and Attachments, 10 July 1968, *FRUS, 1964–1968,* vol. 31, *South and Central America; Mexico,* doc. 112.

58. CIA Intelligence Report, "Obstacles to the Andean Subregional Integration Movement," July 1968, NSF, CF Latin America, box 4, LBJL; Leonard, "Meeting in San Salvador," 128.

59. Covey Oliver Oral History, LBJL; Memo, Rostow to Johnson, "Javits Amendment to the Foreign Aid Bill," 19 July 1966, NSF, Memos to the President, box 9, LBJL; Memo, Gordon to Rostow, "Comments on BOB Reductions of Alliance for Progress FY 1968 Appropriations," 7 December 1966, NSF, AF, box 5, LBJL; Memo, Bowdler to Rostow and Attached Circular, 19 September 1968, NSF, CF Latin America, box 4, LBJL.

60. Memo, Marks to Rostow, "Latin American Press on Aid Cuts," 30 September 1968, NSF, CF Latin America, box 5, LBJL; "Statement by the President upon Signing the Foreign Assistance Act of 1968," 9 October 1968, Office Files of the White House Aides, Office Files of Harry McPherson, box 30, LBJL.

61. For an exploration of such issues, see Christopher Darnton, *Rivalry and Alliance Politics in Cold War Latin America* (Baltimore: Johns Hopkins University Press, 2014).

62. Lyndon B. Johnson, "Remarks at the Chamizal Ceremony, Juarez, Mexico," 28 October 1967, APP, PPP, http://www.presidency.ucsb.edu/ws/index .php?pid=28509.

63. Memo, Rostow to Johnson, 24 June 1967, and State Department Intelligence Report, "Crisis Management in Bolivia," 23 June 1967, both NSF, Intelligence File, box 2, LBJL.

64. Memo, Rostow to Johnson, 23 June 1967, *FRUS, 1964–1968,* vol. 31, *South and Central America; Mexico,* doc. 164; Memo, Rostow to Johnson, 24 June 1967, NSF, Intelligence File, box 2, LBJL; Memo, Helms to Various, "Capture and Execution of Ernesto 'Che' Guevara," 11 October 1967, *FRUS, 1964–1968,* vol. 31, *South and Central America; Mexico,* doc. 171.

65. Memo, Rostow to Johnson, "'Che' Guevara," 14 October 1967, *FRUS, 1964–1968,* vol. 31, *South and Central America; Mexico,* doc. 173; State Department Intelligence Report, "Guevara's Death—the Meaning for Latin America," 12 October 1967, NSF, CF Bolivia, box 8, LBJL; "Guevara: Man and Myth," *New York*

Times, 12 October 1967; Joseph Kraft, "Che Guevara's Death Is Step in Decline of Revolutionaries," *Washington Post,* 12 October 1967; Memo, Bowdler to Johnson, "Covey Oliver's Trip to Venezuela, Bolivia, Peru, and Colombia," 1 March 1968, NSF, CF Latin America, box 3, LBJL.

66. Memo, Rostow to Johnson, 6 July 1967, NSF, CF Latin America, box 3, LBJL; Memo, Rostow to Johnson, "Death of 'Che' Guevara," 11 October 1967, National Security Archive Electronic Briefing Book no. 5, "The Death of Che Guevara: Declassified," http://nsarchive.gwu.edu/NSAEBB/NSAEBB5/index.html; Memo, Helms to Rostow, "The Political Role of the Military in Latin America," 1 May 1968, NSF, CF Latin America, box 4, LBJL.

67. Memo, Bowdler to Rostow, "Alleged U.S./Cuban Rapprochement," 26 June 1968, NSF Intelligence File, box 10, LBJL.

68. Lawrence A. Clayton, *Peru and the United States: The Condor and the Eagle* (Athens: University of Georgia Press, 1999), 245; Walter, *Peru and the United States,* 135.

69. Memo, Rostow to Johnson, "Peru—PL 480 Agreement for Rice," 2 October 1968, and Editorial Note 505, both *FRUS, 1964–1968,* vol. 31, *South and Central America; Mexico,* doc. 508; Memo, Rostow to Johnson, "Peru Coup," 3 October 1968, and Memo, Rostow to Johnson, "Peru Coup," 4 October 1968, both NSF, Memos to the President, box 40, LBJL.

70. Telegram, Department of State to the Embassy in Peru, 6 October 1968, *FRUS, 1964–1968,* vol. 31, *South and Central America; Mexico,* doc. 512.

71. Editorial Note, *FRUS, 1964–1968,* vol. 31, *South and Central America; Mexico,* doc. 446; The Department of State during the Administration of Lyndon B. Johnson, Administrative History, vol. 1, box 2, LBJL; Telegram, Rostow to Johnson in Texas, 12 October 1968, *FRUS, 1964–1968,* vol. 31, *South and Central America; Mexico,* doc. 450.

72. Notes of Meeting, 22 October 1968, *FRUS, 1964–1968,* vol. 31, *South and Central America; Mexico,* doc. 519; Michael L. Conniff, *Panama and the United States: The End of the Alliance,* 3rd ed. (Athens: University of Georgia Press, 2012), 126; Memo, Rostow to Johnson, "Panama," 21 October 1968, *FRUS, 1964–1968,* vol. 31, *South and Central America; Mexico,* doc. 452.

73. Special National Intelligence Estimate, "The Situation in Panama," 1 November 1968, Memo, Lewis to Rostow, 29 October 1968, and Memo, Rostow to Johnson, "Panama," 9 November 1968, all *FRUS, 1964–1968,* vol. 31, *South and Central America; Mexico,* docs. 454, 453, 455.

74. Memorandum for the File, "Panama," 9 December 1968, and Memorandum, Rostow to Johnson, "Military Assistance for the Panamanian National Guard," 30 December 1968, *FRUS, 1964–1968,* vol. 31, *South and Central America; Mexico,* docs. 457, 458.

75. Richard E. Feinberg, *Summitry in the Americas: A Progress Report* (Washington, DC: Institute for International Economics, 1997), 33.

76. Memo, Rostow to Johnson, 15 November 1968, NSF, CF Latin America, box 5, LBJL; Lyndon B. Johnson, "Toasts of the President and President Diaz Ordaz at the Luncheon in El Paso Following the Chamizal Ceremony," 13 December 1968, APP, PPP, http://www.presidency.ucsb.edu/ws/index.php?pid=29276; Memo, Rostow to Johnson, 14 October 1968, and Memo, Rostow to Johnson, 9 December 1968, both NSF, CF Latin America, box 5, LBJL.

Conclusion

1. Mark A. Lawrence, "History from Below: The United States and Latin America in the Nixon Years," in Fredrik Logevall and Andrew Preston, eds., *Nixon in the World: American Foreign Relations, 1969–1977* (Oxford: Oxford University Press, 2008), 269–88, 269, 274 (quotes).

2. McPherson, "Latin America," 400.

3. Mann Oral History, DDEL; Remarks before Foreign Policy Discussion Group, 5 March 1969, Thomas Mann Papers, box 304, TC; Journal Entry, 17 September 1983, Schlesinger, *Journals,* 555.

4. LaFeber, "Thomas C. Mann," 198; Speech to the Dallas Council of World Affairs, "Non-Intervention and Self Defense in Our Latin American Policy," 14 February 1969, Thomas Mann Papers, box 304, TC.

5. Mann Oral History, JFKL; Memo, Mann to Bundy, "NSAM 333: Follow-Up on the Miller Report," 17 June 1965, Memo, Mann to Bundy, "International Sugar Conference," 13 September 1965, and Editorial Note, all *FRUS, 1964–1968,* vol. 9, *International Development and Economic Defense Policy; Commodities* (Washington, DC: Government Printing Office, 1997), docs. 173, 285, 114.

6. Bowdler Oral History, LBJL.

7. The Department of State during the Administration of Lyndon B. Johnson, Administrative History, vol. 1, box 2, LBJL.

Selected Bibliography

Archives

Butler Library, Oral History Research Office, Columbia University, New York
Dwight D. Eisenhower Library, Abilene, KS
John F. Kennedy Library, Boston
Library of Congress, Manuscripts Division, Washington, DC
Lyndon B. Johnson Library, Austin, TX
New York Public Library, Manuscripts and Archives Division, New York
Sterling Memorial Library, Manuscripts and Archives, Yale University, New Haven, CT
The Texas Collection, Baylor University, Waco, TX
US National Archives, College Park, MD
US National Archives, Washington, DC

Select Published Sources

Beschloss, Michael R., ed. *Taking Charge: The Johnson White House Tapes, 1963–1964.* New York: Simon & Schuster, 1997.
———, ed. *Reaching for Glory: Lyndon Johnson's Secret White House Tapes, 1964–1965.* New York: Simon & Schuster, 2001.
Chester, Eric Thomas. *Rag-Tags, Scum, Riff-Raff, and Commies: The U.S. Intervention in the Dominican Republic, 1965–1966.* New York: Monthly Review Press, 2001.
Clayton, Lawrence A. *Peru and the United States: The Condor and the Eagle.* Athens: University of Georgia Press, 1999.
Cohen, Warren I., and Nancy Bernkopf Tucker, eds. *Lyndon Johnson Confronts the World: American Foreign Policy, 1963–1968.* Cambridge: Cambridge University Press, 1994.
Dosman, Edgar J. *The Life and Times of Raúl Prebisch, 1901–1986.* Montreal: McGill-Queen's University Press, 2008.
Engerman, David C., Nils Gilman, Mark Haefele, and Michael E. Latham, eds. *Staging Growth: Modernization, Development, and the Global Cold War.* Amherst: University of Massachusetts Press, 2003.

271

Field, Thomas C., Jr. *From Development to Dictatorship: Bolivia and the Alliance for Progress in the Kennedy Era*. Ithaca, NY: Cornell University Press, 2014.

Gardner, Lloyd. *Economic Aspects of New Deal Diplomacy*. Boston: Beacon, 1964.

Gellman, Irwin F. *Good Neighbor Diplomacy: United States Policies in Latin America, 1933–1945*. Baltimore: Johns Hopkins University Press, 1980.

Gleijeses, Piero. *The Dominican Crisis: The 1965 Constitutionalist Revolt and American Intervention*. Translated by Lawrence Lipson. Baltimore: Johns Hopkins University Press, 1978.

————. *Shattered Hope: The Guatemalan Revolution and the United States, 1944–1954*. Princeton, NJ: Princeton University Press, 1991.

————. "Hope Denied: The US Defeat of the 1965 Revolt in the Dominican Republic." Cold War International History Project Working Paper Series, no. 72. Washington, DC: Wilson Center, November 2014.

Goodwin, Richard. *Remembering America: A Voice from the Sixties*. Boston: Perennial, 1988.

Grandin, Greg, and Gilbert M. Joseph, eds. *A Century of Revolution: Insurgent and Counterinsurgent Violence during Latin America's Long Cold War*. Durham, NC: Duke University Press, 2010.

Grow, Michael. *U.S. Presidents and Latin American Interventions: Pursuing Regime Change in the Cold War*. Lawrence: University Press of Kansas, 2008.

Harmer, Tanya. *Allende's Chile and the Inter-American Cold War*. Chapel Hill: University of North Carolina Press, 2011.

Johnson, Lyndon B. *The Vantage Point: Perspectives of the Presidency, 1963–1969*. New York: Holt, Rinehart & Winston, 1971.

Johnson, Robert David. "Constitutionalism Abroad and at Home: The United States Senate and the Alliance for Progress, 1961–1967." *International History Review* 21, no. 2 (June 1999): 414–42.

Keller, Renata. *Mexico's Cold War: Cuba, the United States and the Legacy of the Mexican Revolution*. New York: Cambridge University Press, 2015.

LaFeber, Walter, and Thomas J. McCormick, eds. *Behind the Throne: Servants of Power to Imperial Presidents, 1898–1968*. Madison: University of Wisconsin Press, 1993.

Latham, Michael. *Modernization as Ideology: American Social Science and "Nation Building" in the Kennedy Era*. Chapel Hill: University of North Carolina Press, 2000.

Leacock, Ruth. *Requiem for Revolution: The United States and Brazil, 1961–1969*. Kent, OH: Kent State University Press, 1990.

Levinson, Jerome, and Juan de Onis. *The Alliance That Lost Its Way: A Critical Report on the Alliance for Progress*. Chicago: Quadrangle, 1970.

Martin, Edwin M. *Kennedy and Latin America*. Lanham, MD: University Press of America, 1994.

McPherson, Alan. *Yankee No! Anti-Americanism in U.S.–Latin American Relations*. Cambridge, MA: Harvard University Press, 2003.

Moyano, María José. *Argentina's Lost Patrol: Armed Struggle, 1969–1979*. New Haven, CT: Yale University Press, 2012.

Rabe, Stephen G. *Eisenhower and Latin America: The Foreign Policy of Anti-ommunism*. Chapel Hill: University of North Carolina Press, 1988.

———. *The Most Dangerous Area in the World: John F. Kennedy Confronts Communist Revolution in Latin America*. Chapel Hill: University of North Carolina Press, 1999.

Rogers, William D. *The Twilight Struggle: The Alliance for Progress and the Politics of Development in Latin America*. New York: Random House, 1967.

Scheman, L. Ronald, ed. *The Alliance for Progress: A Retrospective*. New York: Praeger, 1998.

Schlesinger, Arthur M., Jr. *Robert Kennedy and His Times*. London: Deutsch, 1978.

———. *Journals, 1952–2000*. New York: Penguin, 2007.

Schmidli, William Michael. *The Fate of Freedom Elsewhere: Human Rights and U.S. Cold War Policy toward Argentina*. Ithaca, NY: Cornell University Press, 2013.

Schmitz, David F. *Thank God They're on Our Side: The United States and Right Wing Dictatorships, 1921–1965*. Chapel Hill: University of North Carolina Press, 1999.

Schoultz, Lars. *Beneath the United States: A History of U.S. Policy toward Latin America*. Cambridge, MA: Harvard University Press, 1998.

Sewell, Bevan. *The US and Latin America: Eisenhower, Kennedy and Economic Diplomacy in the Cold War*. London: I. B. Tauris, 2016.

Taffet, Jeffrey F. *Foreign Aid as Foreign Policy: The Alliance for Progress in Latin America*. New York: Routledge, 2007.

Index

Studies in Conflict, Diplomacy, and Peace

Series Editors: George C. Herring, Andrew L. Johns, and
Kathryn C. Statler

This series focuses on key moments of conflict, diplomacy, and peace from the eighteenth century to the present to explore their wider significance in the development of U.S. foreign relations. The series editors welcome new research in the form of original monographs, interpretive studies, biographies, and anthologies from historians, political scientists, journalists, and policymakers. A primary goal of the series is to examine the United States' engagement with the world, its evolving role in the international arena, and the ways in which the state, nonstate actors, individuals, and ideas have shaped and continue to influence history, both at home and abroad.

Advisory Board Members

Books in the Series